THE MOVIES AS A WORLD FORCE

THE MOVIES AS A WORLD FORCE

American Silent Cinema and the Utopian Imagination

RYAN JAY FRIEDMAN

RUTGERS UNIVERSITY PRESS

New Brunswick, Camden, and Newark, New Jersey, and London

Library of Congress Cataloging-in-Publication Data

Names: Friedman, Ryan Jay author.

Title: The movies as a world force : American silent cinema and the utopian imagination / Ryan Jay Friedman.

Description: New Brunswick : Rutgers University Press, 2018. | Includes bibliographical references and index.

Identifiers: LCCN 2018007355 | ISBN 9780813593609 (cloth) | ISBN 9780813593593 (pbk.)

Subjects: LCSH: Utopias in motion pictures. | Silent films—United States—History.

Classification: LCC PN1995.9.U76 F75 2018 | DDC 791.43/672—dc23

LC record available at https://lccn.loc.gov/2018007355

A British Cataloging-in-Publication record for this book is available from the British Library.

∞ The paper used in this publication meets the requirements of the American National Standard for Information Sciences—Permanence of Paper for Printed Library Materials, ANSI Z39.48-1992.

www.rutgersuniversitypress.org

Manufactured in the United States of America

Contents

THE MOVIES AS A WORLD FORCE

Introduction

MOTION PICTURES AND MODERN COMMUNION

An empire built of shadow glories has prospered and its boundaries are the limits of earth.

—Terry Ramsaye, *A Million and One Nights: A History of the Motion Picture*[1]

Writing at the close of the twentieth century, media theorist John Durham Peters notes the remarkable intellectual and cultural power that attaches to a certain notion of communication in the modern United States and Europe. He traces the emergence of "the dream of communication as the mutual communion of souls" through the late nineteenth and early twentieth centuries, highlighting the speed with which this idea installs itself at the center of Western conceptions of human existence.[2] As Peters remarks, "communication" becomes the defining paradox of modernity. It is simultaneously a magnet for the most intense "longings"—"a utopia where nothing is misunderstood, hearts are open, and expression is most uninhibited." And it acts as a source of fear or even despair—the very thing that seems to elude all kinds of social relationships, the very thing that is "always breaking down."[3]

The Movies as a World Force explores the way in which this particular idea of communication shaped American silent cinema culture. Looking at the period between the beginning of World War I and the mid-1920s, the book traces the mutually reinforcing relationship between the perception of cinema as a universal medium and deep-seated longings for "the communion of souls" both national and international. *The Movies as a World Force* is concerned with how, why, and to what ends what I call a utopian-universalist discourse of cinema presents the motion-picture medium as the concrete realization of the ideal of the universal—of totality, of wholeness, of human life in an integral state.[4] To that end, the book examines the extensive body of writing in which such an understanding of the medium developed and through which it was disseminated. And it tracks the ramifications of this theory throughout the broader American cinema culture of the silent-feature-film era, examining its manifestations in particular productions, in the marketing campaigns around them, and in a range of texts that, for reasons of genre and style, do not typically qualify as works of film criticism or history.[5]

As Peters emphasizes, the "experience of the First World War" brings to light the powerful linkages between "novel instruments" for the dissemination of verbal and pictorial symbols and the forms of social organization that characterize urban modernity ("crowds," "masses").[6] Throughout the 1920s, "large-scale communication" and, in turn, the possibilities and dangers of propaganda, persuasion, and public-opinion formation come to dominate the debate about the concept in philosophy and social thought.[7] In the United States, these debates both provided the context for theorizing about film's nature and significance as a medium and were marked by its seemingly unparalleled cultural influence. For its defenders, both inside the industry and on its fringes, the very mass appeal of film warranted an insistently positive account, one in which the medium's astonishing progress seemed to bring the dream of perfected communication within the reach of living human beings.

Living after or through the time of cinema's death—a period when the physical material that once supplied the medium with its presumed ontology disappears and the amorphous universe of on-demand digital content displaces the theatrically exhibited, feature-length motion picture—such an account is liable to strike readers as at least quaint, if not wrongheaded.[8] That anyone would have pinned such lofty hopes to the movies seems to indicate a naïve point of view, one alien to our more skeptical and technologically sophisticated era. And yet there is something tremendously *familiar* about the particular confluence of cultural phenomena that *The Movies as a World Force* explores—longings for an end of conflict, the response to media novelty, and the understanding of communication as a soluble, technical problem—as well as the contexts that shaped them.

For many intellectuals and political journalists in the late 1990s, the demise of Soviet communism and economic globalization seemed to herald the end of history—the cessation of any substantial resistance to Western sovereignty and, in turn, of major armed conflicts between states.[9] The rise of the European Union seemed effectively to further the project of supranational government, which had begun with the attempts to form a League of Nations after World War I.[10] As the de facto center of the new "Empire," the United States appeared to assume the role of world police, treating conflicts happening outside of its borders merely as threats to its own "internal order."[11] And yet, we find ourselves seemingly again in a moment of intractable world conflict, with "the global war on terror" continuing indefinitely, racist nationalism experiencing a resurgence, and international coalitions fraying under the pressure of cyclical financial crises.

In the domestic U.S. political context, the 2008 election of President Barack Obama seemed also to carry decisive historical significance, leading to proclamations of a "postracial" era.[12] This view was staked in part on Obama's wide support among millennials, a generation more diverse than its predecessors and popularly assumed to be the driver of major social changes—both because of its presumed lack of concern with traditional racial categories and because of its being "native" to the digital space.[13] The national news media devoted considerable attention to examining the implications of social media for political organizing, getting caught up in fantasies about the online world (a boundaryless space of fluid identities, where a new, cosmopolitan youth culture was taking hold) as the template for a new electoral culture.[14] As a former campaign strategist for Hillary Clinton marveled, Obama's millennial supporters "looked like Facebook."[15]

In the American context, it is clear that the concept of communication, in the precise sense that Peters delineates, has lost none of its potency. More than a decade and a half into the twenty-first century, it remains true that "the chief dilemmas of our age, both public and personal turn on communication or communications gone sour."[16] Across the political spectrum, one hears continual laments about the polarization of American political culture: the sense that partisan divisions have solidified to the point that people on opposing sides have altogether stopped talking to one another. Sometimes these laments are accompanied by calls for simple listening, for paying heed to disagreeable points of view in an effort to at least respect the legitimacy of one's opponents' concerns and beliefs. Even more to the point, major crises, especially episodes of mass violence, prompt calls for "national conversation," with such frequency this phrase has come to sound like a tired cliché.

To advocate for dialogue in this sense does not presume that the conversation will yield ideological agreement or even that participants will be prompted to alter their points of view. Rather, it reflects a faith that the structure of the conversation will yield mutual recognition and empathy—the awareness that, as President Obama is fond of saying, "the forces that divide us are not as strong as those that unite us."[17] Obama's "belief in the power of national dialogue" represents a centrist-liberal version of the ideal of communication.[18] When in the wake of the 2011 mass shooting in Tucson, Arizona, Obama praised the beginning of a new "national conversation" about gun violence, he seemed less confident that the dialogue would yield a new consensus about firearms legislation or mental health care policy than that it would serve as an antidote to "polariz[ation]."[19] In this case, Obama recommended conversation as therapeutic exercise and as a possible means of reframing intractable social divisions within a broader narrative of commonality.

As an enactment of democratic deliberation, the idea of national conversation has obvious appeal, and yet the overuse of the phrase has prompted critiques from both the right and the left. Those on the right are typically more skeptical about the value of conversation, dismissing it either as an empty display of warm feeling or as a front for liberals' desires to lecture to and indoctrinate their fellow Americans. In the case of the so-called national conversation on race, conservatives object on the grounds that it is self-defeating, "liv[ing] off of the [very] divisions [it is] intended to mend."[20] An authentic national conversation would, from this point of view, exclude "protest" and the airing of "grievance[s]" by racial minorities—"race talk"—in general so as not to alienate the white majority.[21] For the left, the insistence on addressing issues of racism through "national conversation" misses the point entirely; it creates a false sense of conciliation, "substitut[ing] rhetoric for actual discourse and urg[ing] placation over protest."[22]

For all the frustration expressed on both sides, the very fixation on the failure of conversation to engender social unity progress exhibits an underlying faith that some sort of authentic, totally open form of democratic communication—one in which Americans may express themselves freely and truly and be heard, in turn—is possible.[23] It is in this context, marked simultaneously by longings for new forms of social unity (both domestic and international) and by the appearance of sharpening divisions, that we reflect on our relationship to the media that we use to communicate. Social media applications and video-sharing sites, in particular, are evaluated in terms of how they impact these dynamics, as if these tools have some innate disposition toward the ideal of perfected communication.

Lamenting that people ideologically self-segregate online, consuming only news and opinion generated by like-minded people, some commentators have begun to regard social media, suspiciously, as a facilitator of political polarization. This relatively new line of argument has perhaps shaken but not yet dismantled the lofty reputation enjoyed by social-networking applications. It remains commonplace to infer from the decentralized structure and easy accessibility that they are threats to repressive regimes, tools of democratic self-expression that empower common people by enabling them to connect and interact. The speed with which certain words and images can spread across the network seems to realize the ideal of a universal plane of cultural experience, one that traverses any kinds of existing barriers. Indeed, these characteristics give so-called new media a powerful ideological rationale, one that suggests that they continue to have an intrinsically uplifting message for humanity, in spite of rising concerns about political divisions and nationalist retrenchment.

There are obvious affinities, as Peters would say, drawing on Walter Benjamin's discontinuous historiography, between the utopian-universalist understanding of cinema in the 1910s and 1920s and the contemporary ideology of the internet that make the former much more than a historical curiosity.[24] Among the main targets of contemporary "technological solutionism" (Evgeny Morozov's term) is human misunderstanding, which the proponents of this ideology, from the leaders of Silicon Valley corporations to theorists of technology, appear to believe can be overcome simply by correcting inefficiencies in and impediments to networked communications. As Morozov argues, "the Internet" has, itself, become a "fuzzy," "all-encompassing" abstraction, with little resemblance to the actual technological infrastructure to which it refers. This rhetorical imprecision is a symptom of our tendency to locate in any new communications medium an inner truth or essence that will become fully manifest over time.[25] In the case of the internet, the presumed message is cosmopolitan. The medium's remarkable ability to put people around the world in contact with one another is a sign of its ability to topple the linguistic, social, and cultural walls that separate them—to reveal or produce a basic human sameness.[26]

Morozov's polemic, *To Save Everything, Click Here: The Folly of Technological Solutionism*, quotes a litany of pronouncements about internet-related phenomena, which sound quite like the things that procinema writers were saying in the early 1920s. For instance, he quotes Facebook founder Mark Zuckerberg asserting in 2008 that a "lack of connectedness and lack of communication," rather than "deep hatred[s]," are to blame in the Israeli-Palestinian conflict—and that, "by enabling people from diverse backgrounds to easily connect and share their ideas, [Facebook] can decrease world conflict in the short and long term."[27] The prevalence of this type of argument—as well as the American news media's tendency to greet any social-media application that becomes popular as unquestionably transformative—reflects the extent to which the internet's innate wisdom, its presumed ability to provide "an intellectual template for how society itself should be organized," has gained traction in contemporary America.[28]

Morozov attributes such "Internet-centrism" to our collective tendency to gravitate toward technologies that seem revolutionary, overstating their novelty relative to the ones that they displace. This "fake novelty" is precisely what allows new technologies to seem like neutral agents of change (as opposed to the products of specific material structures) and to be granted relevance in a range of contexts (especially politics) outside of the one in which they originally operate.[29] Importantly, the desire for "epochal" technologies produces a kind of amnesia about the history of technology.[30] Internet theory, for one, seems remarkably ignorant about those early epochs in which new technologies have been greeted with triumphalist rhetoric and utopian projects that, in time, proved unrealizable.[31] Ironically in this case, the new technology derives its governing ideology from one of the very older communications media—cinema—that it is meant to have killed off in the very process of staking its claim to historical finality.

One goal of *The Movies as a World Force* is to provide a corrective to this historical amnesia by showing how, with the utopian-universalist cinema discourse, a fully elaborated idea of media essence arose for the first time. Reflecting the Enlightenment's faith in the progress of knowledge as a means of perfecting human conduct, the reduction of strife and war to effects of distance and disconnection emerged, of course, well before the time period being examined here. And cinema was by no means the first industrial technology to be treated as a means of overcoming separation and, in turn, misunderstanding. Similar prognostications about the transformative impact of the new forms of connection, exchange, and dialogue had greeted the emergence of railroads, electrical power generation, and telegraphy in the nineteenth century.[32]

Likewise, photography preceded cinema in being regarded as a universal alphabet, a picture language intelligible to speakers of any language—and as a means for humanity to represent itself to itself as a totality.[33] What cinema did that so excited its observers was to merge photography's magical imaging function with large-scale industrial production and global networks of distribution. As novelist Jack London put it in 1915, the American cinema of the silent-feature era seemed to "annihilat[e]" all forms of "time and distance," "bring[ing] together the peoples of the world."[34] Uniformly distributing images to large, geographically disparate audiences, it was a medium of mass communication with a cosmopolitan message encoded in its very workings, promising to bring in a final, perfected state: communication, the end of history, a single empire that could span the globe.

Writing in the *Atlantic Monthly*, essayist Agnes Repplier noted the ways in which, by 1925, the theoretical discourse on moving pictures—just like the discourse on "the internet" would, decades later—had floated free of the material structures of cinema, allowing them to be treated as plausible instruments of all kinds of social reformation. Repplier begins her piece by dividing the "people who write about moving pictures" into "two classes": "The first class tells us of the marvels of the mechanism and the dizzy cost of production; the second class, of the lofty ideals which animate producers, and of the educational value of films."[35] Repplier acknowledges that she can understand the appeal of the reports belonging to this first category. Detailing the expenses lavished in making particular films, such stories, a contemporary fixture of both film-fan and popular-interest magazines, offer the reader a highly "satisfactory" opportunity to contemplate vast sums of money.[36] Anticipating Morozov's reaction to contemporary internet theory, Repplier is, however, bemused by what the second category of cinema "enthusiasts" have to say. Discussing the "benefactions" rather than the "business" of motion pictures, these writers espouse their transformative intellectual and cultural influence.[37] And while the second class of writers' estimate of the medium's value is even higher than that of their business-minded counterparts, it is immeasurably more abstract.

Of course, Repplier's summary includes only procinema writers; she altogether ignores those detractors who saw motion pictures as morally corrupting and called for them to be more rigorously censored. In limiting herself to writers characterizing cinema as an educational and peacemaking force, Repplier registers the fact that a highly utopian discourse about cinema had captivated the medium's American partisans in the mid-1920s. Attempting to make sense of this discourse, Repplier astutely discerns that the second class of cinema enthusiasts always make one or more of three claims about the medium. First, these writers assert that motion pictures are the most powerful mechanism of instruction available to humanity because they are more efficient than any other existing medium of communication (this is a scientific notion) and because they leave an especially profound mental "'impression'" (this is an aesthetic notion).[38] I call this "the gnostic claim" about cinema.[39] Second, these writers argue that, because motion pictures are universally understandable (accessible to all and unencumbered by any barriers of language, class, or nationality), the movie theater becomes the ultimate educational institution, a veritable "people's university."[40] I call this "the cultural democracy claim." Third, these writers conclude that, by virtue of their gnostic and democratizing tendencies, motion pictures intrinsically promote understanding among the varied peoples of the world and, in turn, international peace. I call this final assertion "the millennialist claim."[41]

Repplier's primary exhibit of the second class of film writing is "Motion Pictures as a Social Force" (1925), by the painter and art historian Louis Weinberg, a text that she reads alongside published statements by Will Hays, president of the Motion Picture Producers and Directors of America (MPPDA), and the screen star and producer Douglas Fairbanks.

She notes that all three men state their claims in a way that is "obviously serious, and obviously sincere," and yet they offer no supporting evidence or explanatory rationale. "What have moving pictures done to so vivify the world?" Repplier wonders. How is it that "the good offices of the cinema" enable intergroup understanding, and moreover, why should such understanding be expected to prevent war?[42] In short, how have these claims become articles of faith among a certain constituency of defenders of the motion-picture medium?

Repplier's piece points to a larger contemporary phenomenon, but mentioning just those three texts explicitly, it only hints at the remarkable quantity of utopian-universalist cinema writing that had been published in the previous ten years. Indeed, by the time of Repplier's writing, the usage of the tropes that she identifies had begun to reach a kind of crescendo, the culmination of a surge that began during the late stages of World War I.[43] Further, it had gained currency with a wide array of constituencies: motion-picture artists, industry leaders, film-trade journalists, cultural critics, and literary authors of different kinds. Labeling cinema an educational "instrument" akin to "the written alphabet and the printed word" and predicting that it will one day supplant these technologies "in the study program of schools and colleges," Weinberg's "Motion Pictures as a Social Force" echoes the gnostic statements confidently made by contemporaries like Charlotte Perkins Gilman, Herbert Francis Sherwood, and the authors of various instruction manuals and behind-the-scenes books.[44] Likewise, Weinberg's celebration of cinema's ability to democratize dramatic storytelling, satisfying on a broad scale the deep-seated, elemental need for "vicarious experience and release for dreams and longings," echoes prominent "cultural democracy" defenses of cinema mounted by Rupert Hughes, Terry Ramsaye, Robert Sherwood, and Hays himself.[45] In both of these respects and in its imagery of a "worldwide audience" coalescing around "glimpses of world events," his essay, finally, follows in the Progressive-internationalist vein of Edward S. Van Zile's *That Marvel—the Movie: A Glance at Its Reckless Past, Its Promising Present, and Its Significant Future*.[46]

Although many of the texts referred to earlier have received little to no scholarly attention, they all traffic in an idea that is, to be sure, familiar to historians of American silent cinema: what Miriam Hansen labeled the "universal-language metaphor."[47] Recent scholarship on American silent cinema has recognized the frequency with which writings about film from "the first [two] decades of the twentieth century and especially . . . the second" make "reference . . . to its potential to serve as a universal language."[48] And the prevalence of this commonplace during the period is widely noted in contemporary film studies textbooks and topical anthologies.[49] The writers that I have identified so far, from the second and third decades of the twentieth centuries, are certainly working in this widely acknowledged tradition. All of them characterize cinema—the medium generally, or American productions specifically—as totally accessible and understandable by all without translation: "[Film] is the long-sought 'universal language,'" writes Gilman, "for it spreads communication world-wide as fast as the eye can follow."[50] In a similar vein, John Amid wonders, "Have you ever happened to think: the world has at last found a universal language? . . . Motion pictures made in one country may be shown in another, and find appreciation. Films produced in America may go to all the countries in the world, and do."[51]

In fact, the universal-language metaphor had become so ubiquitous in discussions of cinema that, in 1924, Fairbanks could begin his essay on the Hollywood film industry with the statement "It's an old story—the one of the universal language of American films."[52] A rote feature of the discourse, the metaphor tended to be accompanied by one or more of three other references: to the Esperanto movement, to the Tower of Babel story in the book of Genesis, and/or to ancient techniques of pictographic communication.[53] Van Zile's phrase "Esperanto of the Eye" is well known, while Amid sees film as having accomplished in a mere twenty-five years what earlier "so-called 'universal' languages" never could.[54] In a piece on the role of American motion pictures in boosting Allied morale during World War I, William Brady writes, "Ever since the dawn of history, the people of the earth have been seeking some common bond of communication. Here it is: the first answer to the Tower of Babel; the Universal Language."[55] Herbert Francis Sherwood employs the latter two points of reference, asserting that "motion pictures might have saved the situation when the Tower of Babel was built" and comparing cinema to the "primitive . . . method" of "picturisation"; he even stakes cinema's universal-language claim on its being "a lineal descendant of the cave man's method of communicating with his fellow."[56]

As much as they gravitate toward language metaphors, the key proponents of the utopian-universalist discourse of cinema during the silent-feature era relate to the idea of language in a novel way. Rather than seeing language as an inert tool or instrument, they begin to treat it as an active force or agency in its own right: as an energy that bonds and melds human beings into unified bodies. In other words, these writers, for the first time, begin to attribute an innate essence or message to the medium, which becomes the warrant for their claims that its growth and expansion will inevitably steer humanity toward the ideal of communication. The idea of language as force represents an insistently modern-technological, machinic rearticulation of the Esperanto metaphor of film. And it is this particular American iteration of that metaphor that film historians have so far overlooked.

In his synoptic study of the literature, philosophy, and criticism published in English during the watershed year 1922, literary scholar Michael North offers the start of a corrective to this oversight. North points out the surprisingly positive manner in which sameness and collective melding are represented during this period—surprising because of the seemingly totalitarian associations that such tropes carry for his own contemporary readers. North's discussions of two key Hollywood novels from 1922, Hughes's *Souls for Sale* and Henry Leon Wilson's *Merton of the Movies*, demonstrates that the film industry's defenders promoted a new model of mass-imagined community formation as a coherent alternative to the one advocated by film censor Ellis Paxson Oberholtzer and other like-minded people. Predicated on an entirely different set of intellectual underpinnings, this alternative model, North shows, made virtues of the very things that, many people feared, the movies demanded of their audiences: standardization and self-alienation. And more than just promoting the movies by making these experiences seem pleasurable, Hughes's and Wilson's novels use the movies to promote what they characterize as new and transformative style of social experience. In a brief but highly instructive moment, North aligns these novels—and, implicitly, nonfiction procinema writings by Van Zile and Hays—with Walter Lippmann's proposals for community formation in *Public Opinion* (1922). Like Lippmann, these writers seem to jettison the idea of a canon of moral imperatives and taboos in favor of a shared "*machinery* of knowledge" that would serve to foster social cohesion at a different mental and spiritual level.[57]

Lippmann proves to be a massively helpful figure to cite here. Even though, by the time Lippmann wrote *Public Opinion*, he had become quite skeptical of commercial mass media, he identified cinema as just such a "machinery of knowledge" earlier on. In a fascinating aside in *Drift and Mastery* (1914), Lippmann, sounding very much like a utopian-universalist cinema writer, declares, "Instruments of a coöperative mind are being forged, be it the world-wide motion picture or some immense generalization of natural science."[58] Within the ambit of liberal political philosophy inhabited by Lippmann at this point in his career, the "world-wide motion picture" (his term for films reaching a global audience) becomes an "instrument" for forging cogent, even enlightened public opinion. According to this way of thinking, standardization becomes salvation.[59]

If the universal-language metaphor discourse is, in its own right, *standardized* by 1915, then it is also subtly revised and repurposed in the decade that follows to fit the emergent forms of social and political thought reflected in Lippmann's paean to the "world-wide motion picture."[60] Lippmann's fusion of the scientific and the mystical in this formation is quite telling, anticipating the ways in which utopian procinema writers during and after World War I would increasingly come to talk about film culture in terms of the production, expansion, and distributions of "forces." As Weinberg's title, "Motion Pictures as a Social Force," indicates, the analogy between cinema and language is increasingly overshadowed by an analogy between cinema and a still more vague, expansive concept of "energy," which appears to straddle the physical and metaphysical realms.

For Weinberg, the historical telos of art is "increase[d] carrying power": every new technology of picture-making or storytelling has served to expand the "circle" of people affected by individual works of art.[61] As the latest step in this historical progression, cinema comes closer than any prior technology in realizing what Weinberg understands as the state of "perfection," that a "single" work will be "carr[ied]" to a global audience: "[Motion pictures] make it more than likely that the whole world will yet respond as one tribe to the picture stories presented by the bards of the future."[62] In this account, the "essentially modern" technology of motion pictures forges a "worldwide audience" in a mystical cultural sense ("as one tribe") that is representable in quasi-scientific terms, global film spectatorship here being compared to a complex circuitry for the transference of binding, magnetic energy.[63] Here Weinberg echoes the pithy phrase of Douglas Fairbanks, who had earlier prognosticated about "the future of the movies as a world force."[64] Speaking the same year as Weinberg's essay was published, Hays describes film entertainment as "rivet[ing] the girders of society," while his interviewer muses on cinema as a "medium of idea-transference."[65] Writing during the war, Herbert Francis Sherwood would wax poetic about the immeasurable "lifting force [and] power" of "the photoplay," predicting that it would serve to "bring all degrees of men together into a co-ordinated organism, working in harmony for the greater things of the world," before chastising would-be "reformers of the drama" for failing to see its remarkable "binding" abilities.[66] In these texts, cinema goes from being a "universal language" to being, as the actress Lillian Gish later put it, "a universal *engine*" that connects and binds.[67]

In the decade after 1915, the American film industry adopted as part of its official self-representation both the universal-language metaphor and this broader vision of the movies as a world. As North emphasizes, the Hollywood film industry was faced with a "moral crusade against the movies in general" touched off by a series of highly publicized scandals involving film stars in 1922–1923.[68] Created in order to mount a public-relations campaign that could mend the studios' tattered image and repel mounting calls for reform and censorship, the MPPDA found it expedient to embrace the idea that, as Repplier puts it, "film is to be the peacemaker of the future."[69] As North writes, "One of the strongest arguments that Will Hays could mount against the forces of censorship was that restrictions on the universal language of the screen would destroy the world's most powerful instrument for international understanding."[70] In other words, the industry's strategy was to overwhelm calls to eliminate morally corrupting representations from films by stressing the medium's international agency—to portray it as mystically bent toward global uplift.

Such portrayals abound in Hays's writings and interviews throughout the 1920s.[71] Repplier quotes a few lines from the 1924 essay in which Hays states, "The motion picture can do more, I believe, than any other existing agency to *unite the peoples of the world* by bringing about better understandings not only between man and man, but between nation and nation, and surely no greater thing can be done."[72] In a 1925 interview, Hays expounds on the theme of international unity at length:

> I do not believe I am too enthusiastic or too visionary when I say that the motion picture may be—possibly will be—the greatest instrument humanity has yet known for the bringing about of understandings between man and man, between group and group and between nation and nation. When we know one another, we do not hate one another. When we do not hate, we do not make war. Wars—and lesser conflicts—are caused because groups and people do not understand each other's ideas and beliefs, each other's background and ambitions . . .
>
> The motion picture knows no barriers of distance. We are apt to look upon the distant group or nation as different from ourselves and therefore as inimical. The motion picture knows no barrier of language. We are apt to regard those who do not speak our own tongue as different and inimical. But a few thousand feet of celluloid film can be sent to the ends of the earth to speak the language which everyone understands, civilized or savage—the language of motion pictures. Or, as a distinguished writer has put it, the Esperanto of the Eye.[73]

In his role as the official spokesperson for the studios, Hays provided a blueprint for other leading industry personnel in their shared efforts to combat calls for industry censorship. Characterizing cinema as a limitless medium, able to surpass every "barrier," Hays allies like William C. DeMille, Charles Pettijohn, and, indeed, Fairbanks conjured a juggernaut that could not be harnessed by existing regulatory agencies.[74]

Considering that Hays was speaking only six years after the end of the First World War, it is remarkable to note the ease with which he seems able to envision a solution to war in general. One might reasonably expect the protracted, devastating, international conflict that was World War I to make this sort of reasoning seem naïve. And yet, it is evident that, for people of a certain cast of mind, the war's main effect was to intensify the longing, as Peters describes it, for perfected communication, reinforcing the underlying assumption that miscommunication was to blame for humanity's gravest problems. Within this intellectual climate, claims about media essence—like the utopian-universalist cinema argument—acquire the mystical status of articles of faith, even as film-industry leaders deploy them for clearly instrumental ends.

During and after the war, the film-as-universal-language rhetoric flourishes, in part, because it acquires a new political resonance, getting grafted onto discussions about the prospects for a "World State." For instance, in 1925, Sydney Cohen, retired president of the Motion Picture Theatre Owners of America, offers an esoteric vision of "the League of Nations" being "developed through a union of the motion picture screens of the world."[75] There is no question that he is repeating a well-worn claim here: "The universal language of the eye will bring with it an era of better understanding, a greater appreciation of one another's needs and problems, and more good will toward all."[76] But somehow, for Cohen, the unfolding of the war and the disappointment of Versailles make these claims seem to him more (rather than less) urgent. Cohen's commentary also illustrates the remarkable extent to which deep-seated belief and professional apologetics become indistinguishable in procinema writings from this period.[77] And yet Cohen concludes "Contribution of the Screen to Public Welfare" by agreeing with French art historian Elie Faure's description of the "religious character" of cinema.[78] With all evident sincerity, he states that, reading Faure's *The Art of Cineplastics*, he feels that he has acquired "a new faith added to that which I already have."[79]

The intellectual genealogy of this belief traces back to two main sources: alternative, neoplatonic spiritual traditions and late Progressive-Era, liberal political thought. On the one hand, the writers of the most substantial and complex utopian-universalist treatises drew terms and concepts from late nineteenth- and early twentieth-century New Age movements like mental science, positive thinking, and theosophy. On the other hand, they capitalized on the idealized view of mass medium as a means of forging "enlightened public opinion" that had been established by Lippmann and the other figures associated with what has been called the "new liberalism" of the 1910s. These two traditions, the book demonstrates, overlap in surprising and significant ways, each one having its own rhetoric of cohesion, of binding forces, and of cognitive transference. Enlightened public opinion is fetishized as a force in late Progressive writings on media, invisible but still measurable (representable in quasi-scientific terms), just as the divine, creative cause of the universe is imagined in neoplatonic spiritualism. To be sure, New Age movements are insistently and exuberantly utopian, whereas the utopian elements of Lippmann and his contemporaries' writings are more subtle, tempered by skeptical and pragmatic elements. And yet both traditions place tremendous faith in the notion of corporate structures, suffused with a single, immanent principle.

To register how novel and significant this belief in movies as a world force is, one has only to consider the kind of resistance that it encountered in the debate over film censorship. North notes, far from "mollify[ing]" advocates of increased industry regulation, procinema writers highlighting the "infinite visibility" seemed to confirm what they most feared.[80] As Ruth Vasey explains, "Many [censorship advocates] felt alarm at the prospect of a new venue for the large-scale dissemination of ideas and standards in which traditional moral guardians—parents, teachers, church leaders had no control."[81] The "very universality of film" threatened to make images of immoral conduct ubiquitous, establishing a "new public sphere" that was, by definition, "heterogeneous and disparate."[82] And at a time of rampant nativism and anti-Semitism, the white, Protestant elites who advocated censorship objected in principle to the "melting pot" cosmopolitanism touted by many in the film industry, seeing it as evidence of an international Jewish conspiracy to undermine "American" identity.[83] When viewed in this most crucial context, their claims for the "infinite visibility" of film—not to mention their rhetorical cosmopolitanism—begin to look fairly radical, complicating our sense of how effectively they might have served to advance the industry's agenda.

The faith that people like Hays and Cohen avow is precisely the idea of a cultural, social, and even cognitive uniformity. During this period, thinkers from a variety of backgrounds and political perspectives advocated shared knowledge and collective mirroring as substitutes for traditional moral standards. Supplanting older forms of collective morality, an ideal of cooperative mind made it possible for film to seem like the basis of a new, universal religion—to become both the presumed instrument for spreading a new gospel of international society and an object of a mystical faith in its own right. In the body of primary materials being examined here, the modern age is defined in terms of collective experience. Distinguished as a period of change and novelty, a site of both crisis and opportunity for human beings, modernity here is insistently *corporate*. Everyday life seems, increasingly, to be conducted within large bodies, both actual and virtual, and yet, for the writers studied here, a binding sense of common purpose seems lacking.

Providing the title of the chapter of *Drift and Mastery* where Lippmann envisions emerging "instruments of a coöperative mind," "modern communion" is Lippmann's phrase for the religiopolitical "spirit" that he finds missing in the contemporary world. Modernity, by his account, has stimulated all kinds of cultural progress but has left people "spiritually homeless," "lacking the one supreme virtue of the older creeds, their capacity for binding the world together."[84] For Lippmann, the primary challenge confronting humanity in "the modern age" is to instantiate some kind of faith that will replace this lost "binding" potential—a religious surrogate capable of promoting community formation on the massive scale demanded by the emerging corporate structures of everyday life. In "Modern Communion," Lippmann describes the binding capacity in a variety of different ways: as an antidote to the modern individual's sense of "feebleness before a brutally uninterested universe," as the "assurance of a communion with something outside of [one]self," and as a sense of being involved "essential[ly] . . . in the drama of eternity."[85] Importantly, the goal of fostering modern communion is the primary goal of Progressivism, as Lippmann theorizes it during this period, hoping to replace the kind of moral censure associated with the earlier Progressive-Era tradition of muckraking with a kind of political journalism focused on outlining positive social goods.

As much as Lippmann associates modernity with "spiritual homeless[ness]," he sees the emerging structures of modern life as incipiently communal. In the case of a "common discipline" like science, with practitioners sharing methods on an international scale, or the "common method of public affairs," in which legislation emerging in one country is imitated in another, the seeds of authentic "cooperation" have been planted.[86] Rejecting a "conservative" skepticism toward the "futurist habit of mind," Lippmann allows himself (at least at this point in his career) to read these virtual collaborations as signs that "the old sense of cosmic wonder, [which] call[s] forth devotion to impersonal ends" is being rekindled.[87]

By looking toward the future, Lippmann catches a glimpse of something ancient. The new communion for which he hopes can, it seems, ultimately be expressed only in antimodern terms. The paradox in Lippmann's argument is one that American procinema writers would echo throughout the 1910s and 1920s. Even as they portray the medium as a quintessential product and expression of modern novelty, they associate it with primordial and mystical states of being (humanity before the Tower of Babel, cave dwellers enthralled by pictograms). Cautioning against simplistic understandings, Ben Singer has noted that, since its very earliest European iterations, the "film-and-modernity discourse" has coincided with a seemingly contradictory characterization, which he calls "broadly neo-Romantic and, at least nominally, antimodern."[88] Underneath the "dominant thrust" of this discourse, which associates cinema with "the novel and dynamic dimensions of [early] twentieth century life," another set of associations persists: "the ethereal, the mystical, the atavistic, and the supernatural."[89] Singer finds examples of this fundamentally ambivalent understanding of the medium's relationship to modernity in the "French Impressionist film theory" of Jean Epstein and Antonin Artaud and in Hugo von Hofmannsthal's portrayal of film as a "substitute for dreams."[90] The material examined in *The Movies as a World Force* represents a parallel articulation of this ambivalent "film-and-modernity discourse," in which the medium's capacity for "metaphysical revelation and spiritual transcendence" is said to make it a force of social binding or communion.[91]

Remarkably in the United States context, assertions of the metaphysical and spiritual qualities of cinema do not remain limited to the aesthetic theorizations of obscure artists and intellectuals working in the neo-Romantic vein that Singer highlights. Instead of being treated as the sole purview of idiosyncratic cinephiles, the promise of transcendence becomes the basis of the industry's understanding of what Lee Grieveson calls the "*social functioning* of cinema" during the silent-feature era: "the uses to which it might be put."[92] In his crucial study of silent-era debates about film censorship, *Policing Cinema: Movies and Censorship in Early-Twentieth-Century America*, Grieveson argues that, after the transitional era (1907–1915), the industry decisively shifted how it talked about its products' social uses, relinquishing any claim that films could be instructive or elevating.

In Grieveson's account, the industry adopted a significantly "delimited" account of cinema's social functioning once it found itself mired in censorship controversies prompted by the cycle of so-called white slave films of 1913–1914.[93] Whereas the studios had sought to promote these as exposés of pressing social problems, which could encourage reform and moral uplift, the outcry they provoked made producers entirely question the wisdom of arguing for movies as promoting the public good.[94] Grieveson finds convincing support for his argument in the shifting stance of the National Board of Censorship—the industry-created self-policing organization. As Grieveson shows, after 1914, the board began to advocate for fictional entertainment films with middlebrow themes and against any effort to stir up controversy and thereby propagandize.[95]

Grieveson's chapter on the "white slave" pictures makes a crucial film-historical contribution, demonstrating how the debate they generated "further clarified the definition of what a 'mainstream' cinema would be, setting in place a by and large institutionally accepted boundary line defining the acceptable and unacceptable social functioning of cinema": "This boundary line marked the establishment of a textual, institutional, and discursive formation central to the founding of what scholars have subsequently termed 'classical Hollywood cinema.'"[96] But Grieveson overstates the case when he concludes that the argument for cinema's educational and uplifting uses was a road not taken by the industry after 1914. Attempting to build on and offer a corrective to Grieveson's study, *The Movies as a World Force* shows that this argument does persist, albeit in a significantly modified form.

To be fair, Grieveson acknowledges that, during the war, a "partial reconfiguration of the relation between state and cinema" occurs, which seems to harken back to the jettisoned (as he sees it) idea that "the power of moving pictures could . . . be harnessed for positive purposes, creating 'good citizenship' and sustaining democracy."[97] Grieveson bases this statement on the wartime collaboration between the Committee on Public Information (CPI) and the National Association of the Motion Picture Industry (NAMPI). Grieveson concludes, however, that this "reconfiguration . . . was severely" delimited due to ongoing concerns about how "cinema screens" were being policed by self-appointed moral guardians.[98] I argue that this reconfiguration is far more significant than Grieveson allows and is articulated, precisely, as a way of pushing back against the efforts of these guardians. In championing a new, progressive ethos—one that simultaneously is novel and taps into premodern wellsprings—the industry argues for the obsolescence of prohibition-based morality in a way that film historians have overlooked. During and after World War I, the industry reclaims an explicitly reformist and instructive posture in the hyperabstracted guise of the discourse of the movies as a force of mystical binding.

Having emerged as the key concept in the federal government's wartime propaganda efforts, *morale* becomes available to the peacetime film industry as a social good to which it can point. Especially in the early and mid-1920s, the industry latches onto a morale-boosting, happiness-promoting function that can be presented as educational, but not propagandistic, because it transcends any particular form of knowledge, morality, or ideology. During World War I, the film industry, now dominated by what Mark Garrett Cooper calls a corporate "managerial class," allies itself with the federal government bureaucracy and the emergent field of public relations.[99]

Not long before Woodrow Wilson hired him to head up the CPI, public relations pioneer George Creel profiled film star Douglas Fairbanks for *Everybody's Magazine*. Creel begins his 1916 "close-up" of Fairbanks by musing on the contagious cheerfulness that radiates from the star's onscreen visage.[100] He suggests that the "Government ought to hire Douglas Fairbanks, and send him over the country as an agent of the Bureau of Grins."[101] However fanciful Creel's opening gambit is, it reflects a belief in "the future of the movies as a world force," wherein mass-produced visual signs will assume a quasi-official function of managing the national—and by the logic of American exceptionalism, international—mood.[102] Fittingly, Fairbanks would reprint Creel's profile as an appendix to his (likely ghostwritten) positive-thinking manual, *Laugh and Live* (1918), a text in which the star presents himself as a paradigm of the happiness and success that can be achieved through the proper management of mental energies.[103]

Hollywood's claiming of this particular social function depends, I argue, upon a middlebrow acceptance of New Age spiritualism that commences with the utopian-universalist procinema writings of the World War I era. In this body of written material, we find a parallel case to that of early twentieth-century German occult literature, as described by Walter Benjamin. In his 1932 essay, "Light from Obscurantists," Benjamin traces the process whereby, "over the last few decades," literature of "the occult sciences" has undergone an "improvement of status," moving "from anonymous obscurity to brightly lit window displays."[104] With its promises that success and happiness are in easy reach of all people, this literature becomes, Benjamin argues, a tool for reinforcing the "meaninglessness of economic struggle."[105] Benjamin theorizes the wide embrace of such magical thinking as a symptom of the loss of public faith in traditional "general education"—and of its ability to foster socioeconomic mobility.[106] The spiritualist texts popping up in fancy shop windows, Benjamin asserts, collectively promote the ideology that the desiderata of "higher class" life can be seized upon directly, independently of any process of acquiring particular bodies of knowledge or forms of material advantage.[107]

Benjamin's essay is useful for thinking about American silent cinema culture because it charts the conflation of mysticism—the faith in the transformative power of "energy," mind over matter—and consumerism within middlebrow culture. The utopian-universalist cinema argument and its deployment by the Hollywood film industry is an emblematic site of this conflation. Its history illustrates precisely the dynamics that Benjamin theorizes: a reciprocal consumerization of spirituality and spiritualization of consumption—to the point that these categories become completely intertwined. Here the economic basis of the circulation of putatively morale-boosting images (publicity) redeems spiritualism by removing its disreputably obscurantist and bohemian associations, while at the same time the evidently noble or lofty aspects of spiritualism elevate the world of consumerism above a vulgar, materialistic footing. In this process, occult meanings and the material object become completely indistinguishable.

The crucial point here is that the revised argument for cinema's elevating and educating function is not merely a marketing ploy. More than an idealized self-representation of how the studios' products might benefit consumers, this argument is an accurate reflection of the industry's real organization—its material involvement with the society it aimed to influence.[108] To exemplify the antimodern tendency within the "film-and-modernity discourse," Singer cites Jean Epstein's statement that cinema is "psychic" and "supernatural."[109] During the silent-feature era, this notion to some extent constitutes the American film industry's organization and its ways of representing that organization to society at large. To put it another way, the history charted through the following chapters is one not just of a shifting view of the social use of cinema but of an effort to reconceptualize society itself. As Cooper points out, "Cinema's rise [in the mid-1910s] encouraged a new kind of argument about the public," the industry's evolving conception of its audiences both influencing and being influenced by contemporary debates in political theory.[110]

Tracing "the 1920s debate between American intellectuals Walter Lippmann and John Dewey" over how "representation [could] serve the public good," Cooper astutely notes the weight that Hollywood's address to its audiences carried at the beginning of the classical era.[111] Conceiving of film viewers as "universalizable abstraction[s]," heterogeneous members participating in a uniform body of putatively unbounded scope, narrative films provided a seemingly viable model of an international corporate society, an ever-growing global public communicating fluidly.[112] Cooper shows that, although the Hollywood cinema of the era did not present itself as "social science . . . it propagated a need for" organized bodies of visual representation capable of forging a true public out of the amorphousness of modern society.[113] Thus he reads Dewey's and Lippmann's arguments about the creation, management, and tendencies of "the public" in light of the American cinema's restructuring of the idea of mass communication during this period. Notwithstanding their significant misgivings about the movies, these intellectuals, Cooper shows, considered the possibility that "shared 'signs' and 'symbols' [could] constitute the public as such, giving it a common basis of 'opinion.'"[114]

Examining the work of the popular commentator and ex-minister Gerald Stanley Lee, chapter 1 demonstrates the discursive machinations whereby public opinion comes to be idealized as a basis of modern communication and communion. Lee, I argue, defines public opinion in terms of the concept of "the Mirror Screen," which he bases in part on actual motion pictures and which, through the subsequent reception of his work, becomes central to early American film theory. Because Lee is not a film theorist in the strict sense, scholars have completely overlooked his influence, even though he is the writer who first synthesizes the New Age and late Progressive intellectual traditions, making moving pictures a metonym for the transformative power unleashed by modern technology. Chapter 2 shows how Vachel Lindsay takes up Lee's terms and concepts, applying them directly to a speculative account of the medium, which, albeit in slightly simplified forms, becomes the industry's dominant self-representation during the silent-feature era.

Beginning with chapter 2's skeptical discussion of Lindsay's theory of film images as national "hieroglyphics," the remainder of the book teases out the paradoxes of utopian universalism, highlighting the violently exclusive structures—racist, sexist, and colonialist—that sustain the quasi-religious ideal of modern communion. Each of these chapters explores one of the many ways in which, during this period, the Hollywood cinema legitimates itself and consolidates its cultural capital by tapping into the power of a mystical faith in the expansive, unifying force of modern power. At the heart of each chapter is a critical analysis of a particular strategy that Hollywood used to espouse an irrational belief in the transformative energies of the new.

Chapter 3 examines D. W. Griffith's multiperiod melodrama *Intolerance* (Griffith Feature Films, 1916), showing how it makes warfare into the esoteric foundation for a new understanding of peace and recasts modern speed as a salvific agency, which stirs inert social atoms into a cohesive mixture. In chapter 4, I show how Rupert Hughes dramatizes the utopian-universalist argument about cinema in his Hollywood novel, *Souls for Sale* (1922), giving considerable credence to the same occult themes that the arch rationalist Hughes elsewhere sought to debunk. The novel affirms the rising consumer culture of the period and stages the replacement of moralism with the building of morale, a concept that, I argue, Hughes developed during his work as a censor for U.S. military intelligence in World War I.

In chapter 5, I turn to *The Thief of Bagdad* (Douglas Fairbanks Pictures, 1924) and to the positive-thinking tracts penned by its star, Douglas Fairbanks. I show that the basic "mind-over-matter" philosophy espoused by Fairbanks in these books determines both the narrative of the film and the publicity campaign that was orchestrated around the film's production—and that this world view takes the form, in both cases, of a white male hero figure's struggle to overcome a frightening, "dark" inertia that envelops him. The film and the newspaper and magazine stories that circulated about life on set draw on a tradition of representing factories as spectacles of corporate modernity, pioneered by Henry Ford, a mutual admirer of Fairbanks and fellow mental science devotee.

Synthesizing the main insights of the five chapters, the conclusion traces the history that the book has assembled forward into the transition to sound and beyond and considers the ways in which mass media institutions reflect on their own histories. It examines two primary texts, Benjamin Hampton's transitional-era study of the medium, *A History of the Movies* (1931), and Universal's part-talkie *Uncle Tom's Cabin* (1927). Reading these artifacts through the lens of Benjamin's "Light from Obscurantists," it explores the extent to which universal-historical concepts and tropes mark film production in the immediate aftermath of talking pictures' rise to dominance and the ways in which the idea of mass-historical education has served the American film industry's commercial agenda.

Taken together, the primary materials at the center of each chapter do not represent a totality or closed system, but my choices of them are by no means arbitrary. They are contingent both on the strong genealogical ties that bind these texts and films together and on my critical methodology. This methodology consists, in the first place, of the recovery of obscured historical contexts, specifically the intellectual tendencies of the period. More than just a matter of filling informational gaps, this recovery serves to provide an entire theoretical framework (both aesthetic and social) that transforms how we understand key artifacts of the period—both those highlighted in the chapters but also potentially many others that, for reasons of limited space, receive only passing attention there.

Although each chapter unfolds through a series of extended readings, the purpose of my approach is not to privilege close textual analysis or to attempt clever exegesis. Rather it represents an effort to reconstruct an intellectual formation involving technology, communication, and social unity (utopian-universalism) that has been ignored by scholars because it appears obsolete, even fanciful—notwithstanding the obvious persistence of the dream of perfected communication tracked at the beginning of this introduction. Inhabiting this formation, each chapter seeks to read a film or text with it, up to the point at which the act of reading reveals its underlying faults and contradictions. Hence each set of readings simultaneously delineates the mystical, irrational tendencies of the artifact at hand and provides a coherent counterformation: a nonutopian faith in the social value of the preservation (rather than the overcoming) of heterogeneity—a perspective that is pragmatic, but progressive. My critical strategy neither redeems nor dismisses utopian-universalist magic but takes seriously the effects it has within the arena of early twentieth-century American cultural history.

1 *Enlightened Public Opinion*

POSTREFORM PROGRESSIVISM, MENTAL SCIENCE, AND GERALD STANLEY LEE'S "MOVING-PICTURES"

> *World-peace is every man's intimate personal peace, his work and play wrought out in his own life and mounting up into other lives until, like some imperious, mysterious floating electric force in the air, it becomes the atmosphere of the world, like ozone, like lightning, becomes a kind of vast invincible storehouse and powerhouse of all life.*
>
> —Gerald Stanley Lee, *We: A Confession of Faith for the American People during and after the War*[1]

In a characteristically rhapsodic passage from *Crowds: A Moving-Picture of Democracy* (1913), Gerald Stanley Lee envisions a "vast white canvas, spread, as it were, over the end of the world, before which we shall sit together, the audience of the nations."[2] On this "screen" is projected "a moving-picture, a portrait of the human race, that shall reveal man's heart to himself": a "vivid picture of our vast desires" that answers the pressing social questions, "'*What do we want? Where are we going?*'"[3] Despite its resolutely idiosyncratic "fus[ion of] impressionistic sociology [and] modern media," Lee's 1913 nonfiction bestseller, as Russ Castronovo explains, typifies late nineteenth- and early twentieth-century American culture's concern with the potential for "aesthetic perception [to] unif[y] people" within the nation and, increasingly, on a "global" scale.[4] Like many American cultural elites during this period, Lee seeks to make democracy "beautiful," capitalizing on aesthetics' presumed ability to foster "universal accord"—to create social attachments, which, in an era of economic internationalism, could ramify beyond the boundaries of the "nation-state" into some kind of "world citizenship."[5]

For Lee, the principal figure of modern democracy is the crowd, a term he uses to refer to actual assemblies of people in a particular place (pedestrians navigating a busy street) and to virtual masses; the "modern reading public" of newspapers and popular novels is his main touchstone.[6] His writings during this period register a thoroughly corporate social horizon: for better or for worse, people experience modernity within and as large multitudes. Although Lee occasionally expresses concern over the possibility of violent group behavior, his work represents an important alternative theoretical model to the period's "crowd psychology." In contrast to earlier theorists of the "mob mind," who believe that mass experience attenuates rational and moral inhibitions and liberate individuals' "savage destructive instincts," Lee is primarily interested in the utopian potentialities of crowds to express new, transformational moments of "collective subjectivity."[7] All that is needed for the inchoate mass to become a purposeful crowd is for it to become "beautiful" in a Whitmanian sense: aware of itself as sharing a common inspiration or viewable as a single, flowing entity.

In Lee's fantastical tableau of the "vast white canvas," the crowd is made beautiful in both of these ways.[8] On the one hand, the construction of the earth-sized screen constitutes the people of the world as a unified collective. The international population is here, first and foremost, an "audience"; the very activity of having their attention drawn to the same point of interest serves to bring them together—even more than the contents of what they are looking at. On the other hand, the image that this audience views is—albeit in some mystical way that Lee is unable to ever really specify—its own all-inclusive "portrait." The passage encapsulates Lee's broader effort to aestheticize politics on a global scale. Exemplified here by the international motion picture, the modern "mechanical arts" promote unity by broadcasting an image of mass desire that is universal—because it lacks any sort of particularity. The global audience is able to see itself as having one, immanent desire; in the experience of sitting before one single screen, the "human race" reveals itself to itself.

Despite its subtitle, Lee's book has little to say about motion pictures as an actual technology, art form, and cultural phenomenon. And yet, as this chapter will demonstrate, his writing provides the obvious outlines for a script that the cinema's most fervent American partisans would embrace throughout the 1910s and 1920s. Lee's precise equation of aestheticized democracy, the international audience, and the dream of social cohesion becomes integral, in time, to the utopian-universalist story that the American film industry wants to tell about itself. Lee arrives at this equation by drawing concurrently on the revised concept of "Progressive reform" formulated by the "new liberal" political journalists of the 1910s and on the neoplatonic doctrine of "mental science." Tracing both of these intellectual influences and situating them within the historical context in which Lee wrote, this chapter demonstrates the formative influence of Lee's "moving-picture" theory on the utopian-universalist understanding of cinema.

A close reading of Lee's foundational works on mass media and public-opinion formation serves to illustrate a unifying critical insight: the utopian-universalist cinema discourse represents an American, liberal-democratic version of the tendency that Walter Benjamin describes in the epilogue to his famous "Artwork" essay. Gilded with New Age tropes, the late Progressive discourse of media as a force of cooperation aestheticizes the political, substituting spectacular representation (the self-expression of each individual) for the accomplishment of "right"—which Benjamin understands as an alteration of "property relations."[9] In the wake of Lee's formulation, it becomes possible for specific silent feature films to be styled as sites of *voluntary* submission to fantasies of collectivity, even as these films serve to promote the *specific corporate interests* with which the institution of the Hollywood studio system is entangled.

Wor(l)d-Picture

In 1896, Gerald Stanley Lee resigned his ministry at the Park Street Congregational Church in Springfield, Massachusetts, in order to pursue a career as a professional writer. He would publish his first book, *The Shadow Christ*, later that year while beginning to contribute essays and reviews on topics like religion, literature, and politics to major magazines.[10] Lee's departure reflected his growing sense that in modern America, the print media and new communications technologies like the telegraph and motion pictures were usurping the clergyman's influence over the "intellectual and spiritual life of the people."[11] Thus Lee turned to the "pulpit of the book" as a way of evangelizing a national and even international audience.[12] He sought to use the "prophetic" powers of print to shape opinion on a national scale while also addressing himself directly to powerful politicians and industrialists (as if they were parishioners sitting in his pews).[13]

In Lee's major works of the 1910s, he fixates on the structural parallels between traditional Christian religious instruction and modern communications strategies like advertising. Both enterprises, he asserts, are guided by an "inspired minority"; both seek to capture the attention of groups of people; both are concerned with influencing collective behavior; and both attempt to persuade an audience to choose a particular "good."[14] In a move that typifies his hyperbolic style, Lee deduces a series of rigid identities from these broad parallels: Christian religion is and has always been protoadvertising; commercial activities, like shopping, are expressions of spiritual energy; and advertisers are ministers, advertisements their sermons.[15]

In *Crowds*, Lee spins these identities into a vision of a new class of social leaders capable of effectively "attracting and holding" the "attention" of the modern masses—"preachers" whose métier is simultaneously commercial and spiritual: "crowd-men." As much as Lee styles himself as belonging to this group, speaking from the "pulpit of the book," his main goal is to delineate the qualities needed by future elite persuaders.[16] The challenge that faces such men, Lee contends, is to "make word-pictures" of abstract ideas, which can be grasped intuitively and immediately.[17] As Lee's biographer, Gregory Bush, explains, Lee would come to believe by 1913 that the majority of people understand ideas and are persuaded of particular opinions only when they can visualize them. Persuasion, then, is a matter of capturing an image and of transferring it to the mental "screens" of one's audience.[18]

Needless to say, the developing medium of cinema occupies a central place in Lee's thinking during this period. On the one hand, he treats "moving-pictures" (he almost always uses the hyphen) as the definitive modern communication technology, the paragon of the "mechanical arts," broadly speaking. On the other hand, he uses "moving-pictures" as a metonym for the process of circulating pictorialized ideas, describing "crowd-men," for instance, as having "moving-picture minds."[19] In *Crowds*, Lee insists that all "sermons" need to unfold in and through "moving-pictures," even and especially those concerned with moral good: the effective preacher "uses[s] . . . maps of goodness . . . [to] make one see each virtue just where it belongs as a kind of dot, like cities in a geography."[20] The fact that Lee conceives of moral virtues as a series of coordinates that can be mapped and presented in the form of a coherent visual image speaks to his investment in what Martin Heidegger called the "world picture": the idea of the world ("the totality of beings taken . . . as standard-giving and obligating") made "graspable as a picture" (present in front of a perceiving subject).[21]

The world-as-picture idea is definitive for Lee's thought during the period in which he wrote *Crowds* and its successor, *We: A Confession of Faith for the American People during and after the War* (1916). Lee understands vision as the primary means of knowing—to see is to "grasp"—and visually based knowledge as the primary means of social formation.[22] By his logic, the members of a society constitute themselves as a unified group primarily by gazing at images of collectively desired "goods" or by looking at idealized images of themselves—images of desiring and desirable crowds. In as much as social cohesion is the primary goal of religious or spiritual life for Lee, moral teaching becomes entirely subsumed within the process of producing, disseminating, and consuming images of shared desire. The highest vocation of the "man of imagination in modern times" is "to conceive a picture or vision for our Society—our present machine-civilization—a common expectation for people which will make them want to live," and there are seemingly no limits to what this "picture" can encompass or to how many people it may influence.[23]

Word-pictures necessarily become world pictures, as the crucial passage about the "vast white canvas" in *Crowds* makes clear. The idea of technologically reproduced images circulating on a global scale is what enables Lee to envision all nations as a single body. The blank canvas is a metaphor for the pages of his own book and represents his ability as a modern thinker and writer to see the people of the world in a picture. In other words, the existence of the mechanical arts (cinema in particular) enables Lee to adopt a quasi-divine perspective, a perspective in which the utopian future of humanity becomes visible and graspable. If anything and everything can be expressed in a "moving-picture" and if all people might view this same picture, then the human race would seem to be on the verge of appearing in a final, essential form.

As Lee readily admits, his notion of the crowd's utopian progress conflates the political and the aesthetic. He takes as a historical given that "politics and aesthetics can no longer be kept apart."[24] In the first place, the mechanical arts are a force of democratization because they make the experience of the beautiful available on a mass scale; "machinery" (like the printing press and the motion-picture camera), Lee argues, is "making all of the arts democracies" by allowing "beauty [to be] indefinitely multiplied . . . produced in endless copies."[25] Through Lee's characteristically circular reasoning, democracy itself becomes an intrinsically aesthetic practice: "Democracy is democracy for this very reason, and for no other: that all things may be expressed at once in it, and that all things may be given a chance to be expressed at once in it."[26] According to the Romanticism of expression as self-fulfillment, to achieve its social and political destiny, the crowd must simply make itself visible (or audible) in a beautiful form.

The particular confusion of self-expression with the exercise of political rights is precisely the logic of totalitarianism as Benjamin would explain it in the early 1930s: rather than granting the masses their "right to change property relations," fascism grants them "a chance to express themselves."[27] In Lee's vignettes, just as in the fascist displays that Benjamin discusses, this self-expression occurs in and through the spectacle of an oceanic mass, its constituent members' personalities subsumed into a totality and basking in the affirmation of the charismatic leader. Aesthetic beauty is, for him, necessarily predicated on a mystical idea of fusion, which is, on the one hand, overtly communitarian and totalitarian and, on the other, related to a complex, gnostic understanding of visual perception.

In his passage on the "audience of nations," Lee speaks vaguely of a "portrait" representing "the human race." Since no human vantage point could encompass every single living person's image in any meaningful way, the unity evoked here is one of affect—"man's heart [as revealed] to himself."[28] In other, rhetorically similar passages, Lee uses the idea of a "composite" face to envision multiple countenances "dissolving" into one, stopping short, however, of explaining how such a process might work.[29] The reader wonders, Does some new face that melds features of the others appear, or are multiple images held in superimposition? Could this unity be not actually graphic at all? For instance, describing a crowd of people gathered to watch an air show, he waxes about "those thousands of faces that had gathered up in some way out of themselves *a kind of* huge crowd-face before [the observer—that is, the writer himself]."[30] In other cases, he will describe a complex, mimetic relationship between American presidents like Theodore Roosevelt and Woodrow Wilson, whereby the faces of these individual "crowd-men" already act as "portraits" of the masses. After "studying" a photograph of Wilson, Lee describes the man's "countenance as a national film."[31]

With its peculiar fusion of aestheticized politics, gnostic revelation, and the concept of the world-as-picture, Lee's argument in *Crowds* has two primary consequences for silent-era procinema discourse. First of all, it turns "expression" into a kind of political, social, and spiritual panacea. Not simply a means of accomplishing particular goals, expression becomes a goal in itself and an intrinsic good. Lee affords utopian potential even to facial "expressions": the "composed" visage manifests the "soul," and once the soul is manifest, the individual or group has achieved essential being, becoming knowable or understandable to the rest of humanity.[32] In his review of the sequel to *Crowds*, *We*, Randolph Bourne aptly noted Lee's tendency to fetishize "expression," chiding him for "present[ing] to the American people the novel idea that inexpressibleness is the root of all evil."[33]

Second, Lee seems to ban negation from instruction and learning, especially in the domain of morality. Because all knowledge is visual, based in pictures transmitted from one subject to another (what he calls "maps of goodness"), and because the irrepressible tendency of all things is toward self-expression, the practice of teaching through prohibitions becomes impossible, inconceivable even. A prohibition or an argument against a particular behavior cannot, within Lee's system, be productively communicated, simply because a negative cannot be *pictured*. Criticisms and reprimands are antithetical to instruction because they communicate no graspable visual knowledge.

With respect to this second point, the phenomena of product advertisement and shopping are definitive for Lee. Just as there is no such thing as a window display of "things one will not buy," so is it impossible to make a person be good by telling her or him what not to do.[34] From here, Lee's propensity for syllogism leads him to conclude that whatever is exhibited (through the various "motion-pictures" emanating from the machinery of modern communication) is itself good. Whatever an individual or group expects, wants, or idealizes must be expressed. Conversely, any attempt to communicate or instruct through negatives not only is bound to fail but also amounts to a failure to embrace expression as a power of/for the good.

Given Lee's background as a Christian minister, it is not surprising that Moses looms large in his thinking about moral instruction. The "contradiction in terms" represented by the window display of "things one will not buy" seems, for Lee, to originate with Moses, "the lawyer," and with "the Ten Commandments, that is a list of nine things they must never do any more, and of one that they must."[35] Moses's "fundamental principle"—"getting people concentrated on not getting concentrated on nine things"—was illogical as a way of promoting the good, unsuited for founding a nation, and ultimately responsible for producing the disproportionate number of "wicked people [there seem to be] among the Hebrews in the Old Testament."[36] And yet Moses is also the archetype of the crowd-man; his leadership of the Exodus is largely responsible for the fact that the Hebrew scripture has "made all other nations the moral passengers of the Hebrews for two thousand years."[37]

In the opening pages of *Crowds*, Lee celebrates "the Bible of the Hebrews" as the definitive expressive portrait of collective desires, using terms that echo his rhapsody on the gargantuan "moving-picture, [the] portrait of the human race, that shall reveal man's heart to himself." The Hebrew Bible, he says, is "the sublimest, most persistent, most colossal, masterful attempt ever made by men to look forth upon the earth, to see all men in it, like sprits hurrying past, and to answer the question, 'WHERE ARE WE GOING?'"[38] Here Lee ventures an esoteric reading of scripture, understanding the text as the repository of a spirit of social bonding. Forced to reflect on the masses of people who have engaged with this text before them, the modern Bible reader is afforded a vision of "all the men" on earth pursuing a shared goal—a "composite" image of the whole of Judeo-Christian civilization. The text is both a representation of mass movement (all of humanity as a single crowd) and an articulation (or exhibition) of a positive goal, ideal, or desire that subsequent masses of humanity can pursue.

Lee's larger point here is that the authentic (though occulted) purpose of traditional Judeo-Christian religiosity has been to provide a socially unifying world picture. Its moral teachings are compelling not because of their specific content but because of their historical efficacy in commanding international *attention*. For Lee, making people "look" is "the secret religion of all the religions."[39] One cannot help but read Lee's statement as a more reductive and rhetorically ostentatious version of the statement from Walter Lippmann's *Drift and Mastery* (1914), cited in this book's introduction: "The one supreme virtue of the older creeds [is] their capacity for binding the world together."[40] Indeed, like Lippmann, Lee emphasizes the historically "binding" effect of religion and argues that the fragmentation and alienation imposed by modern life urgently necessitates that a substitute for this lost capacity be found.

Postreform Progressivism

Upon the publication of *Crowds* in 1913, Lee wrote to Theodore Roosevelt to express his hope that the book would come to be viewed as "the textbook of the Progressive Movement. . . . The Uncle Tom's Cabin of American business."[41] Illustrating his grandiose sense of himself as a would-be "crowd-man," Lee here envisions his book as the first to totally capture the one fundamental problem of his era (the need for a single direction for humanity to pursue) and, therefore, to be capable of providing a solution to it. Cast here as a text with a universal readership—it is important here to recall that it was still commonplace at this time to rank Stowe's novel as the most widely read book in the United States, *after the Bible*—*Crowds* here aspires to make people of all nations its "moral passengers." Such a characterization raises the question, however, of what sense it makes for Lee to call his work "Progressive." Lee opposes negative instruction in principle, sees prohibitions as discouraging good behavior, and looks with suspicion at narrowly focused projects of moral improvement. Is he not, then, opposed to the project of reform, which we tend to see as synonymous with the Progressive movement? Under what definition of the term could *Crowds* be counted as a Progressive "textbook"?

Lee's work reflects and, to some extent, participates in the transformation of Progressive intellectual culture that occurs between 1910 and 1917, the period that sees the rise of the "new liberalism."[42] The new liberalism is historian Charles Forcey's term for the joint efforts of Herbert Croly, Walter Weyl, and Walter Lippmann to "move liberalism in a new direction" through the books of political philosophy that they published and through the magazine that they founded in 1914, the *New Republic*.[43] Forcey notes that the three writers sought to fill the void left by the demise of the muckraking exposé and, thereby, steer the Progressive movement away from what they saw as its outdated belief in a "Jeffersonian" ideal of individual freedom.[44] In spite of the significant ideological differences among them, Croly, Weyl, and Lippmann shared the sense that earlier Progressive political thought was weakened by its essential distrust of consolidated power—its tendency to want to place restrictions on any kind of large organization, especially corporations.

The new liberals espoused a contrary, "Hamiltonian" view of "conscious, co-operative" action as a means of effecting "Progressive" social change and saw the federal government as capable of harnessing and directing (rather than just checking) the power of industrial and other large-scale organizations toward democratically agreed-upon goals.[45] From Weyl's emphasis on commodity consumption as the single activity that binds all Americans together regardless of class position to Croly's commitment to strong nationalism, these writers envisioned progress as occurring through the harnessing of new, distinctly modern social forces—even though such collective action might be seen as encroaching on the freedom of the individual.[46] The constraints of this chapter will not allow me to go beyond such a terse and admittedly simplified discussion of the basic tenets of the new liberalism, nor will it permit any kind of in-depth exploration of the distinct versions of this broad philosophy articulated by Croly, Weyl, and Lippmann, respectively.

These broader concerns aside, what is most significant here is how the new-liberal confidence in the "organizations that [keep] modern society from flying apart" impacts Progressive thinking about reform.[47] During this period of ferment, Forcey notes, all three writers began not only to oppose antitrust legislation as a feature of economic policy but also to view efforts to curb the expansion of corporate-industrial power as symptomatic of an outdated concept of reform as affected only by restraining mechanisms.[48] As Lippmann puts it in *A Preface to Politics* (1913), "If corporations and government have indeed gone on a joy ride, the job of reform is not to put up fences, Sherman Acts and injunctions into which they can bump, but to take the wheel and steer."[49] For the new liberals, the Sherman Antitrust Act of 1890 would become the paradigmatic case of an approach to reform that is essentially, as Lippmann puts it, repressive or "taboo" based.[50]

For Croly and Lippmann especially, the focus of the reformist project shifts broadly from moral restriction (the fight against crime and corruption) and checks on socioeconomic power (trust busting) and toward creatively "extricat[ing] the forces that move" the world, guiding them to worthy ends.[51] Along with this shift away from repression, Croly and Lippmann (though not Weyl) embrace an aestheticized view of social "cohesion" and an almost mystical faith in the unity of values.[52] In their work, national unity becomes a good in and of itself, a reformist goal subsuming all others. More specifically, Croly calls for business tycoons and other kinds of inspired leaders—much like Lee's crowd-men—to take a leading role in national regeneration; these "half-saint, half-hero" figures, as Forcey calls them, are meant to help promote such cohesion by articulating the will of the people.[53] Lippmann similarly charges "far-sighted businessmen" and "statesmen," those people (like, in his view, Roosevelt) closest "to the original forces of public opinion," with guiding and enhancing, rather than damming up, "the motor currents in social life."[54]

In Lippmann's writing, the characterization of these "currents" verges on what Forcey calls the irrational or anti-intellectual.[55] Lippmann seems at times to abstract his key terms from specific political-economic contexts, describing instead a generalized struggle between the repressive tendency (antidemocratic, artificially imposed law) and the expansion of vital forces (organic human needs and wants).[56] Lippmann's antipathy toward taboo and repression in his 1913–1914 writings reflects his reading of Freud, Nietzsche, and Bergson. As Forcey shows, Lippmann construes human "instincts" as vital forces that need to be affirmed rather than denied while at the same time projecting what Freud says about the individual psyche onto a collective horizon.[57] What Freud says about the dangers of repression vis-à-vis "individual instinct" Lippmann applies directly to "social forces."[58]

For instance, prohibitions placed on gambling or alcohol consumption, which Lippmann abhors, leave the "deeply rooted" desires for stimulation or companionship that drive these practices unsatisfied, driving them toward more destructive ends.[59] What is needed instead is some kind of substitute, more salutary means of satisfying these desires, which would serve to affirm the principle that "human nature seems to have wants that must be filled."[60] Hence Lippmann's blanket critique of traditional reform campaigns: "Unless the reformer can invent something which substitutes attractive virtues for attractive vices, he will fail. He will fail because human nature abhors the vacuum created by the taboo."[61] In his criticism of "liberal" churches (by which he means churches espousing the Social Gospel), Lippmann takes this emphasis on the need for "attractive"-ness a step further. He says that these churches' efforts to minister to the needy and to fight civic corruption are all fine and good but ultimately reflect a "shallow," impoverished view of the religious mission.[62] For a church to focus on "serving everyday needs"—doing good in specific, local ways—is for it to neglect the deeper "need" to "paint a background for our lives, to nourish a Weltanschaung [*sic*], strengthen men's ultimate purposes and reaffirm the deepest values of life."[63]

As for Lee, the objective in religion for Lippmann is the creation of social cohesion—the beautiful crowd—by tapping into latent, collectively held ideas; he uses H. G. Wells's term "mental hinterland" here to refer to such unconscious ideas held by "the collective mind," which must be given "ultimate" expression.[64] The modern masses need some kind of suitably compelling ("attractive") target of desire on which to fixate. Privileging sublime inspiration above pragmatic acts of benevolence and abhorring the "vacuum" of desire left by "taboos," Lippmann sounds very much like Lee in these statements. The two writers' work converge around the effort to divest reform from the effort to place checks on other people's behaviors: it is in this specific regard that it makes sense to call both "Progressive."

In spite of all these obvious parallels, Lee's brand of Progressivism remains, in many ways, quite different from that of Lippmann and the other new liberals. It is crucial to remember that for all his criticism of the repressive tendencies of the Jeffersonian individualist model, Lippmann's primary criticism of the Progressive movement in its initial phase is that it assumes progress to be inevitable. Lippmann and Croly both reject the belief in "pervasive economic prosperity guaranteed by free institutions": the idea that as long as large structures of power are broken up, the rest will "take care of itself."[65] For Lippmann and Croly, this attitude has created an excess of "freedom"—the state of "chaos" that Lippmann labels "drift."[66] For Weyl, Croly, and Lippmann, all of whom support varying degrees of nationalization of "major industries," the nation's social and economic destiny must be secured through active, conscious work—"mastery," to use Lippmann's keyword.[67] From this perspective, Lee's rejection of such governmental involvement in economic planning looks like a tacit embrace of "drift." Moreover, his uncomplicated faith in crowd-men acting on their own instincts to pursue social good makes him neither liberal nor Progressive in the alternative sense defined by these writers.

From the new liberals' standpoint, Lee's inability to see a significant role for organized labor in the business-driven transformation of American society that he promotes would seem also to give his thought a paternalistic, conservative edge. In fact, in *Drift and Mastery*, Lippmann offers just such a critique of Lee as a naïve optimist, underneath whose "mystic and rhetorical commercialism" lies an unfortunate fatalism: "Nothing would be easier than to shout for joy, and say that everything is about to be fine: the business men are undergoing a change of heart. That is just what an endless number of American reformers are shouting, and their prophet is Gerald Stanley Lee. The notion seems to be that workers, politicians, consumers and the rest are to have no real part in the glorious revolution which is to be consummated for them."[68] Reflecting a vital strand of pragmatism running through Lippmann's writings, this criticism appears warranted, highlighting as it does a major limitation in Lee's thinking about "reform." At the same time, we must be careful not to let a statement like this obscure the extent to which Lippmann himself is prone to doing the very thing that he charges Lee with doing. Notwithstanding Lippmann's greater hesitancy to declare victory, he shares Lee's habit of "disentangling" a single "hopeful thread" from the "brain-splitting complexity" of the "modern world" and "calling it the solution of the problem."[69]

As for Lee, the possibility of widespread change lies, for Lippmann, in delineating some kind of "general process of thought" that can propel reform on any number of fronts.[70] He calls for a spiritual transformation that addresses the need not for "a special reform embodied in a particular statute, but a way of going at all problems."[71] In its fixation on totality, Lippmann's critical approach to reform is, in the end, scarcely less utopian than Lee's. In Lippmann's contemporaneous writings, "enlightened public opinion" becomes the would-be "solution" to the modern "problem"—the social fragmentation caused by the failure of existing institutions to articulate a sufficiently sublime, unifying world-view.[72] During this period of his career, Lippmann treats "public opinion" as the expression of "the real impulses of men."[73] Coming out of Lippmann's reductive Freudian model, public opinion possesses an intrinsic positivity—it is akin to desire or instinct—and cannot be checked with prohibitions. By contrast, "public opinion" must be liberated, augmented, and guided by those institutions and their leaders who are able to intuit the will of modern crowds.[74]

To become "enlightened," "public opinion" must be expressed, turned into a series of guiding "social myths."[75] The term "myth" carries a positive significance for Lippmann who, drawing on Nietzsche's *Beyond Good and Evil*, makes the case that "opinions" should not be judged on the basis of their truth or falsehood but in terms of whether or not they enhance the vitality of human beings as a species.[76] The form of creativity and binding afforded by "enlightened public opinion" then trumps the content of specific opinions (what groups of people actually think about this or that issue). In the end, Lippmann's "public opinion" is quite like Lee's "attention," a concept meant to capture the ways in which patterns of thinking "express aspiration" (Lippmann's phrase), reflecting deep-seated ("mythic") impulses. The particularities of what the public forms opinions about, or of what it focuses its attention on, become less important than the impulse or force of attraction ("motor current" in Lippmann's terms) expressing itself through them. Therefore, the enlightened control of the force or impulse promises decisive change beyond all "shallow" efforts at reforming society—what Lippmann calls "modern communion."

The intellectual history of this later strain of Progressive social thought helps to explain how Lee can be considered to belong to this movement. It serves further to illuminate the "Progressive" elements of the utopian-universalist cinema argument, whose mature, post-1915 version Lee's work helps to shape. With their mystical faith in cinema as an instrument of social cohesion and animosity toward film censorship or any kind of regulatory legislation, the utopian-universalist writers examined in this study mirror the "Progressive" reaction running through Lee's middecade tomes and in the new liberalism—minus, of course, the latter's interest in the nationalization of industry. For writers like D. W. Griffith, Rupert Hughes, and Douglas Fairbanks, censorship becomes a characteristic instance of negativity and legislation through taboo, making earlier Progressive efforts to reform cinema seem out of step with the realities of modern society.[77] Granting that these writers are self-interested in their efforts to protect the industry from regulatory scrutiny, the kinds of arguments they want to make clearly gain authority and legitimacy from the new liberalism's theorization of mass media's role in producing "enlightened public opinion."

Prior to the moment of Lee's *Crowds*, "Progressive" reactions to motion pictures had run in a variety of opposing directions.[78] The notorious vagueness of that term—the fact that individuals and groups of all different political persuasions "liked the ring of [it]" and applied it to themselves during the first two decades of the twentieth-century—means that it is not possible to speak of a single "Progressive" stance toward cinema.[79] For instance, the National Board of Censorship (NBC), founded in 1909, was a creation of the New York–based People's Institute, a self-styled Progressive organization.[80] Under the guidance of reformer Frederic Howe, the NBC acted "as an industry self-regulatory body, specifically designed to ward off escalating calls for greater official film censorship and the resulting rise in state and municipal control over motion picture exhibition."[81] Howe's board screened and discussed films voluntarily submitted by producers, judging what, if any, elements of their content might be inappropriate for the nickelodeon's demographically diverse audiences and advising necessary changes.[82] Through this method, the NBC sought to gradually shape cinema into an effective tool of moral instruction (according to elite, Protestant norms) while also offering the industry a means of "bolster[ing] its reputation"—protecting itself against accusations of moral corruption.[83]

At the same time, one of the most influential proponents of federal censorship and regulation—and an outspoken critic of the NBC—the Rev. William Sheafe Chase, also donned the mantle of Progressivism.[84] For the Protestant clergyman Chase, the power of the photographic visual image made it uniquely dangerous: what is shown on screen, in Chase's reasoning, affects the viewer in the same way as real-life actions do.[85] Chase saw the moral threat posed by the movies as sufficiently urgent as to require a federal supervisory commission; control of the medium simply could not be left in the hands of motion-picture producers concerned only with profit or of a supervisory board that they funded (and whose decisions were not binding).[86] It should be noted here that Chase's suspicion of producers stemmed largely from his anti-Semitism. Chase bemoaned the "despotic control" of the industry "by four or five Hebrews" and gave credence to the libels contained in the specious *Protocols of the Elders of Zion*, seeing the film industry's growing social influence as evidence of a plot by an international Jewish elite to abolish all world governments and establish their own world "supra-government."[87]

From this racist and religious-elitist stance, Chase argued in favor of regulatory legislation in standard Progressive terms: "New occasions make new duties. . . . We must have new laws to meet new conditions," he told Congress in 1914.[88] The proposed Federal Motion Picture Commission, on behalf of which Chase was there to testify, was, in his view, a well-reasoned political response to material developments that had no precedent in the history of the nation. It was an effort at moral "progress" commensurate with rapid technological and economic progress.[89] Regulating the film industry was akin, then, to inspecting meat and poultry production facilities: Chase wanted to see Congress enact a cinematic equivalent of the Pure Food and Drug Act of 1906, a signature piece of Progressive reform.[90]

Other Progressives like Howe and the settlement movement leader, Jane Addams, viewed the relationship between cinema and moral "progress" in obviously different terms. These figures were less alarmed by the pervasive influence of motion pictures over modern Americans and sought incremental improvements in their quality.[91] Recognizing "the value of commercial leisure in working people's lives and . . . cinema's cultural potential," Addams, along with Howe's NBC, detected in motion pictures an uplifting potentiality that needed to be encouraged; the mass public could be trained to appreciate a higher quality of motion picture.[92] For Chase, the "most irresponsible and weakest elements in the community" ("the young, the curious, the inexperienced") simply could not be trusted to pick "clean" films and, therefore, were totally at the mercy of the predations of a new (Jewish, amoral, putatively "anti-American") business elite clamoring for their money.[93]

In the work of Lee and of those proponents of the universalist-utopian ideal of "moving-pictures" who follow his lead, the medium's progressive potential becomes an unquestioned article of faith, to the point that it becomes possible to talk about cinema as, *in essence*, an "agency" of reform.[94] Indeed, Lee's influence on this ideological shift seems crucial. Opponents of film censorship had long argued that public opinion was largely against the regulation of the content of motion pictures and therefore that governmentally mandated censorship would violate popular will. But after 1915 or so, procinema writers begin to portray the medium as the ultimate index and promoter of enlightened public opinion (in the more generalized sense the term carries in Lippmann's early work).[95] Already stigmatized as antidemocratic, film censors become, in this modified discourse of public opinion, purely "destructive" political entities, contributing nothing to national life and clinging to the outmoded spirit of "Thou shalt not!"—at the very time when positive inspiration is what American society most needs.[96]

In light of the new liberalism's redefinition of reform as collective inspiration, the idea that cinema is a repository of thought and soul (rather than merely entertaining spectacle or a commodity like any other) seems to give the medium an exalted stature. Indeed, for MPPDA President Will Hays, this concept would enable him to forcefully reject the early Progressive analogy between motion pictures and foodstuffs, which censorship proponents like Chase and Ellis Paxson Oberholtzer had often invoked. "Motion pictures are not dead things," Hays wrote in 1927, "to be regulated like commodities like freight and food":

> They are not wares, to be monopolized and traded in by tickets and statutes, or marked like iron and soap. They contain a potency of life in them to be as active as the soul whose progeny they are . . .
>
> Motion pictures are more than foodstuffs. They are more than a few thousand feet of celluloid film on which a series of photographs have been recorded. They are evidence of human thought; and human thought, on which all progress depends, cannot be tampered with safely.[97]

The belief in this spiritual surplus residing within the celluloid strip (a mere physical container) opens up several rhetorical strategies to later proponents of the utopian-universalist view of cinema.

First, it encourages them to employ Lippmann's "futurist habit of mind," of looking ahead to the glorious epoch of understanding and peace that the international film promises to usher in and, therefore, ignoring whatever limitations it might presently have.[98] From this "visionary" standpoint, the actual vulgarity or even immorality of motion pictures seems a trivial matter.[99] Second, it enables them to dispense with the pragmatic concerns about the structure, business practices, and underlying motives of the industry. The likelihood of studio executives wielding despotic power over the public comes to seem small given the relative insignificance of any one person with respect to this universally accepted medium of communication.[100] (On a related note, Lee's prophecies of the "crowd-man" set the stage for a particularly utopian-universalist means of celebrating film stars—rather than producers—in the 1920s.[101]) These concerns recede into the background as the medium is increasingly conceptualized as a mystical (quasi-divine) force placed directly in the hands of "man," something that cannot be repressed and must be allowed to do its assigned work.[102] Third, insofar as this work is that of forging social bonds, the cinema can expediently be portrayed as an agent both of strong nationalism and of international harmony. Cinema is the ultimate enemy of "provincialism" in both arenas, promoting communication (and, in turn, cohesion) on both the domestic and global stages.[103]

All of this is to say that film history needs to add an expanded sense of "Progressive" to its array of concepts, counteracting what has been the tendency—visible in Lary May's foundational work—to equate Progressivism with a repressive "Victorianism." In what is perhaps the most comprehensive attempt to situate the development of U.S. cinema culture in terms of the Progressive Era, May's *Screening Out the Past: The Birth of Mass Culture and the Motion Picture Industry* focuses on D. W. Griffith as the figure who decisively translates the idealism of early twentieth-century reform movements into film entertainment. The title of May's chapter on Griffith, "Apocalyptic Cinema: D. W. Griffith and the Aesthetics of Reform," stresses the way in which Griffith coopted earlier reformers' spirit of moralism and idealism for the project of improving cinema—of restyling it as a promoter of righteous conduct and bourgeois values. May's adjective "apocalyptic" refers to Griffith's religious sensibility as encapsulated in the director's millennialist vision of the movies as bridges "beyond Babel," and the phrase "aesthetics of reform" captures what May sees as Griffith's attempt to sermonize via the screen.[104]

Even as May's analysis convincingly demonstrates Griffith's role in enhancing cinema's cultural respectability, it tends to reduce Progressivism to a generic concern with "moral order"; the word becomes synonymous with the semantically capacious and elusive term "Victorianism"—a term of which May proves tremendously fond.[105] For instance, May uses the phrase "anxious Victorians" to refer to a contingent of Progressive reformers—civic leaders, "muckraking journalists," and members of various "voluntary associations" and "religious groups"—who, around 1905, begin to raise alarms about the corrupting effects of moviegoing on community morals.[106] Some of these figures, May explains, would come to admire the work of Griffith (circa 1908–1915)—whom May also characterizes as thoroughly "Victorian," albeit for somewhat different reasons.

May's characterization proves fruitful in highlighting Griffith's interest in certain kinds of "vice crusading," as seen in the temperance and antisaloon themes of some of his earlier films. But it also forces May to obscure Griffith's clashes with the film censorship community following the release of *The Birth of a Nation* (Griffith Feature Films, 1915), not to mention the vitriolic resentment that he subsequently bore against reformers of all kinds.[107] Indeed, in defending *The Birth of a Nation* against calls for censorship and outright suppression, Griffith squared off with the same "anxious Victorians" whom May highlights, Addams and Howe, donning the mantle of free-speech advocate fighting against government overreach. May's account, further, obfuscates the sense in which Griffith's utopian-universalist vision of cinema—one especially pronounced in a film released after his presumed rift with Progressive reformers, *Intolerance* (Griffith Feature Films, 1916)—is, at heart, "Progressive" in the sense being explored in this chapter.[108] The term "Victorian" (in all of its possible meanings) does not capture this version of Progressivism, and as Nancy Rosenbloom has noted, the tendency to portray Progressives as "nostalgic, backward-looking reformers" and as "vice crusaders" leads to a falsely homogenized understanding of how people belonging to this category responded to the cultural challenges posed by cinema's immense popularity.[109]

Moreover, May's equation of Progressivism with Victorianism lends itself to a simplistic way of periodizing early twentieth-century American culture. In May's account, Griffith's work represents the last gasp of a Victorian concern with moral order, giving way to a nascent "Hollywood" culture embodied by film stars Douglas Fairbanks and Mary Pickford. Because the ascendancy of these stars coincides with Griffith's demise in popularity, May is able to tell the story of a clear, definite shift from the Victorian era to a new era of "mass culture."[110] Itself a capacious concept, mass culture encompasses, in May's understanding, a range of developments, economic (the rise of consumer culture), cultural (hedonism, the worship of youth), social (sexual liberation, challenges to gender norms), and political (conservative reaction, quietism, the spread of corporate ideology). Representing mass culture as the basis of the "Jazz Age" or "roaring twenties," May emphasizes its therapeutic and hedonistic elements.

In the following chapters, I challenge this simple binary scheme of periodization. It is crucial, I argue, to distinguish the threads of continuity that run through the significant historical changes that mark this period. The utopian-universalist understanding of cinema is "Progressive" but not "Victorian" (whatever that is ultimately taken to mean); it is concerned with moral reform and uplift but also insistently modern in its emphasis on new social "forces." It is, further, therapeutic in character and congenial toward the culture of consumption, advertising and the stoking of the desire for goods being one of its constant points of reference—but in a way that is thoroughly moralistic.

We see the full extent of Lee's traversal of this binary in his "war book," *We*, which offers his explanation of World War I's causes, his account of what the war means for Americans, and his prescriptions for how the United States might stay out of the war and hasten its end. Lee adamantly rejects the notion that World War I contradicts his belief in historical progress, continually reaffirming his commitment to the corporate utopianism of *Crowds*. At the same time, in *We*, Lee gravitates toward the terms and concepts of "alternative" or New Age spiritualism like mental science and positive thinking—those offshoots of the nineteenth-century "New Thought" or "mind-cure" movement that had come to permeate business culture during the time of Lee's writing—and projects them onto a collective social horizon.[111]

Consider the arresting passage from *We* that serves as the epigraph to this chapter. Affirmative thinking extrapolated to a mass scale, peace becomes an energy or force that, although essentially spiritual, can, as Lee puts it elsewhere, "make things happen" in the material world.[112] Lee is careful to stress that peace is not an absence of strife, not "a negative thing—a pale, scared, not-fighting," but a "force of nature" that is inherently positive and productive.[113] Peace binds crowds together into ever-larger aggregates, and as in Lee's earlier book, machines—specifically machines that direct attention (like the cinematic apparatus)—have the crucial function of making this binding energy visible and knowable. Hence in Lee's more succinct formulation, "Peace is an energy of mutual attention": attention that has been directed toward humanity's capacity for the good.[114]

Hence the importance of self-assertion in Lee's brand of "peace talk." Whereas the assertion of multiple, contending wills would appear to promote conflict, Lee calls peace "every man's assertion of his larger self."[115] Just as the expression of all things in democracy seemed, in Lee's *Crowds*, to engender social harmony, here aggressive self-assertion promotes bonding at an ethereal level. Conflict never becomes a possibility because the "larger self" being asserted by true believers in "peace-energy" is

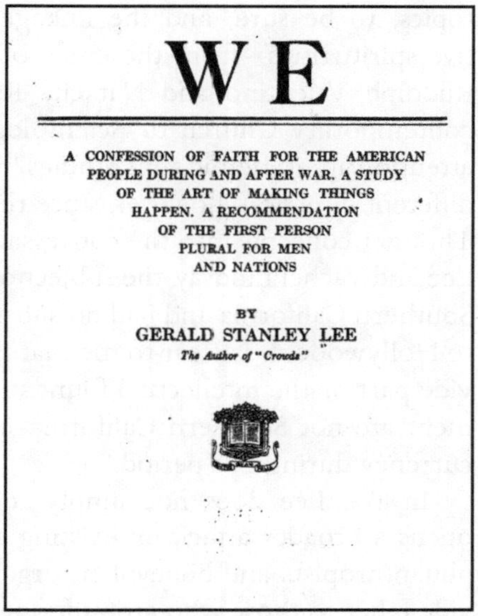
WE

A CONFESSION OF FAITH FOR THE AMERICAN PEOPLE DURING AND AFTER WAR. A STUDY OF THE ART OF MAKING THINGS HAPPEN. A RECOMMENDATION OF THE FIRST PERSON PLURAL FOR MEN AND NATIONS

BY

GERALD STANLEY LEE

The Author of "Crowds"

Figure 1.1. Title page to Gerald Stanley Lee's *We*.

always essentially same: the one and only divine source of all things, in which individual people fully participate.

Although Lee largely avoids using overt religious rhetoric in *We*, it is clear that he sees "peace-energy" as an emanation of what Mental Scientists like Fenwicke Holmes call the "Divine Will" or "Cosmic Mind."[116] To channel the "floating electric force in the air" is to commune with this spirit, to experience "oneness," as Holmes's predecessor Ralph Waldo Trine would put it.[117] Trine's foundational positive-thinking tract, *In Tune with the Infinite* (1908), is crucial for understanding Lee's discussion of peace as a form of divine power channeled by the individual soul. For Lee, as for Trine, the self, having escaped material limitations (which are merely apparent, illusory) and entered the realm of pure "soul," experiences an "inflowing tide of peace."[118] Promoting this experience of *influx* (a key concept in Swedenborgianism and other neoplatonic philosophies) over the advocacy of specific moral virtues, Lee signals his sharp break with the moral reform ethos of the early Progressive Era, even as he remains essentially concerned with the uplift of society at the national and international levels.[119]

In drawing attention to Lee's investment in the neoplatonic spirituality—and that of other writers who take after him—one important disclaimer is in order. This book does not aim to tell the story of New Age sects and communities in Southern California during the 1910s and 1920s or to chart the longer history of the esoteric traditions that have taken hold in the Hollywood movie colony. These are interesting topics, to be sure, and the linkage between film actors and alternative spiritualties—from the circle of Theosophists that formed around Rudolph Valentino and Natacha Rambova in the early 1920s to the contemporary Church of Scientology—has perhaps received too little attention in academic film studies.[120] My research necessarily goes in a different direction, however, since the two thinkers who introduce New Thought concepts into the conversation on cinema during this period—Lee and Vachel Lindsay, the subject of the next chapter—never resided in Southern California and had no substantial ties, professional or personal, to Hollywood. It is clear to me that the New Thought concepts that provide part of the intellectual foundation of the utopian-universalist argument are not Southern California–centric, but enjoyed broad, national currency during this period.[121]

In *We*, Lee does not simply reject conventional "peace talk" but opens a broader attack on existing social reform projects. He criticizes philanthropists and benevolent organizations for their attempts to provide relief to those who are suffering, to resolve specific social problems, and to preserve their ideals of the true, good, and beautiful in cultural institutions like libraries and museums. These benevolent actors, Lee argues, are too insulated in their own wealth to understand what people in general need or want and tend to focus on enshrining the ideals of the past.[122] Clinging to "dead" cultures and obsolete methods of instruction, contemporary elites ("millionaires" in Lee's shorthand) succeed only in making the masses of people *bored*.[123] And this boredom represents the millionaires' lack of inspiration and their concomitant failure to inspire the larger publics whom they seek to help. In this misconceived attempt to "do good to or at" people—Lee's unusual way of describing moral pedantry—elites actually end up oppressing them further.[124]

For Lee, the thing that makes benevolence a "dangerous influence on the world" is its tendency to keep the attention of its ostensible beneficiaries fixated on the mundane rather than on the sublime, to make people fearful of bold action. Any project of uplift that does not begin and end with inspiring scenes of humanity's future ("where we are going") will have the opposite of the desired effect, just like any "peace talk" that does focus entirely on the "infinite" will sow strife.[125] Taken out of context, Lee's construal of boredom as the cardinal sin of contemporary humanity—as both a cause and an expression of moral failure—seems strange, indeed. But in terms of Lee's larger discussion of "moving-pictures" as a gnostic tool, this notion of boredom makes obvious sense.

For the gnostic thinker, the goal of transcending the constraints of material reality and accessing the realm of spirit trumps localized ethical imperatives. Lee uses this same standard to evaluate social elites' relationships to the larger publics whom they seek to assist, reform, and educate. Insofar as "being done good to or at" promotes an awareness of worldly limitation, it is a form of repression, a way of being kept from thinking in the sense that Lee considers authentic. Lee finally makes entertainment into morality, sanctifying stimulation and making hedonism compulsory. Insofar as good feeling alone will save the world, human beings must be made to feel good; this is the ideology that will prove irresistibly attractive for the Hollywood film industry and its defenders after World War I.

2 "The Occult Elements of Motion and Light"

VACHEL LINDSAY'S UTOPIA OF THE MIRROR SCREEN

Whereas the ancient churches were representative, therefore the men of those churches made to themselves sculptured things and images of various kinds, which represented and thence signified things heavenly, and the ancients were delighted with them on account of their signification; wherefore when they looked upon those things they were reminded of the heavenly things which they represented, and inasmuch as they were such as appertained to their religion, they used them in worship; hence came the use of groves and high places, and also of sculptured, molten, and painted figures, which they placed either in groves, or upon mountains, or in temples, or in their houses; hence in Egypt where the science of representations, which is the same as the science of correspondences, flourished, they had images, idols, and sculptured things, whence also came their hieroglyphics.

—*A Dictionary of Correspondences . . . Extracted from the Writings of Emmanuel Swedenborg*[1]

Because ten million people daily enter into the cave, something akin to Egyptian wizardry, certain national rituals, will be born. By studying the matter of being an Egyptian priest for a little while, the author-producer [of motion pictures] may learn in the end how best to express and satisfy the spirit-hungers that are peculiarly American. It is sometimes out of the oldest dream that the youngest vision is born.

—Vachel Lindsay, *The Art of the Moving Picture*[2]

In *The Art of the Moving Picture* (1915), Vachel Lindsay's habit is to treat his own, idiosyncratic interpretations of other texts as self-evident, asserting what seem like highly esoteric affinities between his way of thinking and that of another writer while treating them as if they are completely obvious.[3] Witness how Lindsay concludes his fifth chapter by presenting Gerald Stanley Lee's *Crowds: A Moving Picture of Democracy* (1913) as the key to understanding "the picture of crowd splendor," one of the six "types" that comprise Lindsay's "photoplay" taxonomy. Lindsay refers to Lee's book as "bear[ing] the title of this chapter"—even though the chapter is actually called "The Picture of Crowd Splendor"—and recommends it to his reader as a primer for understanding films belonging to that category.[4] In other words, Lindsay treats *Crowds* as if it already was what he intends *The Art of the Moving Picture* to be: a programmatic articulation of concepts for understanding and passing critical judgment on photoplays or fictional narrative films. He even describes *Crowds* as containing "a score of future [photoplay] scenarios," listing a number of Lee's section headings (such as "Crowds and Heroes") and calling for films to be made "in the spirit of these titles."[5] Masking the obvious differences between their two books' subject matter and ignoring the fact that *Crowds* does not purport to make any kind of contribution to filmmaking or film criticism, Lindsay simultaneously cites and radically revises Lee's work.

Although scholars have so far ignored the crucial influence of *Crowds* on Lindsay's film theory, this passage makes clear that *The Art of the Moving Picture*'s central thesis about the historical significance of cinema depends heavily on Lee's gnostic and utopian ideas of mass portraiture. *The Art of the Moving Picture*, it becomes clear, is an attempt to theorize the aesthetic properties and social effects of contemporary cinema (specifically the feature-length films being produced by the emergent Hollywood studios) in the prophetic terms elaborated in *Crowds*. If Lee appropriates "moving-pictures" as a generic trope for the modern "mechanical arts," then Lindsay borrows this trope back as a way of describing the innate tendencies of actual moving pictures, as he sees them.

Lindsay concludes his brief discussion of *Crowds* by making the cryptic suggestion that films based on Lee's ideas "would help to make world-voters of us all": "The World State," Lindsay writes, "is indeed far away. But as we peer into the Mirror Screen some of us dare to look forward to the time when the pouring streets of men will become sacred in each other's eyes, in pictures and in fact."[6] Making its first appearance in *The Art of the Moving Picture*, the phrase "Mirror Screen" here establishes the crucial point of connection between the section of the book dealing with aesthetics (where this chapter appears) and the following section, which deals with the social effects of cinema; the trope anchors Lindsay's attempts to theorize the medium going forward. Although "Mirror Screen" is Lindsay's coinage, it functions in this passage as a synonym for Lee's "vast white canvas." Elevating the physical medium of the projected image to superhuman dimensions, the Mirror Screen acts as unifying mechanism, binding people around the world into an idealized corporate structure—a "crowd," in Lee's terminology.

In addition to their abiding faith in the possibility of immanent, millennial transformation, Lindsay and Lee also share a strong interest in the therapeutic, mentalist ethos of what in the late nineteenth century had been termed the "New Thought." And while both writers portray this transformation as ultimately social, it takes place, fundamentally, at the level of consciousness. Lee and Lindsay envision a change in and through mental activity, a shift toward "positive thinking" that is, in one way or another, bound up with the emergence of mass-media images in general and motion pictures in particular. For his part, Lee makes a simple call for economic and political elites ("inspired millionaires," "crowd-men") to create and broadcast images of collective good and, thus, to sow an uplifting "energy" in the world. These positive images overcome the trap of self-limitation inherent in negative forms of instruction, stimulating desires that become unifying forces in their own right. Assuming a privileged relationship between seeing and knowing, Lee wants to see abstract lessons conveyed through visual media, inventing the compound "word-pictures" to capture the desired phenomenon.

Lindsay, however, envisions a different, more complex relationship between vision and gnosis. For Lindsay, each film image potentially functions as a "hieroglyphic," possessing both a surface meaning and a "representative," spiritual significance. Lindsay draws this theory of hieroglyphic signification from the "science of correspondences"—developed by of one of his intellectual heroes, the eighteenth-century scientist, theologian, and mystical philosopher Emanuel Swedenborg.[7] Articulated in terms of an esoteric approach to scriptural exegesis, Swedenborg's "science" gives Lindsay a way of theorizing film images as "representative" symbols: visual emblems possessing tremendous occulted power, whose revelation could serve to unite masses of people in spiritual harmony in the way that the sculptural objects and painted emblems of the "ancient churches" once did.[8]

Reading *The Art of the Moving Picture* in terms of Lindsay's Swedenborgian affinities, it is clear that there is a tension between the two layers of meaning supposed to be inherent to each filmic sign. He sometimes treats signs as having obvious meanings that are universally accessible; other times, he treats the "primary form" of signs as a material envelope that must be cracked open in order to reveal their true "spirit-meaning" (Lindsay's self-consciously Swedenborgian coinage).[9] And Lindsay equivocates on the question of how widely held in contemporary society are the tools required to see past mere appearances. Whereas the historical narrative that Lindsay draws from Swedenborg presupposes that only the "ancients" had the ability to think in terms of "correspondences," his radical faith in the democracy of cinema leads him to write *as if* spirit-meanings are self-evident for present-day motion-picture audiences. Lindsay clearly wants this to be true but, as the second epigraph to this chapter indicates, is forced to acknowledge that, in 1915, cinema hieroglyphics still exist in a provisional state. Film producers "may [yet] learn" to craft resonant symbols like "Egyptian priest[s]" once did, and film audiences might one day be able to recognize these for what they are (which is to say, be able to interpret movies like Lindsay himself does); but it is not at all evident that cinema has reached its goal (as Lindsay sees it) of recapturing these ancient, ritual powers.

Lindsay is inclined, then, to flip the two terms in Lee's compound "word-pictures," referring to cinematic images as "picture-words."[10] A "picture-word" is a hieroglyphic in the Swedenborgian sense: a visual sign that has "representative" power, directly conveying a spiritual significance that provides the recipient with an experience of transcendence. Lindsay enacts this shift in service of the book's hopeful and prophetic argument that the movies in their current form are about to become world-spanning, unifying, sublime objects of shared attention that Lee had speculated about in *Crowds*. As a "Mirror Screen," cinema is the inspiring engine of "public opinion" (the religious substitute that Lee, like Walter Lippmann, was looking for) and the portal to spiritual transcendence envisioned in various New Age discourses.

But in his second, posthumously published book of film theory, Lindsay goes beyond such a provisional understanding of filmic "picture-words."[11] In this important but largely overlooked extension of Lindsay's initial speculations about the medium, he begins, first, to characterize it as a magical, "transfiguring" mirror and, second, to see any and all images that appear on this surface as *already possessing* a correspondent, spiritual meaning. In his effort to provide evidence for the claim that the screen has this transfiguring effect, Lindsay is forced, ironically, to fall back on its merely visual properties: the "glittering" quality of the projected image on screen, the glamour projected by certain beautiful filmed faces, and the "splendor" of crowd scenes (especially scenes illustrating American historical subjects).

Therefore, what Lindsay identifies as cinema's "occult elements of motion and light" are shown ultimately to be the obvious, sensible qualities of the image, rendered through the magic of Hollywood studio film production.[12] In a way that follows the broad trajectory of the utopian-universalist cinema discourse, Lindsay reconciles Swedenborg's science of correspondences with the logic of commodity fetishism. The ultimate correspondence he imagines is between the technologically enhanced aura of the object on screen and the highest-imaginable, suprasensible qualities. Anything that shines, glitters, or appears splendid in its motion is deemed suitable as a ritual symbol of national and international binding. The version of Swedenborg's "science of correspondences" that underwrites Lindsay's film theory ends up being a structural one: between mundane perceptual phenomena and a series of increasingly immaterial and grandiose concepts—American unity and self-understanding, international utopia, and the fourth dimension. Indeed, Lindsay will privilege the attractive white female film star as his symbol of the spirit ascending into higher realms; the image of what Mary Ann Doane has called "narcissistic consumption" suffices, for him, as an ideal of modern American social progress. Likewise, he will seize on apologetic images of American settler colonialism as symbols of a communal movement toward utopia. Practicing a kind of "positive thinking" at the level of critical exegesis, Lindsay is able to satisfy the late Progressive call for new, socially transformative myths by simply turning backward to the most well-worn icons of nationalist prestige and power.

"The Film of Light" and Cinematic Transfiguration

An imagined composite of all existing cinema screens, Lindsay's "Mirror Screen," like Lee's world-spanning canvas, exemplifies the medium's ability to depict masses of human beings in a vivid or dramatic fashion and, at the same time, to reach viewers in large numbers. Lindsay is fascinated by the film camera's ability to capture vast "mobs and assemblies . . . [as] they wave their characteristic flags, rags, and torches."[13] Crowds give film its most striking visual material, while film activates the power and significance of crowd movements that even traditional dramatic formats employing actors in large groups—like civic pageants—cannot.[14]

Over the course of Lindsay's two film books, the "epic" historical film, with its extensive crowd spectacles, becomes the defining genre, the one that best illustrates the medium's properties and potentialities. In Lindsay's first treatise, *The Birth of a Nation* (Griffith Feature Films, 1915) receives special attention, indicating the emergence of a new type of American film and pointing the way toward "the great photoplay of tomorrow"—the film that explicitly illustrates the millennial reign of peace.[15] Lindsay's unpublished sequel to *The Art of the Moving Picture* treats *The Birth of a Nation*'s descendants—epics like *Intolerance* (Griffith Feature Films, 1916), *The Covered Wagon* (Paramount, 1923), and *The Thief of*

Bagdad (Douglas Fairbanks Pictures, 1924)—as realizing this potential in part, if not entirely.

For Lindsay, the specific visual quality of cinematic crowds is the same "liquid" flow—with its connotations of organic beauty, fusion, and loss of individual distinction—that characterizes Lee's utopian descriptions of urban masses. Throughout *The Art of the Moving Picture*, Lindsay attempts to verbally translate the oceanic movements of crowds on screen: "masses of human beings pour like waves," "tremendous armies [move] as oceans move," a "population flow[s] like a sluggish river."[16] Cinema's defining attribute for Lindsay appears to be its making visible of the "sea of humanity"—the oceanic crowd—and, in so doing, to make this unified collective body beautiful and awe-inspiring.[17] Lindsay credits cinema with making "the pouring streets of men sacred" first "in pictures" and then "in fact": the crowd's splendor on screen reveals the utopian possibilities that Lee understood to be inherent in the everyday phenomenon of modern street life.[18]

Likewise, Lindsay imagines the world's cinema screens attracting ever-expanding masses of spectators, offering yet another image of bodies flowing together into a virtual crowd of potentially limitless scope. In this way, Lindsay conceives of the overall film audience as a nascent global political body, a "World State," invoking a central concept from World War I–era liberal political philosophy.[19] Lindsay's interest in the aesthetics of unified crowds stands in tensions with the political dynamics of film narratives focused on the actions of large masses of people. For Lindsay, it is an article of faith that the crowd-splendor film genre promotes the idea of international harmony, making viewers see themselves as "world-voters."

In the most fundamental sense, Lindsay's composite screen is a "mirror" because it is an instrument of crowd portraiture, in some manner reflecting the mass audience's image back to itself. Based on the immediate context for this passage, it would appear that Lindsay, like Lee, associates this reflection with the crowd's coming to self-knowledge. On the two previous pages, he discusses the famous scene of Lincoln's assassination in *The Birth of a Nation*, concluding that the "terror" expressed by the members of the intradiegetic audience so "touch[es]" the "real crowd" (the film's own audience) that "it beholds its natural face in the glass."[20] The screen, at that moment, reveals to the audience how it looks and feels, affording them an otherwise impossible experience of gnosis.[21]

Several pages after his initial reference, Lindsay returns to the Mirror Screen trope in the context of a call for "Whitmanesque [film] scenarios": "The possibility of showing the entire American population its own face in the Mirror Screen has at last come," he writes.[22] For Lindsay, the cinema naturally shares a particular "idea of democracy" with the poet, the same idea that Lee has in mind when he defines "democracy" as an imaginary space in which "all things may be given a chance to be expressed."[23] Being universally accessible (as far as Lindsay is concerned) cinema even extends this idea further, making "democratic" art available not just "to our sophisticated literati" but to "the democracy itself"—to the very multitudes whom Whitman famously celebrates in his poems.[24] Thus Lindsay envisions films in which what Lee would call the composite or "crowd face" of the American people appears. These "American patriotic crowd-prophecies," as Lindsay calls them, would represent something like a "hieroglyphic" image of the "entire" American people. Possessing religious or ritual power, such an image would providing the nation with the opportunity to discern its own "spirit-meaning"—visualizing and, thus, understanding itself in a way that, for both Lee and Lindsay, represents utopian self-fulfillment.[25]

Even as it is supposed to reflect the people who gather in front of it, this mirror, in Lindsay's rendering, also possesses the qualities of a magical looking glass. It affords a glimpse of the future—the spectators "peer" into it and "look forward," Lindsay says—and, therefore, shows human beings the way to an achievable utopia, or "where we are going," as Lee had put it. The "Mirror Screen" in this sense has the properties of a shop window, an artifact that Lee also uses to exemplify how objects put on commercial display elicit desire.[26] In his second film book, *The Progress and Poetry of the Movies*, Lindsay establishes the kind of "analogy" between "the show window"—the store display window staged as a "proscenium for commodity display"—and "the cinema screen" that Anne Friedberg famously discusses in *Window Shopping: Cinema and the Postmodern*.[27]

In order to explain the aesthetic and spiritual properties of the Mirror Screen, Lindsay appeals to "transfiguring" qualities that it shares with shop windows—and the other plate-glass surfaces that he sees blanketing American cities. He bookends *The Progress and Poetry of the Movies'* lengthy commentary on the Rudolph Valentino-Bebe Daniels picture, *Monsieur Beaucaire* (Paramount, 1924), with musings on glass like this one: "If you walk down a prosperous street toward evening, you will be interested to note how very many of the stores and window exhibits are rendered beautiful because you view them through crystalline plate glass, that catches the light a little. More and more there is an effort to give this effect even in the corner groceries, meat markets, garages, and hotel elevators. . . . We seem to be looking into very still water or into a mirror everywhere in commercial America."[28] Lindsay marvels at the number of different kinds of establishments using plate glass—noting also the time that Americans spend looking through automobile windshields and Pullman car windows—and surmises that "the American eye" is becoming habituated to looking through this "mysterious surface" all the time.[29]

In Lindsay's estimation, this "mysterious surface" has a number of paradoxical qualities. While plate glass's "predominant function . . . was its transparency," its tendency to catch light makes it reflective like a mirror.[30] The window is a partition or mediating surface, yet it has the effect of seeming to bring forward the goods placed behind it, making them desirable and graspable to such an extent that only in this environment do they become "real."[31] (We might add that the window-mirror makes these goods in some sense a reflection of the person peers into it.) Although plate glass is meant to enhance the appearance of the displayed objects, acting as a kind of ornament, becoming ubiquitous and transforming perceptual habits, it becomes charged with desire in its own right. Or, rather, as Lindsay puts it, the "film of light upon the surface of the glass" (rather than "the glass itself") becomes the symbol of desire, "luxury," and "glamor" for the average American.[32]

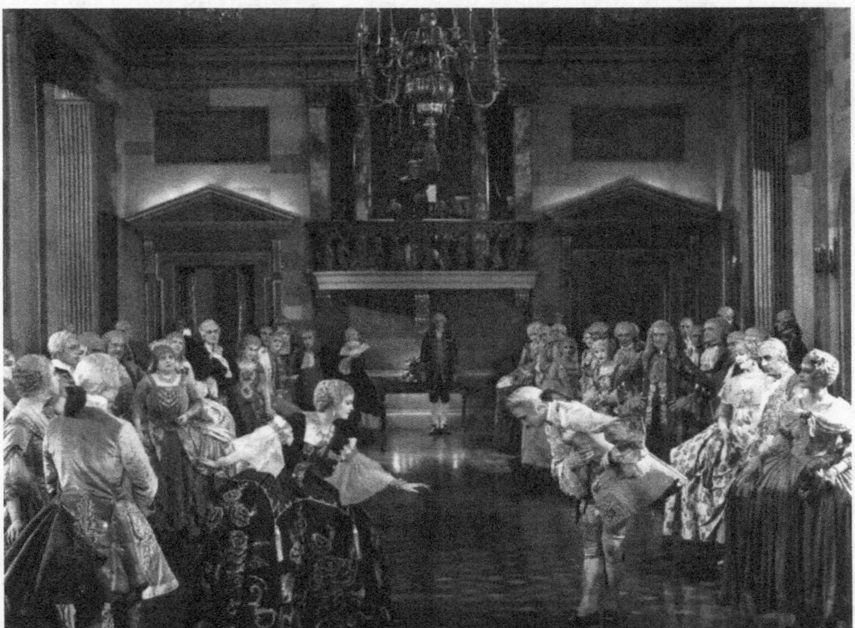

Figure 2.1. Glittering surfaces in *Monsieur Beaucaire* (Paramount, 1924). Courtesy of the Academy of Motion Picture Arts and Sciences.

Lindsay's description of reflected light as a "film" is highly resonant in this context; the entire discussion of plate glass is prompted by Lindsay's lavish praise for *Monsieur Beaucaire*. *Monsieur Beaucaire* is a production that does what, Lindsay feels, a "true movie" should: it "conveys the impression of looking into a crystal, which gives a mystical glitter to everything within it."[33] A characteristic instance where Lindsay combines the descriptive and the programmatic, Lindsay treats this film as if it realizes his dream of the "photoplay of tomorrow" articulated in *The Art of the Moving Picture*. Given that *Monsieur Beaucaire* is an eighteenth-century French costume drama, a Valentino star vehicle set in the court of Louis XV, the choice seems odd. Focused on fashion and manners, the film has no obviously "American patriotic" themes; further, Lindsay seems greatly to exaggerate the part played by crowds in the film.[34]

Lindsay judges *Monsieur Beaucaire* a "masterwork" entirely on the basis of its lighting effects: the film "appears to us as though viewed in a gigantic mirror of the most beautiful and magical quality" and "glitters like a ballroom chandelier."[35] To be sure, Lindsay's chandelier image alludes to a specific scene in the film—a ball, the setting of the obligatory Valentino seduction dance—and his comments accurately highlight *Monsieur Beaucaire*'s striking lighting effects, which result from the filmmakers' innovative use of directed lighting. The film's cameraman, Harry Fischbeck, described using "a preponderance of spotlights" to create painterly and sculptural effects: "The basic idea is to make each picture scene look like a painting, with the characters standing out in bold relief."[36] In almost every scene, the characters are, indeed, sharply highlighted, their white costumes, wigs, and made-up faces seeming to glow within otherwise dark spaces.

At the same time, as on the American Main Street that Lindsay describes, the proliferation of "glass" tropes in Lindsay's own discussion of *Monsieur Beaucaire* becomes dizzying. To paraphrase Lindsay, the film is like a chandelier, so the viewer sees it as if in a mirror, but this mirror is really the simultaneously reflective and transparent glass of the shop window. With such a complex chain of associations, Lindsay makes explicit the associations between visual splendor or magic and the cinema's prophetic function as a window that allows society to peer into the future. Whereas these associations are implicit in *The Art of the Moving Picture*, Lindsay's unpublished sequel grounds the "mirroring" function of the screen in its basic visual qualities, which he articulates in terms of contemporary innovations in commercial-product display.

For Lindsay, the light that catches these "crystalline" surfaces transforms the objects on view into metaphysical signs—into Swedenborgian hieroglyphics. In one instance, Lindsay goes as far as to use the word "transfiguring" to characterize this "mysterious" visual effect, thus invoking the moments in the Synoptic Gospels when Jesus appears "transfigured" before his disciples.[37] In all three tellings of this event, Jesus leads Peter, James, and John "up a high mountain" and then appears alongside (the reanimated) Moses and Elias, his face and "raiment" becoming radiant, "white as the light." Glowing with almost blinding effulgence ("as the sun"), Jesus appears both in his recognizable physical body and as a glorified or perfected (fully divine) being.[38] As in orthodox Christian theologies, in Swedenborg's mystical, neoplatonic doctrine, "transfiguration" refers to the union between the human and the promise of eternal life.[39]

Lacking any evident irony or hyperbole, Lindsay's use of the term "transfiguring" to describe the shop window and the film screen typifies the logic and rhetoric of early twentieth-century technoutopianism, an ideology of which both he and Lee partake. In Lindsay's treatment, these emergent visual technologies become spiritual technologies. Turning what appears like a superficial similarity between the new phenomenon (the glitter of plate glass) and the scriptural image (the heavenly light of transfiguration) into a firm identity, Lindsay assumes the re-enchantment of everyday life; he begins to see signs everywhere that a future-oriented spirit of collective dreaming is ascendant in contemporary America.[40]

One striking thing about Lindsay's favorable treatment of "luxury" and "glamor" in the arena of modern commercial display is how diametrically opposed it seems to his generally ascetic temperament. In his second film book, as in much of his poetry and fiction, Lindsay celebrates a mythic American character—self-reliant, austere, in tune with nature, rooted in the "primitive" conditions of the "frontier"—and those historical figures who, he believes, have best embodied it (like Abraham Lincoln and John Chapman, a.k.a. Johnny Appleseed).[41] Likewise, Lindsay was a longtime Anti-Saloon League member and an outspoken critic of what he saw as the "lax morality" of 1920s American life (especially jazz music and the various dance fads that went along with it). Bearing these points in mind, Lindsay's reader might expect to find him casting a skeptical eye on the material excesses of the modern commercial district, sharply criticizing his contemporaries for becoming, as he himself puts it, "slaves . . . to this glamour."[42]

One finds Lindsay, instead, judging this apparent enslavement to be a positive condition, evidence of a collective fixation on utopian goals. Instead of treating the glittering appearances in the shop window and on the film screen—appearances that he readily concedes are carefully engineered effects—as illusions, Lindsay treats them as reliable hieroglyphics, which possess occulted religious significance. From this standpoint, the apparent vanity or narcissism that seems to grip society—Americans "seem [always] to be looking into still water"—becomes a progressive act of self-study and self-visualization. Lindsay elaborates this theme in a poem titled "To a Lady before Her Mirror," which he interpolates into his discussion of *Monsieur Beaucaire* and plate glass.[43]

The poem's eponymous "lady," whose actions are described in a more or less stereotypical fashion, personifies the nation. She appears to be a white-collar worker (her job requires her to "typewrite all day") who fills her leisure hours with movies and magazine "fashion-plates."[44] And yet her behavior—and the desire for beauty that lies behind it—becomes an extended metaphor for the nation as it moves from a state of youth and innocence into a glorious future. Updating conventional feminine metonymies, Lindsay presents the reader with "Columbia" or "Liberty" in the guise of a mid-1920s "flapper."[45] By emphasizing this figure's intense self-regard—she spends "endless hours" gazing into the mirror—Lindsay echoes period advertising and film-industry discourses, which, as Mary Ann Doane has put it, envisioned "the prototype of the spectator-consumer [as] female."[46]

In her classic of feminist film theory, "The Economy of Desire," Doane explains that the American cinema has historically constructed "the woman" as the subject of consumer culture but only insofar as "she is the subject of a transaction in which her own commodification" is the "ultimate goal."[47] In other words, the cinema's emphasis on women's supposed need to protect and enhance their own feminine appearance idealizes a particular brand of "narcissistic consumption," positioning women as desiring spectators of their own self-images.[48] Doane's work is especially instructive here as she illustrates that, during the teens and twenties, the same association of the screen and the shop window (as well as the corresponding idea of spectatorship as a kind of "window-shopping") that Lindsay discusses was articulated in terms of the female consumer as narcissist.[49] In its early stanzas, Lindsay's "To a Lady before Her Mirror" elaborates on this gendered portrayal of consumer culture, gently chiding the young woman for spending time admiring her "profile" and "silhouette."[50]

Although the description of the young woman's primping suggests vanity and excessive concern for appearances, the speaker counsels her to continue the process of self-study through gazing into mirrors. But in this case, she is to "study [her] soul's air."[51] In the metaphorical register, the poem, then, prescribes a period of education and self-cultivation for "young America," a shifting of focus onto "deeper" questions of the spirit. The nation must spend time getting to know itself and composing its "soul's face" in the magical glass that lines "Main Street" and in the "photoplay," "the land's mirror screen."[52] The poem exhorts the "lady" to climb "up the heavenly way" by studying the "reels" on view in the movie palace: "Dreams look out from films as from a glass—/ Thousands of dreams, a thousand years may pass! // Dreams that will teach us, writing, painting, song—/ And plans for building lovingly and long."[53] These "plans for building," the speaker asserts, are plans for "our future"; as the mirror "where Liberty may dream and preen," the screen assumes this prophetic function.[54] In this part of the poem, Lindsay repeatedly associates dreams with the future, the movies (as mass dream images) taking the central role in the nation's effort to script its future "glor[ies]" and "wonders."[55]

In the poem and throughout his body of work, Lindsay associates the "seeking" of future "wonders" with the transcendence of material constraints. As the nation scripts its future, it will rise into a state of pure spirit or soul, becoming what Lindsay, using an image inspired by Poe's "Ulalume," calls "the Psyche-Butterfly."[56] At this point in the poem, Lindsay fuses his idea of the cinematic Mirror Screen with his theory of hieroglyphics. The process of self-reflection that the poem describes allows the nation to get into the "proper" state of mind, in which the spiritual disposition of the American people comes into line with their outward appearance.[57] In turn, the nation's face becomes a hieroglyphic for itself—its "soul's face," in Lindsay's peculiar extension of Lee's physiognomic concept. The national face acquires an occulted "spirit-meaning," one that is, of course, entirely positive. Showing the nation "transfigured," having reached its glorious destiny, the mirror image is a mystery eminently worth probing; by no means is it an inducement to harmful narcissism.

The poem's resolution illustrates the basic ideological weakness of Lindsay's film theory, one that follows directly from its conceptual foundation, Swedenborg's "science of correspondences." Lindsay's theory ultimately enshrines visual appearances as reliable indicators of truth and endows existing objects of attraction or desire with a surplus of meaning that is entirely in the eye of the beholder, if not arbitrarily determined. In "To a Lady before Her Mirror," Lindsay makes a conventional distinction between body and soul, only to nullify this distinction by insisting that the soul is always something that can be visualized—and by fully equating transcendence with beautiful appearances.

Lindsay's Lee-esque declaration in *The Art of the Moving Picture* offers an important point of context for this poem; there he states, "America is in the state of mind where she must visualize herself again."[58] Self-visualization here carries utopian potentiality; utopia, for Lindsay (and for Lee), is something that happens as "we" watch "our" own reflections.

The concluding sections of Lindsay's poem return to the image of "Columbia" as a woman beautifying herself at "her glass," the process of her "preen[ing]" having become a metaphor for the nation's preparing itself for its apotheosis ("visualizing herself").[59] But the reader is uncertain what the poem's final images—which again have to do with a person examining her physical features in a mirror—really "mean" on this second, spiritual level. How are these concluding images different from the images of "merely" physical "preening" presented in the poem's opening stanzas? If traditionally accepted beauty of appearance already signifies transcendence, then what sort of project of growth and change (at the level of "soul") is really being prescribed here?

The poem seems ultimately stuck on the imagery of physically beautiful outward shows. Columbia's destiny is to become something like a screen idol, singing, dancing, "her beauties with sweet vanity all burning." And yet the public's enjoyment of this performance is supposed to carry deep, transformative spiritual significance.[60] As chapter 4 will illustrate, this is the precise theme of Rupert Hughes's *Souls for Sale* (1923), a novel that traces the rise of a Hollywood film star. In Lindsay's poem and Hughes's novel alike, the beautiful white female face on screen becomes the nation's "soul's face," a magical object or a thing to be worshipped in its own right.

Moving "Toward Utopia . . . West of the West"

Lindsay's "Psyche-Butterfly" forms part of a larger pattern of flight imagery in his discourse on film spectatorship, which, in turn, typifies his emphasis on various forms of movement whenever he comments broadly on American society, past, present, and future. In fact, Lindsay assumes a deep-seated affinity between the American nation and the motion picture on the grounds that both are fundamentally movement based. He elaborates this affinity by focusing on three distinct movement tropes, all of them in some way pertinent to film experience, and each one corresponding roughly to a temporal phase in the nation's development.

The movement of westward pioneering is the keystone of Lindsay's understanding of the American historical past. In a totally conventional fashion, he celebrates the "romance" of white colonial settlers caught up in the "west-going dream," people prompted by a "vague yearning" to leave "civilization" behind and to explore new frontiers.[61] Consequently, his national history is a compendium of hackneyed Americana, a series of mythic images in some way related to the motif of westward pioneering: the wagon train, the locomotive entering the "wilderness," Johnny Appleseed's peregrinations, "the leaping flame on the hearthstone of the [log] cabin," and so on.[62] And in turn, Lindsay's film criticism privileges epic American history films like *The Covered Wagon* and *The Iron Horse* (Fox, 1924). The central image of movement in each of these films—the westward incursion of settlers along the Oregon Trail and the construction of the transcontinental railroad, respectively—carries potent ritual-symbolic meaning for Lindsay. He repeatedly endorses the viewing of *The Covered Wagon* and *The Iron Horse* as an exercise in civic education.[63]

More than simply dramatizing the pioneering adventure, the motion picture seems, for Lindsay, to reveal historical "west-going" to have had the esoteric purpose of inspiring (of moving, we might say) subsequent generations of Americans to undertake journeys "toward utopia": "It is part of the function of the motion picture to lead us that way."[64] Therefore, Lindsay concludes, "all American history, past, present, and to come, is a gigantic movie."[65] Ironically highlighting the extent to which Lindsay's knowledge of American history seems derived from period films, this statement seems at first like a throwaway. But Lindsay is actually reaching for a fairly complex point: that American history is cinematic because it is always already staged as a spectacle for an audience—an enactment of founding ideals (like the "pioneer spirit") as visual symbols or hieroglyphics. Lindsay refers collectively to the repertoire of historical images that he cites as the nation's "west-going pageantry."[66]

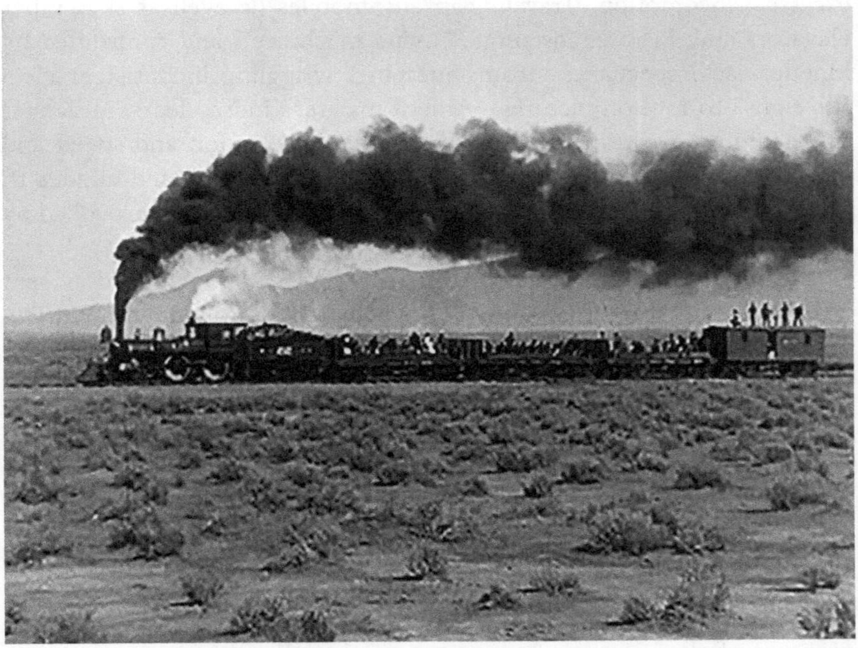

Figure 2.2. Cinematic history in *The Iron Horse* (Fox, 1924).

It must be pointed out that Lindsay's view of American history as a "gigantic movie" has the primary consequence of imbuing a mythic version of the past with a utopian significance. Whatever happened in the sphere of westward pioneering can be consumed by contemporary Americans as the manifestation a single "eternal dream" and as an image of the nation moving inevitably toward glory.[67] Such mystique authorizes, in turn, the most blatant revisionism—already the stock-in-trade of Hollywood's historical films, the western in particular. According to Lindsay's method, events from the past must be idealized, to the extent that such idealization is the means of revealing their hieroglyphic truth. And the sense that a film feels "American" to its audience—that the audience wants it to be so—becomes a reliable index of its being true, or "real."[68] Likewise, images of violence and destruction can be willfully misread as emblems of "eternal dream," as Lindsay does when he reduces images of Native Americans—the ostensible targets of colonial oppression in several of the films he cites—to hieroglyphics of American nationalism.

In terms of the present day, Lindsay fixates on the rapid "locomotion" of modern life. He represents the contemporary United States as gripped by a "rampant speed-mania," symbolized by the "all-conquering Ford car."[69] As the term "mania" suggests, Lindsay, far from immediately according utopian meaning to it, worries with the negative effects of excessive locomotion. Traveling in automobiles (as well as skyscraper elevators and, in rarer instances, "flying machines") and confronted by kinetic visual spectacles—from "jumping, wriggling inconsistent electric signs" to motion pictures—Americans are, Lindsay fears, in danger of becoming overstimulated.[70] He stresses that "action and speed and blazing light must alternate with mellowness and rest" and alludes to cases of actual disturbances in "nervous psychology" being provoked by excessive driving or film viewing.[71]

Assuming that such excess can be contained, however, Lindsay sees a positive, liberating effect in America's "fanaticism of motion."[72] "The most inert soul in the world," Lindsay writes, "once learning to drive a car, even a Ford car is swept relentlessly past his own resolution and convictions."[73] While this rapid psychological change yields careless drivers, it also, Lindsay speculates, can produce dramatic social changes. He credits speed with "making one nation of all the tribes and tongues under this government, and really making them one separate tribe"—that is, with producing a distinct, unified, but internally heterogeneous American people.[74] Therefore, constant car driving is a kind of incipient national ritual. Although the average driver (unlike the west-going pioneers of the past) is not engaged in a long-distance journey, she or he nevertheless participates in a virtual collective movement, one that expresses an intrinsic national restlessness. And of course, for Lindsay, the motion picture, "closely akin" to the Ford car, has this same beneficial "speeding-up" effect; film "does the same thing to the human-mind," liberating "souls" from a state of inertia.[75]

Articulated in terms of the analogy between cars and movies, the nervous agitation of film spectatorship (the physical and mental state induced by the viewing of filmed motion) gives way, in Lindsay's account, to his third and final type of historical movement. In making his prescriptions for the near future, Lindsay stresses the need for *imaginative* travel. Whatever dangers motion pictures may pose in terms of overstimulation, they are, he believes, the most effective basis for reflecting (and producing) collective dreams. And these dreams, of course, are enactments of and opportunities for utopian journeys; they allow for virtual movements, the flight of the "Psyche-Butterfly," or what Lindsay calls the "leap" into the "fourth dimension." Throughout *The Progress and Poetry of the Movies*, Lindsay talks about "stepping through the mirror screen into the fourth dimension."[76] He uses the argot of theosophy to name the realm of existence that supposedly lies, in the words of P. D. Ouspensky, "outside of three-dimensional space" and portrays the film screen as its portal.[77]

Although Lindsay's third type of movement, imaginative transport, is quite different from the other two, he sees it as their historical successor and as superior to them in terms of transformative power. In essence, the movement of dreams recapitulates the movements of westward pioneers and speed-crazed drivers on a higher level. Because this movement is totally ethereal—in fact, it is not movement, in the spatial sense at all—it becomes paradoxically perfect: movement through time and directly into the "mystical future." As Lindsay's repeated references to the fourth dimension indicate, "in the hands of the right dreamer" (the suitably inspired producer), the motion picture "can transport us instantly to the end of the world, to the depths of the ages, and forward into the millennium," just as it transports spectators to imaginary places.[78]

To bolster his claim that film activates the inert soul, Lindsay leans heavily on Hugo Münsterberg's *The Photoplay: A Psychological Study* (1916), a work of applied psychology that closely followed Lindsay's *The Art of the Moving Picture* into publication. Specifically, Lindsay concentrates on those passages in which Münsterberg describes the film spectator's "soul" as becoming empowered to shape "reality," such that she or he feels a sense of liberation—"*the massive outer world has lost its weight . . . mind has triumphed over matter.*"[79] While Münsterberg and Lindsay no doubt reach significant shared conclusions, it is important to note the crucial differences between their respective theoretical aims and emphases.

First, Münsterberg's account of film spectatorship comes out of early cognitive science. He attempts to describe how formal devices in film (like flashbacks or variations in camera distance) activate particular parts of the viewer's own mental apparatus (like memory or association), allowing her or him to feel like an active participant in the process of giving coherence and continuity to the events unfolding on screen. The film, he argues, seems to be the product of the spectator's imagination. Then Münsterberg construes the spectator's sense of freedom from mundane "laws," in neo-Kantian terms, as a pleasurable escape into an autonomous realm of aesthetic experience. In his view, the "unique satisfaction" of "the photoplay" is that it renders human actions in beautiful, unified forms existing in *"complete isolation from the practical world."*[80]

In Lindsay's reading of Münsterberg, we see him, again, stretching to assert not just a common project but a total harmony of ideas—indeed, a kind of mental cooperation—with another intellectual.[81] Reading Münsterberg's psychological and neo-Kantian study selectively, Lindsay seizes on a few striking phrases and recasts them into his own Swedenborgian, mystical framework, then insisting, hyperbolically, that "every page of Münsterberg implies the philosophy of the fourth dimension."[82] In other words, Lindsay takes Münsterberg's words as an endorsement of the logic of theosophy and mental science.[83] Lindsay understands Münsterberg as saying that cinema moves the spectator into what Fenwicke Holmes called *"an idealistic universe"*: *"a universe in which in its essential nature is purely spiritual and therefore subject to"* the "law" of "creative mind."[84]

Portraying the mind's triumph over matter as the culminating form of utopian American movement, Lindsay's discussion of Münsterberg offers the theoretical basis for his analyses in the second film book's central chapters. There Lindsay engages in extensive "hieroglyphic" readings of and critical commentaries on what he takes to be the two most important films of the present moment—"the greatest pictures now playing," to use his projected title—*The Covered Wagon* and the Raoul Walsh–directed, Douglas Fairbanks vehicle, *The Thief of Bagdad* (United Artists, 1924). As we have seen, Lindsay lavishes praises on the first of these films. He treats it as *the* film of American history—the film that demonstrates both the "fundamental" plots (what he calls "Pilgrim's Progress" and the "hurdle-race") underlying national history and the essentially cinematic character of that history.[85]

But having seemed to anoint *The Covered Wagon* as the apotheosis of photoplay aesthetics, Lindsay makes the surprising move of judging *The Thief of Bagdad* to be an even better film—superior, precisely, as an American utopian prophecy. Lindsay's judgment appears odd at first glance, given the film's milieu. *The Thief of Bagdad* is an expressionistic fantasy that weaves together characters and plotlines from the *Arabian Nights*; as such, it explores a decidedly "foreign," "exotic" setting, one deliberately removed from the homely Americana of *The Covered Wagon* or Johnny Appleseed, for that matter. It makes obvious sense, however, once we grasp how fully Lindsay associates *The Thief of Bagdad* with the central themes of his second film book.

For Lindsay, this film is a kind of waking dream that takes place entirely in the glittering surface of the Mirror Screen, which permits entry to a fourth-dimensional reality.[86] Evoking the thrills he experienced as a child reading the *Arabian Nights* tales, the film, Lindsay is certain, will transport contemporary audiences into what, in *The Art of the Moving Picture*, he calls "Ali Baba's cave."[87] As chapter 5 will illustrate, Lindsay's approach to *The Thief of Bagdad* is tremendously instructive in how it highlights the film's own underlying mentalist ("mind over matter") ideology—its appeals to positive thinking and the harnessing of invisible forces. It is also notable for being the most extensive performance in Lindsay's critical oeuvre of his esoteric, hieroglyphic-analytical technique.

In Lindsay's reading, the film's Baghdad represents the eternal "dream city," which then represents, relative to existing American cities (with their ubiquitous glass surfaces, visual emblems, and miraculous new modes of transportation), a transfigured, prophetic self-image.[88] Lindsay treats the film's fictional Baghdad as a veritable "utopia" while also suggesting that it remains a somewhat provisional image, a precursor of the real thing. The cinema's vocation ("the function of the motion picture") is "to lead us," Lindsay asserts, "past Bagdad and on toward Utopia."[89] This latter (non)place becomes visible or accessible in and through motion pictures, in that they allow us to watch ourselves (in fictional, representative form) enacting "dream" journeys.

Here linear temporality collapses: Lindsay seems to imagine a kind of pageant being staged in the present, a historical "pioneer" journey reenacted, but also introducing the technological anachronism of the film image ("dream picture")—covered wagons fronted by, or moving toward, the projected image of a steam train. At the same time, this imaginary pageant represents the "hieroglyphic" meaning of prior American history while also showing the way forward for the nation. The historical "west-going spirit" has been a protocinematic movement toward and through "dream pictures," a movement that the moving pictures of the present distill into essential forms. The cinema allows the contemporary public every day to take a saving journey, a journey at the level of "wisdom." It allows audiences to move "west of the west," as Lindsay puts it, to the Orientalized space of screen fantasy ("the East" that is "Bagdad") but also to the realm that lies altogether beyond geographical space, the fourth dimension.[90]

Not surprisingly, Lindsay does not explain what the fourth dimension is, in any definite way, maintaining the mystical vagueness that accompanies the term in much of the period's occultist literature. It is clear, nonetheless, that Lindsay understands the fourth dimension as a place of liberation from material constraints, spiritual truth, and time travel; the fact that cinema experience, in his view, takes place within this dimension solidifies the medium's claim to spiritual or religious transcendence. By adopting this perspective, Lindsay again takes a cue from Lee, whose philosophy underwrites the notion of the Mirror Screen as both a machine of collective self-visualization and as a portal into a dematerialized plane of existence.

In *Crowds*, Lee describes a utopian social process involving some degree of temporal delay and discernable material change: the "inspired" leader produces "moving-pictures" of the crowd's desires, goals, and ideals, and the crowd refashions itself according to these pictures, thereby becoming a spiritualized body. This is the basis for Lindsay's initial account of the Mirror Screen in *The Art of the Moving Picture*. By contrast,

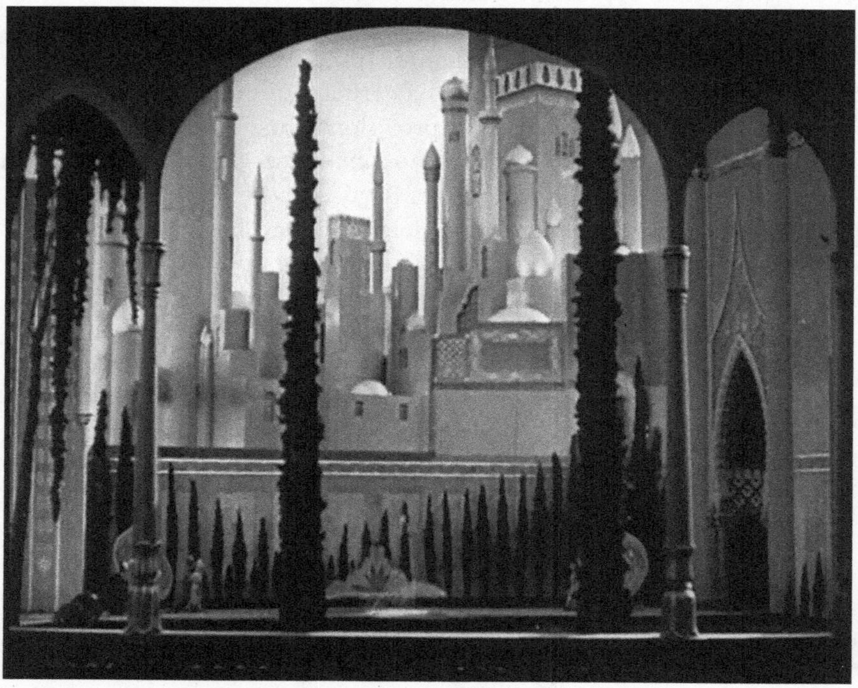

Figure 2.3. Bagdad as "dream city" in *The Thief of Bagdad* (Douglas Fairbanks Pictures, 1924).

in *We: A Confession of Faith for the American People during and after the War* (1916), Lee seems to eliminate all kinds of mediation and agency from the process. As my discussion of that text at the end of the last chapter showed, Lee's assertion is no longer that the "mechanical arts" promote the formation of a utopian community over time by altering the way that modern crowds live but rather that they provide *immediate* transcendence of material constraints. This is Lindsay's view of the Mirror Screen in *The Progress and Poetry of the Movies*.

By the time of Lindsay's writing of his second film book in 1925, he has made a basic shift in how he conceptualizes the screen. At this point, he sees its function as one of directly shifting the audience's thinking onto a plane of pure spirit, where invisible but real bonds can be forged. From this perspective, spectatorial attention becomes a conduit for a force that Lee had earlier called "the unseen or the intangible—the spiritual—as especially typified in electricity, in the wireless telegraph, the aeroplane."[91] In a seemingly tangential passage from *Crowds*, Lee starts to describe thinking ("imagination") as a way of harnessing the metaphysical forces that undergird the material world. The spiritual, in this formulation, is a field of forces, very similar to electricity, and new technologies are instruments of spiritual measurement, insofar as they register and display the presence of the unseen energy. Lee points here to the "mastery of spirit over matter" and indicates the crucial role that modern machinery plays in making this mastery evident to human beings—in fact, he goes as far as to say "chang[ing] the structure of the brain."[92] Representing a miraculous invention (an indication of "what is going to happen next in the world") and allowing communication across great distances, the telephone, for instance, mystically enables people to experience future times as "an organic part of [their lives] today" and to break free of constraints on their imaginations ("to think in larger figures").[93]

In all of these ways, Lee signals his early interest in a type of thought that is insistently "positive," possessing the power to transform matter and subject to quasi-scientific study (spirit being a form of energy, force, or even electricity).[94] Lindsay follows Lee, especially in the second film book, in giving autonomy and priority to all things mental. Therefore, his account of the Mirror Screen ends in exactly the ideological paradox that Lee's "moving-picture" theory does. It ends up simply fetishizing existent reality, imbuing the act of its consumption as spectacle with the importance of utopian social transformation. Indeed, Lindsay explicitly refuses "economic revolution," or, for that matter, any kind of "public act" as a means of bringing about the "New Jerusalem."[95] He makes this statement in the context of endorsing national self-visualization, proposing something like an endless civic pageant or "Perpetual World's Fair"—the exhibition of ideals as commodities—as a means to resolving national problems that exist, first and foremost, in the material realm of production.[96] The New Jerusalem, for Lindsay, is crucially not about universal property ownership or even expanded leisure opportunities. It is, to borrow Lee's phrase, about "changing the structure of the brain."

Likewise, the spiritual journey afforded by motion pictures is not a process of development in the sense of change that takes place over time and in the material world but rather an upward flight through increasingly elevated states of mind. As the religious historian Robert Ellwood says apropos of Lindsay's intellectual hero, Swedenborg, "only motives, not acts are saving."[97] In both Lee's and Lindsay's writings, the basic gambit is, if we can just set about turning everything that exists or has existed into visual emblems of desire—"moving-pictures," reality viewed through the rose-colored glasses of advertising and mind-cure doctrine—then we can reach the millennium here and now, even though (or perhaps because) nothing outwardly changes.

3 "The Motion Picture Is War's Greatest Antidote"

RESCUE AS RELEASE OF FORCE IN D. W. GRIFFITH'S *INTOLERANCE*

The people in Ford cars are not the only ones that enjoy them. They fly through the streets addressed to all of us—happy valentines about the world and about the way things are going in it. . . .

Instead of merely founding another university for the world with ten million dollars, Mr. Ford is making the world a university. Ten thousand factories have gone to school and the streets are full of people learning. He has arrested the attention of us all.

—Gerald Stanley Lee, *We: A Confession of Faith for the American People during and after the War*[1]

Many amusing incidents crept in to relieve the tension under which Griffith and all his workers labored. On one occasion De Wolf Hopper [a renowned actor playing a small role in the film] came out to look things over. Standing on the director's platform with Mr. Griffith, he observed an automobile passing through the streets of Jerusalem; its only occupant was a man clothed in a snow-white robe.

"That's far enough!" shouted Griffith. "You may enter the scene from there!"

Hopper turned a puzzling face toward Griffith.

"Who is that?" he asked.

"That is Jesus of Nazareth," answered Griffith.

"Well!" exclaimed Hopper, "I have lived to see Christ entering Jerusalem in a Ford!"

—Robert Long, *David Wark Griffith: A Brief Sketch of His Career*[2]

Between June and September 1916, two of the major producers of the early part of the silent-feature era released epic melodramas with pacifist messages. Both films announced their lofty ambitions through titles composed of single abstract nouns, and both appeared to align themselves with the anti-interventionist stance toward the Great War then maintained by President Woodrow Wilson. The first of these films, Thomas Ince's *Civilization* (Triangle), tells the story of a fictional kingdom, Wredpryd, that becomes embroiled in a destructive, technologically enhanced conflict, only to be saved by the second coming of Jesus Christ.[3]

Focusing on the devastating impact of the King of Wredpryd's (Herschel Mayall) warmongering, the greater part of *Civilization* is a traditional war film, featuring long and spectacular battle scenes. At the start of the film, the king ignores the pleas of Christian peace advocates, including his own daughter, Katheryn (Enid Markey), refusing to sign a treaty that would preempt such carnage. One of the king's initial allies, Count Ferdinand (Howard C. Hickman), a submarine inventor who is in love with Katheryn, becomes the vehicle of his eventual conversion.

After shipping out to the war, Ferdinand refuses an order to torpedo a passenger ship believed to be carrying enemy munitions. Ferdinand is critically injured in a scuffle with his own men, and as he lies near death, Jesus returns to inhabit his "earthly body." Now the leader of the movement for "Universal Peace," Ferdinand gathers an enormous crowd, led by the mothers of soldiers, in front of the palace; they pray, sing, and plead for an end to the war. When visiting Ferdinand in the cell where he has imprisoned him, the recalcitrant King suddenly finds himself in "the presence of a higher power." Jesus's spirit emerges from the count's body and summons the king's spirit to follow him. The wall of the cell breaks open, and using double exposure, the film proceeds to show Jesus and the king observing various scenes of carnage and grief, themselves unseen. Awakening from his "trance," the king repents and immediately signs the peace treaty that he previously spurned. The film concludes with joyous scenes of soldiers returning to Nurma and reuniting with their families. An intertitle asserts, "The cry of woe is forever hushed," before the capitalized word "CIVILIZATION" flashes on screen, to end the film.

Released just a few months after *Civilization*, D. W. Griffith's *Intolerance* (Griffith Feature Films) also concludes with a hopeful vision of the end of the contemporary conflict and the dawn of perpetual peace.[4] Both films frame their overarching theme in broad, dualistic terms.[5] In *Civilization*, the story is meant to illustrate that only when human beings obey "the command of the Prince of Peace . . . 'Love thy neighbor as thyself'" and overcome all the impulses that lead to war ("Hatred—Greed—Envy") can they achieve a state of "Civilization." Short of a state of permanent "Universal Peace," modern society is undeserving of that title.[6] For its part, *Intolerance* aims to tell the story of "how hatred and intolerance, through all the ages, have battled against love and charity," and it presents World War I as the latest instance of this eternal metaphysical struggle.[7] Like *Civilization*, *Intolerance* equates the swift ending of the contemporary conflict with the arrival of the millennium ("perfect love," "peace forevermore" are its key phrases), suggesting that this international conflict has a final or apocalyptic (in the strict sense of the term) historical significance.

Unlike the Ince film, the Griffith epic limits its actual representation of the Great War to a few shots that come at the very end.[8] These shots form the core of *Intolerance*'s narrative coda, which immediately follows the resolution of the four "parallel" plots comprising the narrative proper, marked by the Boy's (Robert Harron) last-second rescue from execution in the modern section.[9] After the final shot of the Boy being reunited with his wife, the Dear One (Mae Marsh), an intertitle appears, reading, "When cannon and prison bars wrought in the fires of intolerance—"; a two-minute sequence set alternately on what appears to be a World War I battlefield and on the grounds of a modern prison follows.

In a series of ominously red-tinted shots that recall combat scenes both in Griffith's own *The Birth of a Nation* (Griffith Feature Films, 1915) and in *Civilization*, two lines of troops charge at one another and begin fighting hand to hand, a tank and large howitzer operating behind one of the infantries. Intercut into this series is a single shot of a group of inmates in stripes angrily clamoring toward the interior wall of a prison. As a cluster of white-robed angels appear in the clouds above, the combatants freeze in place: several soldiers shown in an iris shot pause, rifles raised, as they are about to bayonet their prone adversaries. An intertitle reading "And perfect love shall bring peace forevermore" marks the transition. Having dropped their weapons, the soldiers all raise their arms toward the angels. Then in a series of trick shots, the inmates appear to pass through the wall, and the prison itself seems to disappear, a field of blooming flowers taking its place. Finally, we see people of varying ages, dressed as if for a Sunday picnic, strolling casually across the site of the former battlefield, the howitzer, now garlanded in flowers, providing a seat for a pair of small children. For the final shot, *Intolerance* returns to its "leitmotif," the shot of the woman who rocks the cradle (Lillian Gish), visible in this version in a medium-long shot that reveals the cradle to be filled with cut flowers.[10]

Civilization's conclusion depicts the triumph of the pacifist movement, enabled crucially by the intervention of Jesus Christ in worldly affairs—it explicitly shows several religious conversions. But the logic that enables *Intolerance* to conclude with a vision of an end to war is far less clear; it seems not to provide any kind of warrant for the coda's leap forward

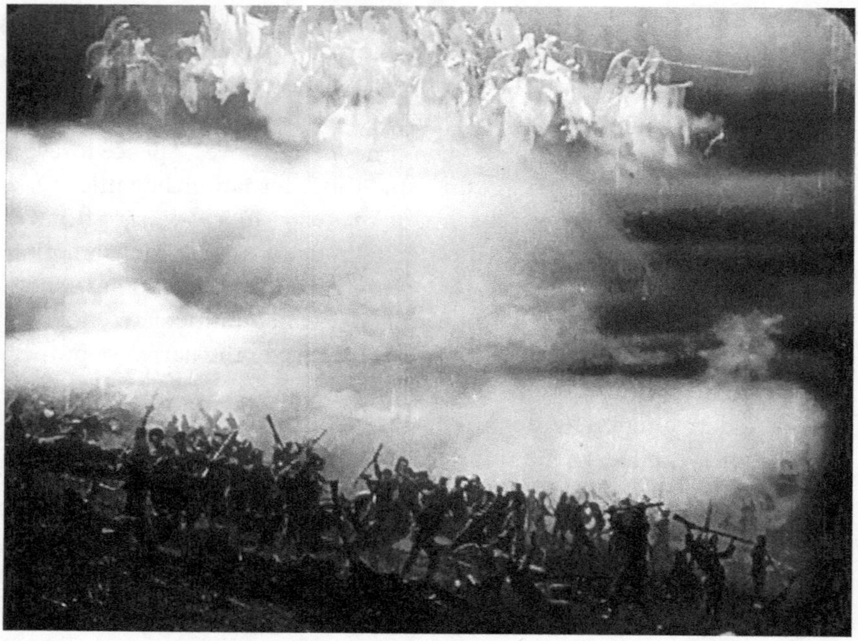

Figure 3.1. Angels appearing above a World War I battlefield in *Intolerance* (Griffith Feature Films, 1916).

into the age of perpetual peace. The warrant for this leap lies not, I argue, in the outcome of the events of *Intolerance*'s narrative, which are, at best, ambiguous. Rather it lies in the film's confidence in its own ability to drive the spectator to a specific "spiritual" disposition. In the transition from the conclusion of the narrative proper to the coda, *Intolerance* implicitly establishes this disposition—an exalted state of mind and feeling—as the basis of the utopian condition that it imagines becoming manifest in the imminent future. And it uses the automobile as the agent of spiritual exaltation. Speeding cars dramatically release forces that the film, self-reflexively, associates with another modern machine, cinema.

In the end, the film takes as its tacit subject the liberating and authentically "uplifting" power of cinema, which this particular film—with its ambition to be all-encompassing—is supposed to have realized. The coda must, then, be read as a visionary enactment of the worldly consequences of the new consciousness that the film itself aims to have elicited from the audience. This consciousness entails simultaneously an expanded optical perspective and a capacity for sublime feeling about "humanity" at large—about the potential for human beings living in the present to resolve the ages-old metaphysical struggle finally and positively.

Aiming to foster enlightened public opinion, *Intolerance* is a film whose audience address reflects Hollywood's early efforts to once again embrace the instructive and uplifting uses of cinema. Echoing prior articulations of the utopian-universalist cinema discourse, the film provides a model for subsequent films and industry marketing campaigns in the way that it allies cinema with the strategies and techniques of the nascent public relations industry and in the particular complex of themes that it assembles. Attacking censorious reformers generally and censorship specifically, Griffith champions a generic, departicularized brand of pacifism, which he links to the ideal of entertainment as a public good. *Intolerance* finally makes a moralistic case for the need for tools that alleviate boredom, locating a mystical unity in forces of social binding that it codes as simultaneously ultramodern and ancient.

"The Whole Picture the War Is Part Of"

As I showed at the end of chapter 1, Gerald Stanley Lee's *We: A Confession of Faith in the American People during and after the War* (1916) conceives of peace as a "sublime, irresistible, implacable burning energy."[11] For Lee, peace is not the absence of fighting but a force in its own right, a focusing of attention on shared goals that accomplishes tangible outcomes. In this self-described "war book," published in the same year as *Civilization* and *Intolerance* came out, Lee very clearly applies the rhetoric and conceptual framework of mental science to the task of rethinking pacifism. As one of that movement's proponents, Fenwicke Holmes, would argue, "*thought produces energy*."[12] A neoplatonic belief system, mental science denies the difference between matter and spirit, asserting that seemingly immaterial phenomena like thoughts actually participate in "the existing visible cosmos."[13] What goes on in one's mind influences the physical environment and is, therefore, scientifically demonstrable; thinking about and willing a desired outcome (prosperity, winning a competition), for instance, releases "electrons," pushing that outcome toward becoming a reality.[14] In this discourse, "force" is not an electrical metaphor being applied to the workings of the mind but a term that captures the fact that the psychic and the physical are inherently indistinguishable.

If peace is essentially positive thinking, then it follows that war is just negative mental energy, like the restraining thoughts against which writers of Holmes's ilk constantly caution. Seeing humanity as disposed to violence, then, is a sociopolitical version of the fears and doubts that keep individuals from achieving their potential. Lee's "war book" essentially advises that Americans should ignore news about the conflict so as to avoid succumbing to negativity and loss of faith. Learning too much about the day-to-day progress of the war, or about its political and logistical aspects, is liable to cause a person to take a dim view of "human nature." Aiming, on the contrary, to "cheer [his readers] up about human nature," Lee attacks conventional "peace talk" for its failure to recognize the positive, transformative power of "peace-energy."[15] Pushing the odd symmetry between "peace" and "war" even further, Lee keeps assuring the reader that he is not a typical "peace person"; instead, he is a "fighter" who aims to "present peace as a better way of fighting"—a benign form of coercion that also raises armies and seeks to conquer.[16]

Certainly, Lee's critique of existing antiwar movements resembles his criticism of prohibition-based moral instruction. In their focus on negating the not good, both promote a counterproductive negativity in thinking. But Lee goes further here, lambasting proponents for portraying peace as a "duty" or a "mere virtue," accusing them of a lack of real faith.[17] In his insistence on a peace as a sublime compulsion, Lee anticipates the argument made a few years later by the psychologist Granville Stanley Hall that "morale" is "the supreme standard of life and conduct," greater even than mere "morality."[18] The only viable concept of peace that Lee could imagine was "a better way of fighting," what Walter Lippmann, drawing on the work of William James, regarded as a "moral equivalent of war."[19]

Like Lippmann and James before him, Lee is concerned with preserving the "ideals of hardihood," group discipline, and manly valor most clearly embodied in "militarism": the goal of peace, these writers believe, cannot lead to the "tabooing" of the martial impulse.[20] Conveniently for Lee—as well as for Lippmann and his fellow new liberals—the corollary belief that the expansion of social "forces" is inherently positive means that actual fighting among nations (as witnessed in the Great War) allowed actual war to serve, at least to some extent, as its own "moral equivalent." The engagement of world powers with one another, however destructive in fact, could be viewed, in theory, as an avenue toward communication and communion; no engagement could finally be bad.

And for those commentators, like Lee, who viewed the United States as crusading on behalf of democracy and free society—fighting, in other words, a war against the *spirit* of militarism—waging war seemed indistinguishable from promoting peace. Just as the new liberals firmly embraced Wilsonian internationalism and the Wellsian logic of "the war that will end war," Lee would quickly get behind the United States' military cause while maintaining the posture of pacifist prophet.[21] By 1918, he would be writing copy for Liberty Bond advertisements and embarking on a series of essays in the *Saturday Evening Post*, which recycled all his arguments from *We* as criticisms of the tepidness of the nation's efforts to "advertise" its goals on the global stage.[22]

Griffith, of course, followed a similar trajectory, moving in step with his political hero, Wilson. Griffith quickly abandoned the proneutrality stance of *Intolerance* and, by spring 1917, was making plans to produce patriotic, pro-Allied films.[23] Juxtaposing *Intolerance* to *Civilization* illustrates the extent to which Griffith himself had already embraced Lee's dim view of conventional "peace-talk" as "a negative thing—a pale, scared, not-fighting" and the ways in which Griffith aspired to use cinema as a means of fostering a better kind of pacifism—peace understood as "an energy of mutual attention."[24]

Although the two films strike very similar final notes, their ways of representing war (and the resistance to war) differ markedly. *Civilization* works as a traditional preachment. It gives diegetic priority to scenes of battle (replete with images of wounded and dead soldiers) and of grieving civilians in order to impress upon the viewer the horrors of modern warfare.[25] In this way, the portion of the film where the king's spirit is treated to a panoply of shocking images (like Scrooge in Dickens's *A Christmas Carol*) reenacts the film's address to the spectator in microcosm. Entreating viewers to undergo a similar kind of conversion, the film relies entirely on warnings and moral chastisement of the sort that Lee rejects as obsolete.

Civilization does briefly portray the antiwar protestors summoned by the count as an oceanic crowd. The film includes one extreme long shot of the assembled mass, taken from a high angle, to indicate the perspective of the people in the palace, looking down at them. Although the panorama includes hundreds of figures, the crowd clearly spills over the boundaries of the frame, conveying a sense of sublimity and anticipating the similarly uncontainable crowds that feature in key moments of later silent epics like *The Thief of Bagdad* (Douglas Fairbanks Pictures, 1924) and *Ben-Hur* (MGM, 1925). But apart from this one moment that evokes Lee's crowd sublime—and one intertitle that, intriguingly, calls the groups a "peace army"—*Civilization* portrays these activists as insufficient to the task of inspiring change, dependent on a the intercession of an *otherworldly* agency. *Civilization* functions as a fairly conventional Christian allegory: belief in the divine Creator alone spares people from folly and damnation, and the eventual reign of the "Prince of Peace" alone brings a final end to war.

To critique the film using Lee's terms, we could say that *Civilization* keeps the audience's attention too closely trained on the brutality of war. It thereby risks confirming the idea of humanity's intrinsic fallenness and fails to provide any worldly vantage point from which salvation could be seen as an immanent feature of historical progress. For Lee, World War I "is and must be a part of a larger vision": "I know that if we can look hard, take our stand back far enough in civilization to get our perspective, see the *whole picture* the war is a part of, the war will cheer us up."[26] The imperative here is to convert one's mind's-eye perspective of the war into an all-encompassing vision that reconciles divisions into unities; from a sufficiently great distance, warring nations become members of a single "humanity," and international war becomes incipient global social communion.[27]

While sharing *Civilization*'s explicit antiwar, neutrality stance, *Intolerance* is distinguished by its "manifest intention" to establish the viewer in a sufficiently lofty perspective to encompass human history as a whole—and, as such, to make the idea of perpetual, universal peace available in an image.[28] As my comments about the film suggest, *Intolerance* barely depicts World War I—and this is crucial. The coda's brief images of that conflict are, as it were, dwarfed by the centuries-wide scope established by the film's four narrative strands. Griffith's comments about the film during and after the production clearly indicate that he intended this broad framing to cheer up the viewer about human nature, to afford the viewer a vantage point from which the film's insistently grim renderings of human cruelty resolve themselves into an image of peace.[29]

This resolution marks a significant reversal because, as many critics have commented, the majority of climactic scenes in the narrative are tragic. Although the focus falls there on the Boy being spared execution in the modern section, the other three sections end in carnage and death (e.g., the St. Bartholomew's Day massacre of Huguenots by Catholic mobs in the medieval-French section). These outcomes would seem to give the upper hand to "intolerance" in the historical and metaphysical struggle that the film takes as its main theme. And even if one sees the Boy's rescue as weighing more heavily than the other results in the film's affective balance, the main narrative conclusion indicates, at least, that the devastation wrought by hatred/intolerance is eternally recurrent, as it battles endlessly with the opposing force of love/charity. And yet with the appearance of the angelic host in the coda, the film stages the decisive victory of peace and love; the ending is *uplifting*, to use a fraught term—albeit one that still had a considerable currency during this period.

Critics have had trouble coming to terms with the seeming disparity between *Intolerance*'s evocation of cyclical struggle and division and the final image of decisive victory and unity. As a result, some want to minimize the importance of this last issue. For instance, Lesley Brill states that the fact that the film offers no explicit "transition" from its narrative climax to the "final sequence" poses an unanswered question of cause and effect.[30] The coda's resolution of the film's historical problem is, I argue, motivated precisely by the formation of the "whole picture of the war," as the film envisions it; the revelation of wholeness *is* the transitional mechanism that Brill struggles to locate. This universal image of humanity is not simply the product of the director's unorthodox decision to tell four separately situated stories in (or as) one film but rather is something that the film visualizes explicitly and signals reflexively as part of the experience it envisions for the spectator. In the film's climactic sequence and coda, unification is something that has to be produced—it is not a given—through the release of an esoteric force of motion, transportation, and finally, inspiration. And in order to keep the focus on this esoteric, distinctly modern engine of transformation, the film goes to some lengths to discount the two traditional agencies at the center of *Civilization*'s narrative.

First, *Intolerance* significantly restricts the role of Jesus Christ. This is not to say that Jesus (Howard Gaye) is merely a character like any other. As Brill persuasively argues, Christ's story "effectively sums up both the lessons taught by the errors and malice of the other stories and the hope that underlies them"; Jesus is, of course, a paradigmatic figure, "the greatest enemy of intolerance" to have ever lived, as the film calls him.[31] At the same time, his agency cannot be said to be the cause of the "peace forevermore" established at the end of the film. The film seems to resist the conclusion that divine intervention resolves the four plotlines or brings about what Brill calls the "lovingly peaceful" apocalypse of the end of the film.[32] Griffith's inclusion of a crucifixion scene (the final shot from the Judean story line) in the climactic montage encourages the viewer to reflect on the Boy's pardon as an instance of proper mercy. But even this lone example of "love and charity" triumphing over "hatred and intolerance" lacks an overtly Christian inspiration.

Second, *Intolerance* is explicitly antireformist, echoing the late Progressive concern with identifying mechanisms of social uplift that go beyond "repressive," legislative approaches to regulating human behavior. Mocked as "ambitious ladies banded together for the 'uplift' of humanity," the reformers in *Intolerance* are shown to be driven by envy and spite. They are women who, having allegedly lost their youth and beauty, begin to channel their frustrated desires toward preventing other people from partaking in harmless amusements.[33] These "vestal virgins of Uplift," as an intertitle calls them, are, further, wealthy women who seek to gain social prestige by controlling the fates of the urban poor. The paradigmatic example of "hatred and intolerance," the film's uplift campaign is a front for persecution: a charitable organization that aims to trounce the virtues of "love and charity."

The actions of the "ambitious ladies" provide the modern image that, by analogy, helps the viewer identify a transhistorical tendency on the part of social elites to legislate morality and to suppress religious and cultural difference—a tendency that the film, then, holds up as the primary cause of strife and war across the ages.[34] One of the fascinating things about *Intolerance* is how quickly it establishes the premise of human history as rooted in this metaphysical conflict. At the outset, "youth"—meaning life, joy, and movement—is confronted by a resentful "age," which, seeing itself as lacking in these qualities, becomes bent simply on checking the vital forces of the world. In the modern section of the film, women's civic organizations concretely embody this modern tendency, offering a simplified, exaggerated version of the conflict at the heart of Lee's and Lippmann's critiques of reform culture as repressive.

Given the film's misogynistic construction of reformist scolds as women who have lost their ability to attract men, it is impossible to imagine *Intolerance* treating a group of female activists like *Civilization*'s Christian "peace army" in a sympathetic way. *Intolerance*'s "vestal virgins of Uplift" are symbolically opposed to Christ himself, who, in the Judean section, rejects the hypocritical teachings of the Pharisees, their historical (feminized-male) counterparts, encouraging festivity and laughter. And the reformers' irrational and excessive persecution of the Dear One makes them enemies of the maternity and fecundity that the film holds up as essential feminine traits. Their move into public life seems to deprive them of the capacity for maternal sympathy that motivates the peace advocates in *Civilization*.

Carrying Power

In his authorized portrait, *David Wark Griffith* (1920), Robert Long tells the story of how the director came up with the idea for *Intolerance*. Upon suddenly recalling scattered lines from Walt Whitman's "Out of the Cradle Endlessly Rocking," Griffith envisioned "a girl seated at a cradle . . . rocking the children of destiny in the cradle of life . . . tenderly watching the human atoms who suffer through intolerance."[35] In this moment of inspiration, Griffith seized on Whitman's phrase "uniter of here and hereafter." Long cites these words, which appear on an intertitle accompanying one of the appearances of the cradle leitmotif in the film, as giving Griffith the idea for "joining the present with the past" in a single film.[36] The cradle is "uniter" here because it is a container. A couple of things are crucial to note here. First, the cradle contains in this sense because it makes unity visible, or at least conceivable in the mind's eye; the "girl" is the ideal spectator of a world picture, her perspective acting as a model for the film's addressees, both in its universal breadth and in its sympathy. Second, the cradle does this because it moves, its incessant rocking causing the infinitesimal particles of all of humanity to intermingle.

Whereas the visibility afforded by the cradle is clearly utopian, its movement proves to be ambiguous here and in the film. Associated with repetition (the endless motion "back and forth—to and fro"), suffering, and entrapment, the rocking cradle seems to highlight the perpetual reign of "intolerance" as well as the difficulty faced by contemporary humanity in trying to extricate itself from this age-old "destiny."[37] As with all of Griffith's complex, contradictory images of maternity in the film, the cradle is here equated with life as such but also shown to be menaced by the transhistorical force that seems bent on thwarting all kinds of vitality.[38] Clearly, in the end, the rocking cradle fails to function as a sufficient hieroglyphic (to use Lindsay's term, frequently invoked in critical discussions of Griffith's technique in the film) standing for the liberation of humanity from the forces of intolerance. Like other figures and concepts presented in the film as uniters, the cradle looks forward but finally gives way to other moving containers, which do succeed in bringing about this desired outcome.

In the Judean narrative, the film highlights Jesus Christ's role as "uniter of here and hereafter" by depicting the miracle of turning water

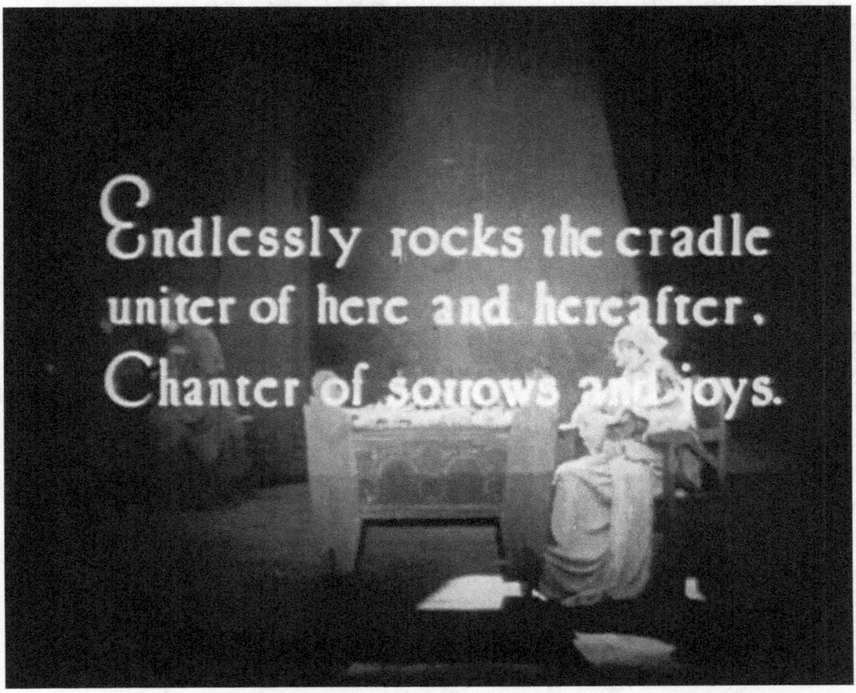

Figure 3.2. Cradle as container of humanity and time periods in *Intolerance* (Griffith Feature Films, 1916).

to wine. Likewise, in the Babylonian narrative, *Intolerance* draws on what Miriam Hansen calls "the Babelistic tradition" to portray Babylon as possessed of a legitimate but eventually suppressed "universal language" (cuneiform), which sustained harmonious relations among rulers and subjects and brought human civilization closer to the heavens.[39] During the film's lengthy climax, the viewer witnesses the destruction of both of these uniters, whereas another, seemingly quite innocuous object succeeds in uniting various elements of the film, with a transformative effect. Like the cradle, this object is also a container that moves: the automobile.

As Julian Smith explains, "The last forty minutes [of *Intolerance*] dramatize the efforts of a young woman to save her husband" from execution by hanging.[40] In order to rescue the Boy, the Dear One avails herself of four automobiles: "She dashes across town in two taxis, first to plead with the governor, and then to confront him with new evidence that will prove her husband's innocence. She then races against a locomotive in a commandeered racing car, and finally, pardon in hand, she races against the hangman in another taxi."[41] Known for chase scenes and the race to the rescue climax, Griffith had, of course, utilized what Smith calls "the 'saved by auto'" theme in earlier films, like *The Drive for Life* (Biograph, 1909) and *An Unseen Enemy* (Biograph 1912).[42] But *Intolerance* seems to portray the "*extra*-ordinary life-and-death utility of the automobile" by inserting several different cars into the protracted chase scene, by staking so much on the rescue of the Boy (he is not just a person being executed by the state but the paradigmatic victim of "civil intolerance"), and by intercutting this race to the rescue with three other tragic climaxes.[43]

As Smith suggests, the juxtaposition of the happy resolution of the modern story to the others may invite viewers to consider the counterfactual possibility that, had cars been available to the protagonists of the other three stories, they might have completed successful rescues or flights to safety. The two of the other three stories that culminate in failed rescues (the Babylonian and the eighteenth-century French) involve people who rely on horses as transportation.[44] It is, for sure, conceivable that the film worked "subconscious[ly]" as "free advertising for the automobile in a world full of danger and intolerance."[45] Whether or not the car's efficacy in the saving of the Boy suggests the possibility of alternative rescues, the sense of an ideally swift, maneuverable, and accessible vehicle certainly points to a narrative of progress through technology.[46] As Francesco Casetti has argued, the viewer's thrill in the pacing of the film's climax hinges in part on the idea of "the speed of progress," the sense that human beings are increasingly able to master and control complex environments.[47] Miriam Hansen, further, stresses how important the film's association of modernity with progress is to the structure of the narrative. Whereas the film establishes an overall "pattern of eternal sameness and cyclical return," the "happy ending of the modern narrative" (as enabled by technologies of locomotion) introduces a "teleological movement" into the film, one that is part "Christian theology of redemption" and part post-Enlightenment progress ideology.[48]

More important still, the car's introduction as a key narrative element marks the crucial acceleration in the film's own pacing (the surge of dramatic physical action in each plotline as well as the more rapid cutting between them). Casetti correctly notes that an element of speed enters the film at this point, a "feverish movement . . . that implicates everyone and everything": "It spreads from Babylon to Golgotha, and from Golgotha to the night of Saint Bartholomew, climaxing in the contemporary story."[49] In and through the arrival of this emblematically modern machine, the film "celebrates the thrill of speed."[50] Automobile engines are shown to overcome distances, moving human bodies through space with ease in order to unite them.[51] It is the thrill afforded by the spreading acceleration within the diegesis and at the level of montage that ultimately allows the previously separate plot strands to seem to weave together—the human atoms of the film's several ages to commingle.

Even though the rocking cradle leitmotif—the supposed "golden thread" linking all four stories—continues to reappear during all of this frenzy, its own motion becomes, by contrast, noticeably slow and unchanging.[52] Casetti argues that this image provides a counterpoint, serving to heighten the sense of "shock" that accompanies the images of mechanical locomotion.[53] Indeed, the film's motion becomes the motion of the car rather than that of the "cradle endlessly rocking," and the viewer is carried along accordingly. In this respect, the film draws on the period's romance of automobiles as agents of physical, social, and spiritual transformation—not to mention early film theory's equation of cinema with a stimulating experience of motion. *Intolerance* associates its eponymous concept with physical confinement, the repression of vital impulses, and the imposition of boredom—what Lindsay calls "inertia" is shown to be the underlying cause of all these things. Only the car and, by extension, the film screen seem able to overcome the *inertia* that is intolerance.

Smith places Griffith's film's celebration of cars' miraculous utility in the context of the lofty claims being made by period car advocates like James Doolittle. Doolittle's 1916 tract, *The Romance of the Automobile Industry*, characterizes the automobile as, among other things, "the most important device ever made by man"; "an always-ready servant that has more strength than Aladdin's genii"; and "the only improvement to road transportation since Moses."[54] Without a doubt, such rhetoric recalls the grandiose claims being made on behalf of the movies around this time. As apt as Doolittle's book is, the "spiritual" discourse around automobiles afforded by late Progressive figures like Lee and Lindsay seems even more helpful as a means of glossing *Intolerance*'s feverish motion.

The first epigraph to this chapter recalls that, for Lee, cars are "moving-pictures" of human striving: they are objects that advertise themselves—that spell out ideals and desires—and, therefore, serve an educational and uplifting purpose within society. They have this capacity because they *circulate*. Of course, for Lee, the Ford is more important than other brands of cars because it specifically advertises the vision of the company's "inspired millionaire" boss. Lee means to celebrate Henry Ford's willingness to pay his workers a fair wage and his design of a vehicle (the Model T) that is ostensibly affordable by all Americans. Although none of the cars featured in *Intolerance* appear to be Fords, Lee's broader point seems to apply here: the on-screen automobile "arrest[s] the attention" and teaches an esoteric lesson in human capability.[55]

As my discussion of Lindsay's comments on the "all-conquering Ford car" in the last chapter indicates, he too was interested how the experience of rapid movement through space could induce spiritual liberation. Lindsay saw car travel and cinema as kindred technologies in terms of their ability provide such an experience. And although Lindsay had serious reservations about the effects of "speed-mania" on contemporary Americans, he seems in his remarks on automobile driving in *The Progress and Poetry of the Movies* (1925), as in other moments in his work, to conclude that the benefits of acceleration outweigh the harms.[56] The collective sense of being swept away in or by the Ford car has transformed the American people into a single, unified community (a distinct "race," even)—with all the utopian connotations that the image of collective movement carries in Lindsay's writing. In seeing the same thing happening at a "mental" level with cinema, Lindsay, further, makes a quasi-scientific claim about "nervous psychology" that seems drawn right from the work of Hugo Münsterberg.[57] As Casetti notes, Münsterberg saw film as mentally invigorating, "stir[ring] . . . personal energies" and "heightening the sense of vitality in the spectator."[58]

Intolerance combines the speed mania of the automobile within the perceptual stimulation of the cinema screen. Even as the car is the ultimate moving and unifying container within the diegesis, the cinematic gaze serves to contain its actions and effects, translating them into a meaningful cognitive (if not spiritual) experience for the viewer.[59] The mobility of perspective afforded by the mobile camera and montage—the unique properties of cinema, according to the (problematic) media-specificity theses that Griffith himself helped originate—makes automotive motion an important theme. It places cars within the "whole [historical] picture," allowing the audience to thrill over the imagery of motion and sweeping them along emotionally. And this last, metaphorical form of moving is crucial in as much as *Intolerance*'s project is to produce a shared experience on a mass scale. As Louis Wienberg would write several years later, picking up on some of Griffith's characteristic procinema rhetoric, film (as a "universal language" and "people's university") brings "the carrying power of art" to its highest known point.[60] With cinema, the "single picture" can be dispersed throughout a "circle" that is, at least hypothetically, as big as "the whole world."[61] It becomes possible for the creators of film like *Intolerance* to see it as one single container carrying humanity—and not simply in terms of its fictional conceit, but in terms of its address to the international audience.

In statements explaining and promoting the film, Griffith tends to insist—in apparent contradiction to his own rhetoric of parallelism—that the four plotlines of the main story converge. The idea here is not just that the stories are truly one story in the sense of being iterations of the same underlying pattern; the description of *Intolerance* as a "drama of comparisons" already affords this perspective. Rather, the idea is that the four stories ultimately *intersect*, resolving themselves into an image of unity that is decisive with respect to human history. This logic is spelled out clearly in the explanation of the "Story-Form of the Play" contained in the program prepared for *Intolerance*'s New York premier. Following a list of the first six scenes of the film according to the story or setting, a quotation appears, presumably from the director himself: "And so the four stories alternate with one another until, in the climax of the last act, they seem to flow together in one common flood of humanity."[62]

Insisting on such a confluence of the four stories, this statement reiterates in condensed fashion a frequently cited Griffith remark that first appeared in Long's 1920 book. Here Griffith uses a visual analogy to better explain the cryptic notion that the four stories might "seem to flow together": "[The stories] begin like four currents, looked at as from a hilltop. At first the four currents will flow apart, slowly and quietly. But as they flow they grow nearer and nearer together, faster and faster, until in the end, in the last act, they mingle in one mighty river of expressed emotion."[63] According to this somewhat mystical scheme, the viewer is able to watch the four storylines unfolding simultaneously and continuously, even though the sequential nature of the medium means that, at any given time, only one story/setting is, in fact, visible on screen. From this sufficiently elevated, distanced vantage point, the film's four streams flow in parallel but eventually converge, revealing themselves to be (and perhaps to always have been) a single liquid flow, which, at the point of mingling, reveals its overwhelming power; they become an overflow. A force of attraction somehow draws these currents together, and the increasing speed of their flow—the result of the film's accelerating parallel montage—causes their convergence.

Picking up on the long-standing liquid metaphors of the crowd or mass, Griffith's unusual glossing of "stories" as "currents" highlights the central role played by this social figure in each of *Intolerance*'s narrative sections and, thus, in their seeming mingling.[64] It is the presence of dynamic, even tumultuous crowds that makes each story visible or conceivable as a flow, and with Griffith's initial description of the film's conclusion, "one common flood of humanity," he imagines a crowd of crowds merging across distances of space and time as the film's climactic effect. That the "flood of humanity" becomes a "mighty river of expressed emotion" in the second iteration indicates not so much a shift in conception as the kinship of these terms in Griffith's thinking. As in the contemporary utopian understanding of crowds, of which Lee was perhaps the foremost American exponent, the moving mass *expresses* deep-seated human longings and aspirations, making visible the transformative energies shaping modern society.

In a brief footnote highlighting Griffith's penchant for liquid metaphors, Hansen has suggested that his "four currents" statement "perhaps invok[es] the four rivers of Eden" mentioned in Genesis 2:10: "And a river went out of Eden to water the garden; and from thence it was parted, and became into four heads."[65] Given Griffith's unorthodox and esoteric habits of scriptural interpretation—witness his statements about the restoration of humanity to a pre-Babelic condition, discussed later—Hansen's suggestion proves compelling. If humankind has been forced out of the Edenic state by historical "intolerance," then this state has become conceivable for the film's spectator as Griffith imagines her.

Indeed, the case for the Genesis allusion is bolstered by the imagery of the narrative coda, which presents a "restored Eden," as Brill aptly terms it.[66] The final series of shots picks up on the crowd motif so important to the four stories, making the harmonious multitude, what Brill calls "humankind as a natural crowd," the central image of peace's epochal victory.[67] The battlefield provides the staging ground for a series of crowd panoramas. Strolling civilians take the place of the soldiers, who, after ceasing to fight, appear to merge with the angelic host in the sky, the light that streams down from the latter eventually resolving into a cross joining the two halves of the frame. Even the field of flowers that replaces the prison and its riotous inhabitants seems to encode the idea of a peaceful, aesthetically pleasing crowd. Given this chain of

Edenic associations, it is not surprising that the children in the penultimate shot exchange flowers or that flowers are the focal point of the final shot of the film, the last appearance of the rocking cradle motif. Here the flowers seem to function like the "atoms" that, Long asserts, Griffith first imagined being contained within the rocking cradle.

In Griffith's commentaries, "humanity" is synonymous with "expressed emotion" to the degree that the film, with its climactic overflow, elicits strong affective response from a viewer properly positioned to appreciate its sublimity. In other words, the overflow that results from the mingling of the film's currents *is* the viewer's sense of exaltation over what she has seen. Channeling Griffith's voice, Long narrates the director's intentions for the film, envisioning this climax's effect on the viewer: the "one swiftly rushing denouement . . . would leave you bigger, broader, happier than you ever had been in all of your life."[68] *Intolerance* can be seen as following the blueprint laid out by Lee in the foreword to *We*. It is an antiwar preachment that sidesteps details of the contemporary armed conflict in order to focus on the "real war—the universal war": the struggle between contending theories of "human nature," one negative and constraining, the other positive and liberating.[69] In Long's explanation, as in Lee's discourse about the "whole picture" of which World War I is but a small part, the experience of a broad perspective (the view from the metaphorical hilltop) correlates to an encouraging sense of humanity.

The pivot that occurs between the "swiftly rushing denouement" of the narrative and the coda depends on the reflection of sublime perspective and spirit back into the world of the film. In this sense, the film's pivot does imply the work of a supernatural or divine agency. It is, however, an immanent (rather than a transcendent) agency, humanity becoming a channel for what Lee would think of as an infinite energy. And the presence of this spirit is registered historically by images of liberated humanity, humanity freed from self-imposed constraints—from "cannon and prison bars wrought in the fires of intolerance." Alternately transformed and removed in the film's final shots, these motifs signify war and oppression as malignant entities oppressing humanity; in fact, the otherwise odd juxtaposition of the prison imagery might be read as equating war with oppression.

Descending on the battlefield and then on the penitentiary, light from the sky seems to make the soldiers freeze and the building disappear. In as much as the "heavenly light" can be seen as representing the light of the film, it associates cinema with transformation, a point underscored by *Intolerance*'s ostentatious use of "trick" shots in this sequence. Images like the angelic host appearing above the battlefield or the prison that fades into a field of flowers showcase the medium's magical properties, which here correlate to its spiritually transformative abilities. Given that the spectator is the intended subject of the spiritual transformation wrought by *Intolerance*'s accelerating parallel montage, it seems apt, then, that the angels appearing in some of these shots are permeated by the light from above. The angels are, in this respect, like ideal film spectators, elevated to a lofty perspective and exalted by the film's earlier rendering of human suffering across the ages, an enlightened multitude imbued with what an intertitle calls a "perfect love." And in the final image of the coda, the light intensifies, becoming a cross that seems to physically link (ex-)soldiers on the ground and the angels above, providing the viewer with a final image of fusion. It allows them in a sense to communicate, the angels looking down and the figures on the ground waving back.

Lest this description of the audience as an enlightened multitude seem exaggerated, let us recall the social importance that Griffith placed on the medium of cinema's ability to operate free of restraint. Responding to criticisms that *The Birth of a Nation* promoted antiblack violence and calls for the film to be censored, Griffith published a pamphlet titled *The Rise and Fall of Free Speech in America* (1916). In the pamphlet, Griffith portrays film censorship as the paradigmatic case of the impulse to "reform," which he sees as nothing but a contemporary "mask" for hatred.[70] Beginning here to articulate the expansive and overdetermined trope of intolerance that animates the film, Griffith adduces that proponents of censorship are motivated by a hostility toward vital human impulses (toward knowledge, love, laughter, and so on), their moralizing being nothing but a form of negativity or repression. Although my critical strategy will be to use this discourse around censorship as a guide for reading *Intolerance*, I must stress that the film's conceptual origins in Griffith's racism—not to mention his fatuous insistence on viewing himself as the victim of hatred—invalidates the film's putative humanitarian ideology, rendering it nonsensical from the start.

Griffith can then, conveniently, define cinema as censorship's opposing metaphysical pole, a pure positivity; it is as if censorship is not just a response to particular images deemed offensive or taboo but a willful opposition to what his early biographer refers to as "life itself."[71] In the pamphlet, Griffith makes the perplexing (but characteristic) assumption that films always teach "the truths of history," the very truths that allow human beings to overcome the "ignorance" of past generations.[72] Leading to intolerance, ignorance is "one of the two chief causes of making war possible," along with "monotony."[73] By Griffith's reasoning, the cinema is crucial not just because it instructs, acting as "the laboring man's university," but because it brightens the "cheerless existence of millions," alleviating a potentially "deadly" boredom.[74] As a consequence, "the motion picture is war's greatest antidote," whereas, in her or his perverse desire to keep the masses ignorant and bored, the advocate of film censorship—indeed, anyone who would have particular images cut from even a single moving picture—invites conflict.[75]

The idea of cinema as an "antidote" to conflict echoes Griffith's earlier insistence that film is a universal language that takes humanity "beyond Babel, beyond words" and has the "power [to] make men brothers and end war forever," indeed to "bring about the millennium."[76] The motion picture, Griffith declared in a 1916 newspaper article, is "the greatest spiritual force the world has ever known."[77] And the persistent inclination to keep "the motion picture under [the] thumb" of censorship only testifies to this force.[78] Given Griffith's confidence in the power of cinema, his evident belief that the medium is absolutely vulnerable to the meddling of the "narrow-minded" censors is paradoxical.[79] Clearly, this paranoid rhetoric allows Griffith to portray the struggle between cinema and the reformist impulse in the same dire, Manichean terms that he uses to structure the film's four plotlines—and, in turn, to make cinema's own "rescue" a subject of dramatic representation.

By Griffith's reasoning, an individual film like *Intolerance* can contribute to bringing about the millennium not by preaching against a particular war (its causes or its prosecution) but by aggrandizing the medium itself, highlighting its structural aversion to limitations (of space, time, and scale). It is as if the struggle between the motion picture and censorship encompasses all other historical conflicts (actually depicted in this film or hypothetically depicted in any other), revealing them to be dueling metaphysical forces. As the defender of positivity in the abstract, cinema is the means through which the metaphysical struggle can be resolved, its rescue from the reformist's tyranny being tantamount to liberating humanity from the yoke of intolerance. *Intolerance* pretends to do this by unmasking moral reformers as mere agents of constraint and negativity while providing a glimpse of cinema unleashed—cinema realizing its full capacity to move the audience with a quasi-divine, spiritual force.

Imaginary Unity

The reading being developed here, no doubt, relies very heavily on the director's stated intentions for how the viewer should perceive and understand the film's multipart narrative. In this respect, it risks presenting the kind of "closed" or "univocal" account of the film that Hansen warns against in her transformative study of *Intolerance* in *Babel and Babylon*.[80] Hansen notes that earlier critics have tended to take *Intolerance*'s "self-definition at face value," "self-definition" referring here to the notion that the film's explicit theme (intolerance as constant across the ages) and its structure (parallel montage) necessarily complement one another. In Hansen's view, critics like Christian Metz have attributed an ideological unity to the film that it ultimately cannot sustain and that is at odds with historical audiences' experiences of it.[81] Hansen grants that Griffith intended to convey a sense of continuity and coherence between the film's segments, ultimately allowing the viewer to understand them as merging into "a metaphysical level" of "narration" where they take on the same thematic significance.[82] But she contends that the parallel structure, in actual fact, creates resonances and patterns that either do not relate to the film's overtly "humanitarian ideology" (Metz's term) or undermine any sense of coherence and clarity of meaning.[83]

For Hansen, *Intolerance*'s parallel design yields "proliferating connotations," which mitigate against easy comprehension and, therefore, against the film's ability to communicate its message.[84] In her brilliant, deconstructive reading of the film, Hansen details these connotations, leveraging them against the "closed" and "univocal" design of the film. In turn, Hansen persuasively accounts for the sense of overwhelming heterogeneity that has confronted viewers of the film since its release in 1916 and for the frustration, confusion, and indeed, *boredom* that many of them have experienced.[85] At the same time, the way in which Hansen contextualizes the film forces her to construe Griffith's gestures of authorial intention (in the film's metatextual devices and in comments circulated in various print venues) somewhat too narrowly, thereby exaggerating the film's evident crisis of meaning.

Intervening in recent debates over "the spectator as a term of discourse," *Babel and Babylon* historicizes *Intolerance* in terms of the rise of the classical narrative paradigm and of the ideal viewing subject established by this paradigm—the unacknowledged addressee sutured into a fictional world made to appear self-sufficient.[86] From this perspective, Hansen reads the director's comments on *Intolerance* as expressions of anxiety about viewers' ability to comprehend the plotlines and synthesize main themes. She portrays Griffith as wanting, on the one hand, to assume the norm of classical spectator for the viewer of the film, while, on the other hand, being compelled to resort to preclassical modes of narrative address. In other words, Hansen projects taxonomies of narrative conventions used by academic film historians in the late 1980s and early 1990s back onto the film's "self-definition"—as if these later constructs were the defining terms of Griffith's own thinking about spectatorship. The film's heterogeneity becomes an effect of Griffith's uncertain, ambiguous position in film history, of his being simultaneously a pioneer of invisible narration (the defining feature of the emergent classical style) and an "archaic" allegorist unafraid to address the viewer directly in a didactic fashion or to revert to a "presentational," spectacle-driven aesthetic.[87] In turn, academic film studies' narrative of historical progression toward the classical paradigm dictates a negative evaluation of the film's efforts at unity as self-contradictory.

I contextualize Griffith's authorial discourse quite differently, focusing on the history of the epic film (of which *Intolerance* is a foundational example) as a fundamentally didactic genre—an attempt to exploit the putatively instructive and enlightening aspects of cinema—and on the development of the esoteric and utopian film philosophies that are the focus of this book. Not surprisingly then, I approach Griffith's discourse of spectatorship very differently than does Hansen. For Griffith, the ideal viewer of *Intolerance* is not first and foremost a person with "expectations of narrative clarity and closure" but a person wanting (or at least needing) some type of inspiration and instruction, like someone who might read a tract or listen to a sermon and who, moreover, is capable of sublime experiences.[88] Individuated but also part of various modern crowds, this imagined viewer is addressed, then, as someone whose disposition relative to the social whole can (and must) be transformed.

Unity is certainly the film's manifest goal, but this unity is not primarily a question of textual coherence and spectator comprehension, as the framework of classical narration and spectatorship would have it. While coherence and comprehensibility are certainly relevant to any analysis of the film, they are, I would argue, secondary to the truly "metaphysical" (to use Hansen's term) notion of unity that animates the film, with its rhetoric of esoteric communication between groups of people and between the cinematic image and its audience. As I have tried to demonstrate, this construction of unity allows us to begin to make sense of *Intolerance*'s otherwise unaccountable ideological mixture—of moral antinomianism, utopian collectivism, millennial faith, and Wilsonian antiwar sentiment—and to illustrate that this mixture is not entirely idiosyncratic. Rather it has obvious affinities with contemporary discourses about cinema as a moral and social instrument.

The labor involved in this process of deciphering perhaps proves Hansen's more general point that the film's rhetoric of universal intelligibility—the premise that it communicates in lucid visual symbols, or hieroglyphics—is ultimately ironic, highlighting the possibility of multiple, divergent readings. But the reading ventured here is meant as a necessary first step in the process of thinking with this film (like the others discussed in this study) as an attempted enactment of a broader cinema theory. To that end, it has been necessary to follow Griffith's statements of authorial intention even deeper, not to enshrine them as the final word on how the film should be interpreted, but to open the film to precisely the kind of analysis foreclosed by any approach that would deem self-reflexivity historically anomalous. Such an analysis articulates the logic of *Intolerance*'s final "pivot," the logic whereby the outcome of the film can be seen as positive and as offering a final sense of *oneness* (again, a form of metaphysical unity). It makes it possible to fathom how the dualism of intolerance versus love should ever be overcome and to grasp why intolerance should not always remain the dominant force historically.

Since its release, viewers of *Intolerance* have been perplexed and amused by the film's climactic sense of historical merging, the sense, as Hansen puts it, "that the Babylonian chariot is racing with the car and train in Modern America."[89] Buster Keaton's wry parody, *The Three Ages* (Metro, 1923), offers surreal instances of this perceived anachronism by projecting distinctly modern phenomena and habits back into the prehistoric and ancient Roman sections. Griffith's film, of course, refuses to actually transgress historical boundaries; a baseline cinematic realism is finally maintained. And yet boundary crossing—the merger of historically disparate cultures—remains a potent ideal, one to which Griffith frequently appealed in his public characterizations of his project. Even before the film was released, the *Intolerance* lot was styled as a space of impossible merger; the mythology that surrounds the film has as much to do with the fantastical scenes of oneness that could be glimpsed there as with the huge sets or the lavish resources expended on the production.

In Long's hagiographic account, the merger is, initially, social: he characterizes the "Griffith lot" as a cross between a social experiment and religious revival.[90] The news that something marvelous is happening on set, in Long's account, spreads across Los Angeles and eventually, around the country; people come to find out the cause of the excitement and sometimes stay to take part: "When the great mob scenes were being photographed, it seemed as though the entire population of Los Angeles had come out to Griffith's place to take part in the various pageants and mighty rushing armies. Actors from other studios—many of them prominent stars—joined in the scenes, anxious to be ever so small a part of this greatest production of modern times."[91] For Long, this "motly [*sic*] gathering" of extras, costumed according to the film's different historical periods, become a mass spectacle, a crowd of crowds acting—to Long's pleasant surprise—in a harmonious fashion.[92] He reports that relatively few people were injured during the production and reflects on the casual "mingling" of "as many as 15,000 men, women and children" during the "luncheon hour": "one of the most picturesque scenes ever witnessed by human eyes."[93]

Long's account participates in shaping a particular way of looking at the production lot as a microcosm that would become important to the publicity campaigns for subsequent epic crowd films, such as *The Thief of Bagdad*. In chapter 5, I examine the staging of that film's site of production as staging of the utopian crowd, laboring under the benevolent guidance of an inspired leader, which is hyperconsumable as a spectacle. Here, as I show, the studio lot becomes an even more pure manifestation of the late Progressive ideal of social cohesion than any scene that might appear in a fictional entertainment film. At the same time, as the third epigraph to this chapter suggests, Long is interested in the imagery of historical merger: "Christ entering Jerusalem in a Ford car" exemplifies the patent anachronism that the film finally keeps outside of the frame.[94]

It is one of the "amusing incidents" available to the visitor to the "Griffith lot" but not the viewer of the finished film. And yet what Hansen calls the "cross-diegetic thrust" driving the *Intolerance*'s climax depends on figurative or impressionistic merger.[95] Because, as my reading insists, physical acceleration becomes the mechanism of this thrust—the speed of the automobile paces the agitation and intermingling of episodes—the specific image that Long chooses ends up being more than a humorous throwaway. It literalizes the possibility of the rescue of the past that the film seems in various ways to evoke for the viewer and provides an interesting gloss on the redemptive meaning of automotive speed.

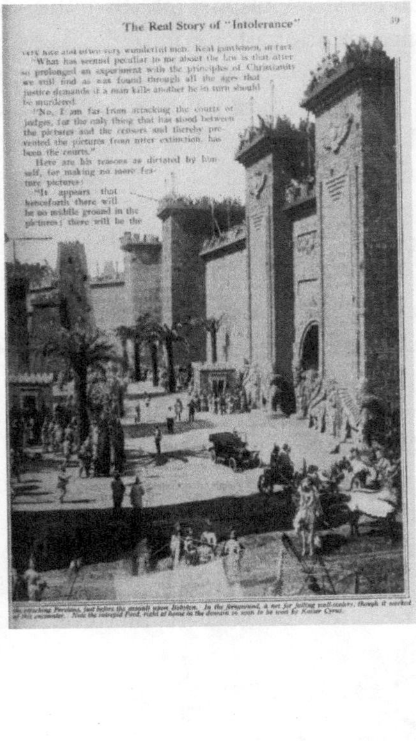
The Real Story of "Intolerance"

"What has seemed peculiar to me about the law is that after so prolonged an experiment with the principles of Christianity we still find as was found through all the ages that justice demands if a man kills another he in turn should be murdered.

"No, I am far from attacking the courts or judges, for the only thing that has stood between the pictures and the censors and thereby prevented the pictures from utter extinction, has been the courts."

Here are his reasons as dictated by himself, for making no more feature pictures:

"It appears that henceforth there will be no middle ground in the pictures; there will be the

Figure 3.3. The Babylon set as featured in "The Real Story of Intolerance," *Photoplay* 10, no. 6 (November 1916).

Customized for maximum speed, the racing car that miraculously appears in time to outrun the train is adorned with the number eight; an intertitle refers lovingly to this swift vehicle as the "no. 8." In its narrative function, the "no. 8" is akin to Jesus riding in the Ford car: not the savior riding in a modern machine ("deus ex machina"?), but the modern machine, as the ultimate "uniter of here and hereafter" (God in or as the machine?), a substitute second coming. At the risk of getting caught up in the film's mystical conceits, it is hard to ignore the significance accorded to the numeral eight by certain Christian traditions of biblical numerology. According to a symbolic interpretation of biblical numerals, eight signifies resurrection or a new beginning, because, to pick a couple of examples, it is the number of people "saved out of the flood to begin the new dispensation" and the number of "cases of resurrection mentioned" in the scriptures (apart from the resurrection of Jesus Christ).[96] Similarly, according to a mystical interpretation, eight is "the dominical number" because the "gematria"—the "interpretation of a word according to the numerical value of its letters"—of "Jesus" is "888."[97]

While the racing car surely carried its number when Griffith's staff found it, these hermeneutical traditions make the fact of it being the "No. 8" very apt in light of the film's pretense of staging a modern second coming, a new beginning for humanity. Given the attention that Griffith himself paid to numerology—witness his usage of the number four as a signifier of creation—the resonance was perhaps not lost on him. More important than this detail, however, is the film's broader presentation of automobiles as expressive emblems, moving images that signify the saving capacity of circulation.

In Lee's *Saturday Evening Post* essays published after the 1919 Armistice, he would reach all the way back to the prophetic vision of *Crowds*. Far from seeing the war as dealing a blow to the dream of international peace, he would simply reassert his belief that the use of "moving pictures" (a term he had by then taken to using in blandly literal sense) by political leaders of all kind will hasten the arrival of this utopian situation. Throughout the magazine series, Lee muses on the phenomenon of the international film star, seeing people like Mary Pickford and Charlie Chaplin as having perfected the art of making "nations want what [they want]."[98] The fact, for example, that Pickford's face is "familiar to everybody in all languages" proves that, by being visualized or dramatized, ideas can be made universally desirable. All ideas, he concluded, need simply be translated into moving pictures for domestic politics to be transformed; "statesmen" need to become "showmen."[99]

One of Lee's warrants for the claim about statesmen as showmen is the career of William McAdoo. McAdoo was secretary of the treasury

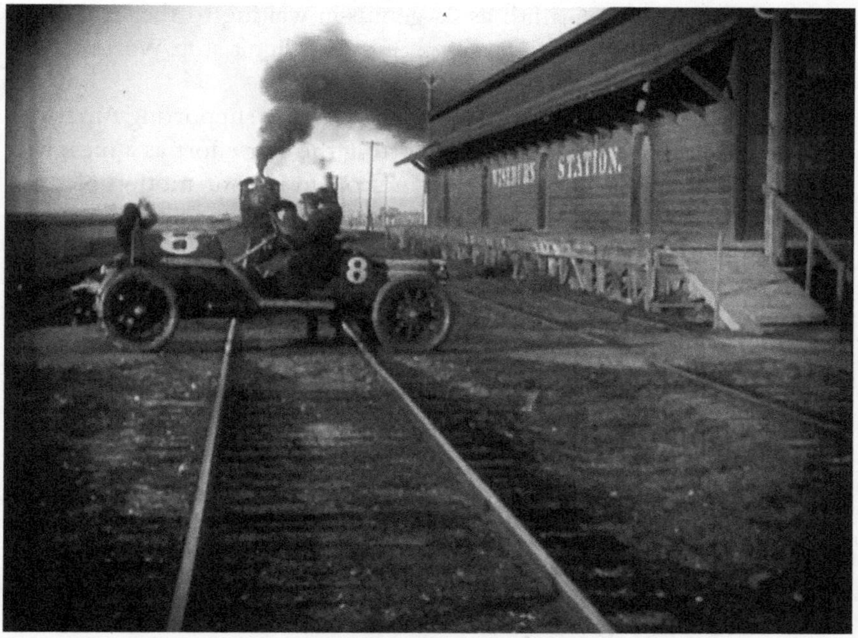

Figure 3.4. The no. 8 racecar in *Intolerance* (Griffith Feature Films, 1916).

under Woodrow Wilson (he was also Wilson's son-in-law), returning to his private legal practice in 1918. In 1919, McAdoo served as legal counsel to Griffith, Pickford, Chaplin, and Douglas Fairbanks in the formation of United Artists.[100] For Lee, who (erroneously) portrays McAdoo as having resigned his cabinet post directly in order to found a film production company, this episode demonstrates the ascendency of motion pictures over conventional politics. In the passage where he talks about McAdoo, Lee predicts that the former treasury secretary, having made sufficient money working for United Artists, will become president of the United States, "tak[ing] all he has learned into the White House to use for the prayers and the hopes of peoples, to use to sell the destiny of America to the people in it, and to sell America to the World."[101]

For Lee, Griffith himself had already come closest to executing this feat. Griffith, who historians credit with helping invent the concept of the film star and who had launched the careers of Pickford and Fairbanks, seemed, to Lee, to have fully grasped the binding power of desirable images. Just as Ford had done with automobiles, creating mobile icons of pleasure and enjoyment that could teach the world "about the way things are going in it," so Griffith had unlocked the power of moving images of faces, circulating freely around the world—hence Lee's seemingly cryptic description of Griffith as "a genius-in-waiting to the League of Nations," even though his *Intolerance* certainly didn't stop World War I, much less end human strife as such.[102]

For Lee, who, like Griffith, quickly moved from supporting American neutrality on pacifist grounds to supporting the war effort as a means of ending war, the continuity of a certain utopian idea of motion pictures was enough to keep faith with the prospect of a harmonious World State. Revealing the full power of moving pictures, achievements in the cinematic realm during and after the war, like *Intolerance*, seemed to make the League of Nations a viable prospect. Such a political body, Lee asserted, simply needed to be reconceived as an organization devoted to the production and consumption of films: its charge was to establish an arena in which nations could reveal their "faces" to other nations, making themselves mutually known and, therefore, beloved.[103]

"With the moving picture," Lee writes, "forty million people can look forty million people in the eye. They watch each other living in each other's dooryards across the sea."[104] Reflecting an emergent view in the late 1910s, Lee's conclusion emerges from a convoluted meditation on film stars, advertising, and political leadership. Within just a few years, the idea that the motion picture was the ultimate instrument for teaching nations to *know* one another would become the centerpiece of the American film industry's official self-representation, an idea that could be repeated simply and straightforwardly, as if it was a matter of common sense. In MPPDA president Will Hays's succinct summary, "When we know each other we do not hate; when we do not hate, we do not wage wars."[105]

4 "Everything Wooed Everything"

THE TRIUMPH OF MORALE OVER MORALISM IN RUPERT HUGHES'S *SOULS FOR SALE*

In the early 1920s, the screenwriter and director Rupert Hughes succeeded D. W. Griffith as the most outspoken critic of film censorship in the industry. Echoing Griffith's descriptions of restrictions on free speech as tyrannical and self-defeating, Hughes assailed "clergymen and moralists" for clinging to this "century-old method of attempting to make men and women good by law" and drew attention to what he saw as the absurdity of some state censor boards' prohibitions.[1] In 1921 Hughes appeared in a short industry propaganda film called *Non-Sense of Censorship*, produced by the National Association of the Motion Picture Industry (NAMPI) in response to Methodist leaders' new practice of designating specific films as suitable or unsuitable for their members to view.[2] Hughes expounded on his critique of the theory and practice of film censorship in his influential Hollywood novel, *Souls for Sale*, originally serialized in *Red Book Magazine* in 1921.[3] An early example of the popular fictional genre of female star making, Hughes's novel is an overt vindication of the industry in the wake of Fatty Arbuckle's rape and manslaughter trial and Wallace Reid's fatal overdose. It is a novel that further travesties clerical cinephobia and enlists the universal language metaphor in the medium's defense.[4]

In the different facets of the public relations campaign it mounts on behalf of the medium of motion pictures, the studios, and the Hollywood community at large, *Souls for Sale* reads like a kind of playbook for the Motion Picture Producers and Distributors of America (MPPDA), whose head, Will Hays, Hughes enthusiastically welcomed to Hollywood in March 1922.[5] In particular, *Souls for Sale*, which was adapted as a film (directed by Hughes himself) by MGM in 1923, propagates the notion of cinema as the most powerful tool of human education and moral instruction that would be central to Hays's discourse for the rest of the decade. Hughes's novel shows the extent to which, having been articulated, first, in the more esoteric writings of people like Gerald Stanley Lee and Vachel Lindsay, this notion had taken hold in Hollywood, becoming integral to the story that the industry wanted to tell about itself. It situates the industry's work within broad historical and metaphysical perspective—as an antidote to the corrupting efforts of "professional soul savers"—proselytizes for the "Esperanto" of the screen and calls Los Angeles both a "new Eden" and a "new Babel."[6]

Hughes, it is important to note, had made his first public comments on the subject of film censorship in the context of a preemptive apology for Griffith's *The Birth of a Nation* (Griffith Feature Films, 1915). Following

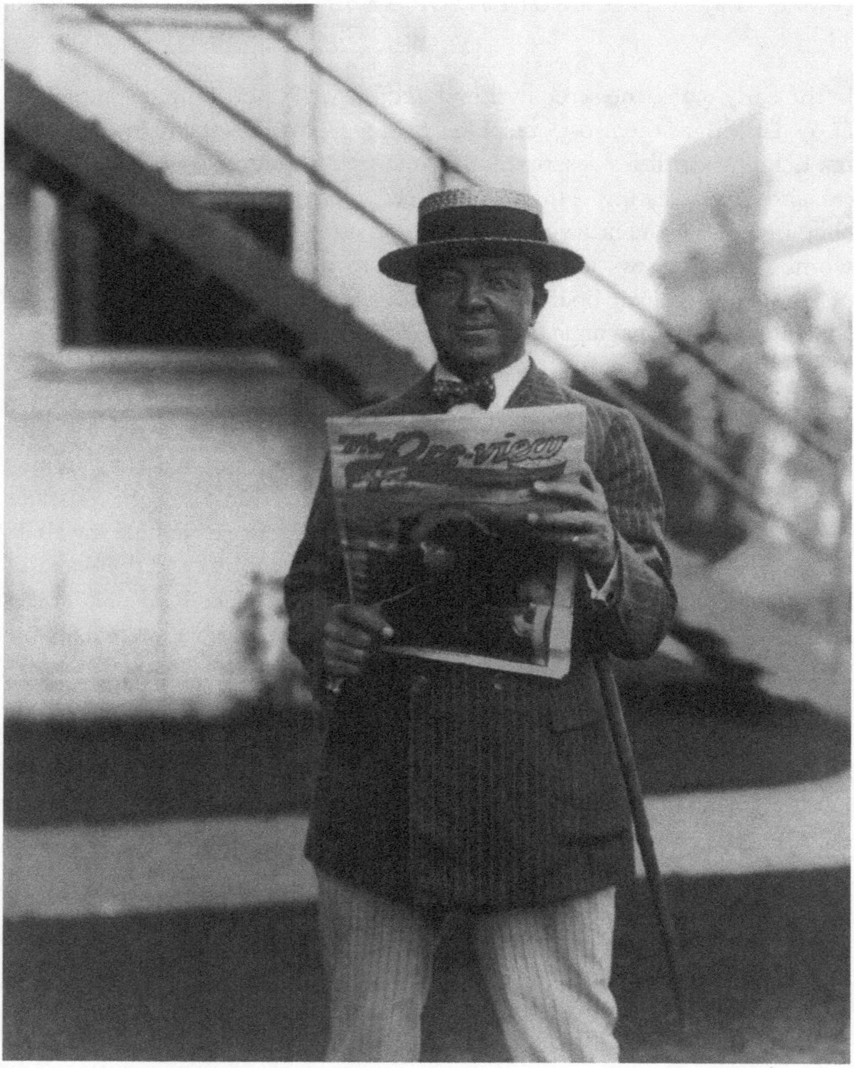

Figure 4.1. Rupert Hughes in Hollywood. Courtesy of the Academy of Motion Picture Arts and Sciences.

the controversy provoked by theatrical performances of Thomas Dixon's *The Clansman*, an important source text for *The Birth of a Nation*, Griffith sought to head off any attempts to cut or suppress the film by building a public case for its artistic and intellectual merits. Eager to capitalize on the weight carried by the opinion of the popular and respected novelist, playwright, and composer, Griffith chose to print Hughes's enthusiastic "tribute" in the program distributed during the film's premier run in New York.[7] Identifying himself as "one who cherishes a great affection and a profound admiration for the negro," Hughes, who was white like Griffith, praised the film for what he saw as its even-handed treatment of both racial groups, calling it factually true, authentic, and "in no sense an appeal to lynch-law." He concluded, "The suppression of [*The Birth of a Nation*] would be a dangerous precedent in American dramatic art."[8]

Like Griffith's, Hughes's own opposition to film censorship would, in time, be fueled by a sense of personal affront at the treatment of his own work. According to biographer James Kemm, the producers of the adaptation of Hughes's World War I novel, *The Unpardonable Sin* (1919), were advised to remove an intertitle in which a young woman announces that she is expecting a child, "any reference to impending motherhood" being "taboo" in certain jurisdictions.[9] Although Kemm does not specify which censor board(s) would have objected, Pennsylvania seems like the (or at least a) likely candidate given Hughes habitual, mocking references in the ensuing years to that state's strict policies: "No mention of approaching maternity is permitted [by the State of Pennsylvania] because it contradicts the legend of the stork."[10]

In spite of the two men's common experiences and early allegiance, Hughes would appear to be a most unlikely successor to Griffith in the roles of censor's scourge and champion of the cinema's utopian-universalist powers. First of all, whereas Griffith was willing to talk about cinema as a "spiritual force" and to depict angelic apparitions in his films, Hughes had long dedicated himself to debunking of spiritualism in all its forms. Hughes applied a rigorous standard of scientific proof to occult phenomena like telepathy, mesmerism, and the communication with and photography of the dead, criticizing in particular the tendency of occultists to latch onto technological developments (like the use of X-rays) as proof of "thought-transference."[11] Second, Hughes rejected the possibility of "perpetual peace" or any organization capable of altering human beings' belligerent nature. Hughes argued that the post–World War I League of Nations would fail in its mission "to 'end war' with a capital W," conflict being a permanent facet of human existence.[12] Whereas Griffith saw "intolerance" as finally conquerable, Hughes assailed millennial peace advocates as deluded—peddling "nostrums," as spiritualists do—and meddlesome soul savers. Hughes, ironically, characterized "Leaguers" in the same terms that Griffith had used to describe moral reformers, decrying their "ferocious *intolerance*" and "witch-burning piety."[13]

Last, and even more to the point, Hughes was, by the time he arrived in Hollywood, experienced in the art of "suppression," having spent the final year of World War I working as a censor in the military intelligence branch of the U.S. Army. In this capacity, Hughes wrote a treatise on the threat posed by enemy propaganda during times of war, which the Department of Justice used to pursue violators of the Espionage Act of 1917. Although Hughes's wartime career might appear to render his vehement opposition of film censorship hypocritical, this chapter argues that Hughes's preference for "expression" over "suppression" was consistent and, in fact, rooted in his work in military intelligence. Specifically, Hughes had absorbed the doctrines of George Creel's Committee on Public Information (CPI), with which his office collaborated, and judged specific acts of speech or representation in terms of their relative enhancement or diminishment of "morale." Hughes came to see cinema (which he reduced to the films produced by the Hollywood studios) as the ultimate tool of morale building during peacetime and, therefore, as existing beyond the pale of censorship.

In *Souls for Sale*, Hughes stakes his defense of cinema as a kind of positive propaganda (meaning, here, a generalized tool promoting collective faith) on the figure of the white female film star. For Hughes, the film star not only embodies a new philosophy of self-advertising but also provides an image that inspires members of the viewing public, mediating their communion. For all his avowed dislike of mystical, pacifistic, and utopian thinking, when it comes to movies and movie stars, Hughes readily embraces the rhetoric of magnetic attraction, telepathy, and unmediated understanding. By attributing this sort of religious vocation to the film star, *Souls for Sale* illustrates the full embrace by the American film industry of the utopian-universalist discourse. A writer and director with experience in government, Hughes fuses the late Progressive and New Age spiritualist elements of procinema thinking with the new star system. His association of the star's screen image with a robust concept of publicity further literalizes Lindsay's earlier poetic musings about the "lady before her mirror"—and in a way that preserves Lindsay's colonialist racial imaginary.

Escape Valves

Souls for Sale chronicles the unlikely rise to film stardom of a young woman named Remember Steddon, called "Mem," who hails from a small Midwestern town and whose father is the pastor of a Protestant church of an unspecified denomination. The Reverend Doctor Steddon is an arch "cinemaphobe" who lambasts the "new Babylon" of Los Angeles from his pulpit, blaming the movies for corrupting the morals of American youth and calling for the industry's immediate "reform."[14] Reflexively contemptuous of all things modern and fun, Rev. Steddon is the butt of the novel's satire.[15] It turns out that he has never actually been to the cinema, and when he finally does see a movie starring his daughter, he instantaneously converts to the procinema camp.

Though Rev. Steddon's hypocrisy and overheated rhetoric make him a comic caricature, *Souls for Sale* has a very serious critical agenda. The novel takes aim at the religiously driven film reform campaigns of the early 1920s by making censorship a metonym for repressive moralism and by blaming people who seek to censor for all kinds of misery and suffering. For instance, the novel blames the destitute condition of Mem's suitor's family on the passage of prohibition, a law widely supported by people of Rev. Steddon's ilk. The ban on the sale of alcoholic beverages has, the reader is told, encouraged Elwood Farnaby's father to devote his native ingenuity to procuring "illegal liquor" while also driving up the price of his supplies, further impoverishing him.[16] Here, repressive legislation serves to make a relatively benign desire for stimulation pathological by blocking any healthy means of satisfying it.

The same pattern obtains in Mem and Elwood's relationship. Rev. Steddon prevents Mem from spending time with the impeccable Elwood—a war hero and fast-rising employee in his company who supports his entire family—simply because he is "the son of the town's most eminent drunkard."[17] By not allowing the two to engage in a healthy courtship and by decrying all things carnal from the pulpit, Rev. Steddon succeeds only in "magnify[ying]" Mem and Elwood's erotic "temptation."[18] With their pathway to marriage blocked and with no "escape valves" available to "divert the strain on their souls" caused by duly enflamed curiosity, Mem and Elwood are doomed to "fall."[19] They meet in secret, consummate their relationship, and conceive a child.

Even as this passage acknowledges the salutary effects of a wide range of "diversions" ("art, theater, dance, fiction"), it lays the groundwork for the novel's larger endorsement of cinema as the ultimate escape valve—a source of "vicarious romance" that deters ardent youth like Mem and Elwood from pursuing the real thing.[20] With the pregnancy plot, Hughes turns the tables on those who would blame the movies for the conduct of wayward youth, presenting a character who is the product of a social environment utterly controlled by soul savers. Even though she has not seen a movie, driven a car, consumed alcohol, or worn a bathing suit, she has, nonetheless—or, in fact, *therefore*—"gone wrong."[21]

Souls for Sale goes as far as to blame the country's postwar economic struggles (including the Hollywood film industry's crisis of 1921–1922, detailed in the novel's final chapters) on the ascendency of the champions of "enforced morality."[22] Elwood's own promising career is interrupted when the adding-machine factory where he works as a foreman is forced to close due to a lack of demand: "People suddenly had ceased to buy adding machines. The world's chief business was subtraction and cancellation."[23] The explanation makes sense only at an allegorical level; literally, it is nonsensical, given that what was called "an adding machine" in this period could perform other mathematical functions, including subtraction. Symbolically, this plot point serves to portray negative thinking as a virus that has spread beyond the religious and moral realms, infecting the nation's very way of doing business.

Hughes is so wary of negativity that, in the passage where Mem begins to plot her elopement with Elwood, he refers to "the arch-realist, the sneering censor, Poverty, slash[ing] at [her]": she realizes that she has no money with which to even purchase a marriage license.[24] Referring to poverty not as the lack of money but as an active force of privation that "censors" Mem's dreams, Hughes reveals his underlying Romantic belief about the nature and condition of the "soul."[25] For Hughes, the soul is less in danger of being corrupted than it is of having its motive energies stifled in the very "attempt to save" it.[26] Given that he does not recognize the possibility of "fallen" souls, Hughes sees no need to erect a hedge of behavioral prohibitions around them; rather, he reconceives morality as a cultivating and liberating—"selling" in the complex sense of the term that he develops in the narrative—of the soul.

Not surprisingly, the fictional vehicle through which Hughes develops his alternative theory of the soul is Mem's journey into the film industry. Her experiences with film production and film viewing introduce her to the broader view of the world that allows her to transcend her father's narrow, judgmental morality while she finds in Los Angeles itself (the putative "New Babylon") a new "Eden" dedicated to the cultivation of healthy instincts and desires.[27] Mem senses early on that her physical attraction for Elwood is innocent, even though it puts her at odds with the norms of her community. She even feels that, in "disobey[ing]" her father's orders not to see Elwood, she "obey[s] a higher duty."[28] Over time, Mem comes to recognize her father's moral imperatives as a form of what the narrator calls the "cag[ing]" of her soul.[29] Mem comes to define the highest good as a kind of Emersonian self-reliance, a fidelity to her own "constitution," without any further attempt to label her conduct as good or evil—as conforming to or violating God's will.[30]

Mem's doubts about her father's understanding of what God does or does not want are reinforced by her first experiences working in the film industry. After arriving in Los Angeles but before becoming a successful film actress, Mem finds herself employed in a studio's "laboratory projection room," screening footage at various stages of the editing process to check for typographical errors and technical flaws.[31] Working at the industry's "spinning wheels" allows Mem to experience moving pictures as a totality, in a way that most viewers can only imagine. As Mem's eyes wander from her own editing machine, she is able to observe the "infinite variety" of imagery represented on the other technicians' screens (a popular serial heroine escaping a flooded canyon, Lon Chaney in "Chinese" masquerade, Tom Mix on horseback, and so on).[32] Taken as a whole, the studio's output comprises a world picture, a composite portrait of human life in its sheer diversity.[33]

Scanning "the magic window[s]" in the projection room and observing the "countless phases of life and emotion and character," Mem achieves what she understands to be a "divine purview of the world": "Life to her looked much what life must look like to God."[34] At this moment, Mem comes to understand God as all-seeing spectator; it follows from this understanding that human beings are actors in ceaseless "processions" staged for his enjoyment: "Humanity must dance before him as before her until each life was cut off or vanished in its final fade-out."[35] The lesson that Mem learns from this momentary experience of godliness is that aesthetic judgment is preferable to moral judgment. The divine perspective allows all things to be seen as balancing one another out across the whole of time, making distinctions between "good" and "bad" finally irrelevant; what God values most is whatever is visually striking—motion, contrast, texture, and so on.[36] Mem's God literalizes Lee's assertion that the only real sin in modernity is boredom ("The main road to hell is paved with being bored"); she or he demands only to be entertained and exhibits a generalized sympathy for all the players who come onto the stage.[37]

As in Griffith's *Intolerance*, the all-encompassing perspective opened up by cinema is meant, in *Souls for Sale*, to promote "a finer sympathy for mankind . . . toward life itself."[38] Given his antispiritualist bent and his skepticism about the possibility of permanent peace, Hughes does not, however, equate the availability of this sympathy with the arrival of a perfected human condition. Although he does not imagine that cinema can altogether eliminate moral condemnation, Hughes provides examples of characters who, like Mem, learn cinema's lessons about God and the human soul. For instance, the town's kindly physician, Doctor Bretherick—a foil for the doctor of divinity, Rev. Steddon—refuses to scorn Mem when he discovers her pregnancy and tries to help her and Elwood elope.[39]

Dr. Bretherick explains to Mem late in the novel that he does not believe that it is possible for human beings to "tell [right and wrong] apart."[40] Culminating in her saving her own family from financial ruin, Mem's own improbable journey from "fallen woman" to screen idol, he argues, contradicts the belief that "good can . . . come out of evil" and, hence, provides a good lesson of the futility of trying to differentiate between the two.[41] The novel implicitly attributes Dr. Bretherick's "almost total abst[ention] from the vice of blame" to his being a movie fan and amateur screenplay writer.[42] Having observed the full panoply of conduct dramatized on the movie screen, Dr. Bretherick has arrived at a wide-ranging sympathy for his brethren (to pick up on what the punning quality of his name), in all their wisdom and folly. From her first day in the studio projection room, Mem has intuitively grasped what Dr. Bretherick is talking about and cannot imagine why someone like her father would scorn the cinematic medium; it has the power to "teach the world a new language" and "open a new world."[43]

Mem encounters this language at its source as she begins to accustom herself to life in Los Angeles. Mem spends her first night in Los Angeles at her friend Leva Lemaire's house and finds herself in the middle of an impromptu party, with music, dancing, and male company—all temptations to sin, from her father's perspective. Mem overcomes her initial hesitancy to join the party and allows one of the young film actors present to teach her how to dance.[44] Her sense of having to learn not simply unfamiliar steps but an entirely "new alphabet of expression" continues when, confused and exhausted, she seeks refuge on Leva's patio.[45] In this paradisal setting of palms and fruit trees, Mem discerns a "lexicon" that contains "no such word as 'Don't!'"[46] With the very means of expressing prohibition being removed from this setting, Mem is free to submit to the "ecstasy" of desire suffusing all the sights, smells, and sounds around her: "Everything wooed everything."[47] Concluding that her "yearning was divine" and that "the great needs of her soul were love, tenderness, rapture," the already "fallen" Mem finds herself in a new Eden.[48] She decides to self-consciously reenact the biblical Eve's gesture of succumbing to temptation, sucking the juice out of an orange whose "luscious fragrance" has caught her attention.[49]

Overcoming her own proclivity to feel "shame," Mem comes to love what Hilary Hallett calls "Hollywood Bohemia."[50] She identifies herself with the young residents of Los Angeles, who have begun to cultivate a salutary "new paganism."[51] Rejecting "outward proprieties," she and her peers remain hardworking, sober, and sexually temperate; it is simply that they cannot abide hypocrisy or any type of artificially imposed constraint on free action.[52] Although the Hollywood film industry has begun to broadcast the tenets of this new freedom on a global scale, it is crucially rooted, for Hughes, in the climate and topography of Southern California. The region's balmy weather and gorgeous light make it an ideal place to care for the body and to cultivate the desires of the soul, a fitting place for people to have discovered that "the enjoyment of life" does not, in fact, lead to depravity.

The Shining Multitude

Souls for Sale repeatedly makes its case for the "noble service" provided by cinema, offering a series of variations on the "vicarious romance" idea.[53] Like all kinds of "dramatic fiction," the movies, the reader is told, have the "honorable . . . pretense" of "divert[ing] someone from his own distresses by exploiting imaginary joys or sorrows."[54] Movies provide a valuable form of therapy, "warming . . . dreary lives" with comedy, distracting the distressed with "pictured problems" other than their own, offering unsupervised young people a safe way of satisfying romantic longings, and so on.[55]

Finding dreariness everywhere he looks in modern America, Hughes immensely appreciates the figuratively brightening effects of the movies, an idea he underscores by repeatedly associating film with the sun. Sun metaphors abound in *Souls for Sale*'s descriptions of cinema. On a single page alone, the reader hears that cinema is a "heliographic" art; that the Hollywood studios are "strange workshops where the enslaved sun and the chained lightning wrote stories in photographs"; and that the films that they produce appear "wherever the sun traveled," "their reeled minstrelsy gleaming for the delight and indignation of mankind."[56] To wit, the novel sees film as originating with the light of the sun and reflecting its brilliance back to the worldwide public. Figuratively blanketing the globe, movies acquire some of the sun's properties, presiding over and providing constant evidence of the eternal human pageant. As in the famous passage from Ecclesiastes, the movies bear witness to the fact that "there is no new thing under the sun."[57]

Souls for Sale, likewise, plays on the trope of the film star, constructing this figure as a small sun, whose vocation is quasi-ministerial, brightening dreary lives by deflecting attention away from ordinary woes. Mem herself discovers the star's therapeutic powers even before she sees her first movie. After Elwood dies, she decides to leave her hometown for Arizona, and the westbound train that she rides also carries a group of film actors, on their way back to Los Angeles. Having descended to the platform during a stop, Mem purchases her first film fan magazines, only to collide a moment later with a handsome screen idol named Tom Holby, famous for his "sad smile" expression.[58] After Tom bends down to pick up the items that Mem has dropped, he stands up, his face appearing in front of Mem's, "like a sun dawning across her horizon": "his eyes beat on her like long beams," making Mem feel "warmed and healed."[59]

In her ignorance of the movies, Mem does not yet "know" that, from screens across the world, the "brightness" and "pathos" of Tom's expression also "pour[s] on millions alike."[60] She experiences the "amazing magnetism" of Tom's countenance as specifically intended for her.[61] As she will soon learn, however, Tom's trademark expression is a carefully manufactured commodity that he "sells by the foot" to millions of fans—one whose essentially impersonal character they fail to perceive.[62] Magnified by the screen and broadcast to all corners of the world, this expression undergoes a sort of mystical multiplication—it becomes "broad enough to circumscribe the world"—and the *attractiveness* that is evident in a face-to-face encounter becomes, in the narrator's account, an unparalleled force of social binding.[63]

Tom's screen image is, as Lee says apropos of famous people, a "peg [on which] to hang the wandering minds of a crowd and pull its attention together."[64] Basking in the star's warming light, the millions of fans not only imagine themselves to be communicating with her or him but, through this process of imagined communication, come to hold a powerful experience in common. The star's image, then, is a "community property" that emblematizes the individual's need for recognition (the bored and lonely person's longing to be noticed) as well as the possibility for unmediated understanding between disparate people.[65] As Hughes puts it in a passage forecasting Mem's own eventual celebrity, the star's image is "always of a more than human sympathy, and [speaks] in a language that men of every nation under[stand]."[66]

Given all of Hughes's skepticism about ecclesiastical structures, the occult, and the theory of human perfectibility, it is remarkable how easily *Souls for Sale* slides into a discourse that is at once overtly religious and strongly utopian when discussing film stars. At such moments, Hughes makes considerable allowances for the esoteric. For instance, Hughes's narrator highlights Mem's transformation from a "shy, frightened girl" into "a shining multitude," through photographic "multiplication," detecting a "diabolic telepathy" in the process.[67] Here "telepathy," the concept around which Hughes focuses his most severe critiques of "occult" beliefs, is invoked to affirm cinema's power to forge invisible lines of communication around the globe.[68]

Although Hughes uses it in the first place to describe Mem's mechanically reproduced image, the figure of the "shining multitude" also applies to the audience, for whom that image provides a point of anchorage: the mass public brightened by the "heliographic" art of cinema and bound up in the magnetism of its various smaller suns. It serves, then, as Hughes's version of the mystical concept of humanity come to a state of full understanding (in the joint cognitive, communicative, and ethical senses of the term outlined in the introduction to this book). In time, Mem the screen idol accepts that "her body and soul [are] the public's" property and treats her "dramaturgy" as a veritable religious vocation.[69] Refusing to marry either of her suitors in Hollywood on the grounds that she is wedded to "Mankind" at large, Mem assumes, in the novel's conclusion, the role of priestess in a new cult religion, one whose global reach and access to universal human problems makes her father's ministry look utterly trivial.[70]

Mem's powers of telepathy are cultivated by the studio system's machinery of beautification and dramatic training. *Souls for Sale* portrays her innate physical beauty (she is "pretty—attractive, compulsive") as a raw material—an "ore"—that must undergo a process of extraction

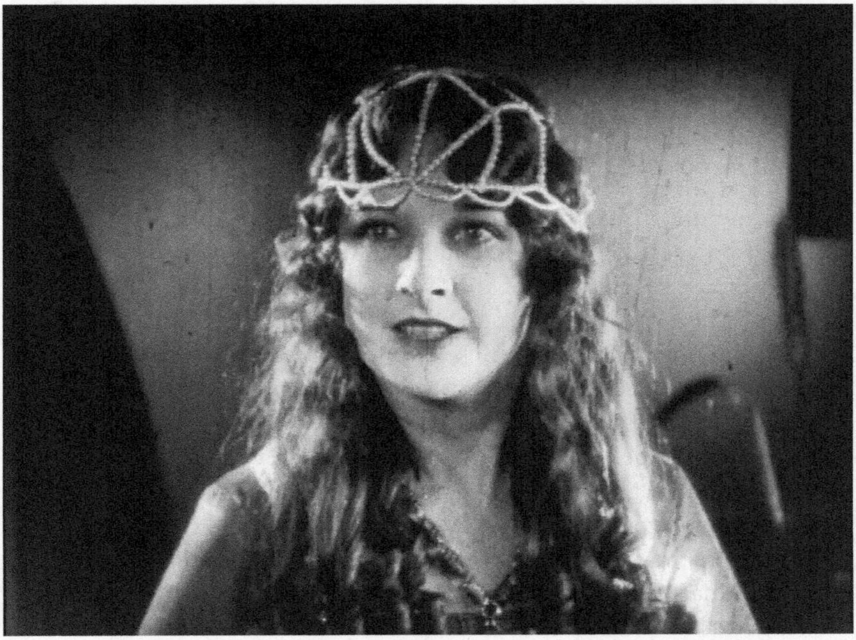

Figure 4.2. Eleanor Boardman as Remember "Mem" Steddon in *Souls for Sale* (MGM, 1923).

and refinement in order to have its potential energy released.[71] When he begins to work with Mem, the eminent director, Tom Claymore, assumes the roles of explorer and industrialist. Claymore, the narrator states, sees himself as "one of those developers of talent who feels a passion for searching out gold where it lies, building roads, as it were, to hidden hearts and giving them expression, making a traffic and commerce of expression."[72] In this analogy, Mem's body is an inert terrain that must be colonized (appropriated, charted, and exploited) before it can become a commodity consumable by the public, and the utopian image of the cinema as global network of "commerce and expression" is revealed to be an image of empire.

Hughes goes beyond describing star making as a process of commodification to suggest that the male director's work is akin to a rescue. Without being tied into the utopian "traffic" of international film, Mem's existence would be valueless; to be sold is to be "saved," albeit in an economic rather than soteriological sense. The narrator explains this counterintuitive concept by expounding on the idea of Mem's body and soul as colonialized territory: "[Claymore] compared the development of an artist with the slow human miracle from the grim bleakness of the desert."[73] In this analogy, Claymore plays the role of the heroic white "pioneers" who have "push[ed] the wasteland back," turning the region into a "pleasaunce" and "paradise."[74] Here Mem is aligned with the physical setting of the film studios, the Southern California landscape, which, in late nineteenth and early twentieth-century settlement mythology, is always portrayed as an arid waste awaiting irrigation to be turned into lush garden.[75]

The narrator's rhetoric highlights the fact that, within the institutional structure of the film industry, Mem herself remains subject to a gendered power differential. As Hallett's work shows, however, *Souls for Sale*'s evident endorsement of this differential is tempered somewhat by the novel's portrayal of Mem as a feminist pioneer.[76] Hughes's mouthpiece in the novel, Dr. Bretherick, attempts to impress upon Mem that she is living in an era of women's liberation and should capitalize on the opportunities that lie therein (such as the right to vote), rejecting her father's outdated belief in female subservience.[77] Further, in the passages depicting Mem's arrival in Los Angeles, Hughes's narrator lauds the young women working in Hollywood for being "self-supporting."[78] In moments like these, Hallett explains, Hughes styles Mem as a representative of the many "New Women" of the 1910s and 1920s, who migrated to Los Angeles and participated in the formation of a "new urban frontier," where the domestic ideal of "true womanhood" could be contested.[79]

As significant as Hughes's celebration of women's political equality and economic independence is his portrayal of the female film star's rise retains troubling sexist and racist-colonialist elements. What really stands out, first of all, about Mem's transformation is that the process being described is, by and large, one of simple beautification. Some of what Claymore impresses upon Mem has to do with expressive movement, but the emphasis in this passage (as well as others dealing with Mem's development into a star) falls on the cultivation of outwardly pleasing qualities; the novel's notion of the visible soul never seems to distinguish itself completely from the body. In this regard, Hughes falls into the same trap as Vachel Lindsay does in "To a Lady before Her Mirror," the poem interpolated into his posthumously published second book of film theory, which I examined at length in chapter 2.

The novel struggles to differentiate Mem's "soul" from her "body," constantly reducing the liberation ("uncaging") of the former to the exhibition of the latter. Like Lindsay, Hughes often seems to attribute unwarranted philosophical significance to commonplace notions of aesthetic and erotic desirability. In short, *Souls for Sale* tries to imbue "attractiveness" (in the colloquial sense of the word) with the nobility that social cohesiveness carries in the late Progressive discourse around media. The novel's fetishization of female beauty, as well as its celebration of bodily self-exhibition as an act of emancipation, suggests another kind of patriarchal ideology, albeit one that is hostile to the "Victorian" patriarchalism that it caricatures in the figure of Rev. Steddon. Mem achieves significant intellectual, sexual, and financial freedom relative to her position at the start of the novel, and yet the vehicle of all these different types of freedom is classical Hollywood cinema's familiar pattern of female objectification: she is locked into the position that Laura Mulvey has famously described as "to-be-looked-at-ness."[80]

More urgently still, the novel theorizes Mem's magnetism through a series of parallels and contrasts between her and Native Americans. The passages containing these parallels subtly but effectively communicate to the reader that whiteness is a criterion for admission into the "shining multitude" of film stars as well as its public mirror image, the enlightened film audience. Here Hughes offers a tacit admission that his universalism is merely rhetorical and suggests that the communion of souls supposedly fostered by motion pictures excludes people of color.

Toward the end of the novel, Mem, now a famous film star on a cross-country tour, encounters a group of young Native American women selling beads and baskets to passengers at a train station somewhere in the Southwestern desert. Gazing through the train window, a surface that the novel has repeatedly associated with the film screen, Mem detects "a resemblance in herself to one copper-colored maid who held up her handiwork": "[Mem] herself, each of her fellow-creatures, white, red, brown, and black was but a poor ignorant savage offering some crude ware to busy strangers drawn past in an express train."[81] But the narrative is quick to curtail this identification: just then another train pulls into the station, "cut[ting] off all communication" between Mem and the Native American peddler.[82]

The brief moment of cross-racial identification proves to be illusory for Mem. Not only is Mem prevented from exploring the evident similarity between herself and the other woman any further, but the sheer scale and efficacy of her particular brand of soul-selling makes the Native American woman's efforts to financially support herself pitiful by comparison. The humble tone of Mem's self-reflection is obviously ironic. She is anything but "a poor ignorant savage," having gained full access to the world of modern mobility—symbolized, in this passage, by her being the passenger in the train and, more broadly, by the unfettered circulation of her filmed image. Even though the initial presentation of the preglamorized Mem carries colonialist overtones, she is shown to possess the power and privilege of historical self-determination necessary to attain the condition of modernity (corporate and otherwise)—one denied to the indigenous community depicted in the novel. The film star's "attractiveness," so frequently invoked by Hughes, is predicated on a whiteness that is taken for granted, treated in the way that Richard Dyer has famously theorized: as the unraced, as what is not remarked as a category of identity, and as what is treated as a state of "being 'just' human."[83] We see further proof of this point in the fact that the star's work often involves cross-racial masquerade, including "redface" performance.[84]

This late passage recalls the fact that Mem witnesses her first motion picture in the company of a predominantly Native American audience. That earlier scene provides a rehearsal for the colonialist optics of Mem's encounter at the train station as well as its manner of conjuring and then cancelling a sense of kinship between Mem and native people. After fleeing home, Mem's first destination is Yuma, Arizona, a town she finds to be "filled with Indians."[85] The text suggests some awareness on Hughes's part of the existence of the a large Native American community in this region; apropos of Yuma, it correctly notes, "An Indian school was there, and a reservation."[86] But as a text ultimately unconcerned with the particularities of tribal history and identity, the novel never names the Quechan people as such; it inaccurately refers to the area around Yuma as "old Apache country" and classifies the people whom Mem encounters as "Hopis" and

"Navajos"—as if any tribal group with a presence in Arizona would likely be represented in this, the far Southwestern corner of the state.[87]

A significant portion of the first chapter set in Yuma consists of quasi-ethnographic commentary on Native American people. Combining Mem's impressions with the narrator's general pronouncements, this commentary creates a dizzying sense of contradiction. Mem's cultural training as a white Midwesterner leads her to expect that Native Americans are dangerous "savages," so she is somewhat relieved to find that the people around her seem very "tamed."[88] At the same time, the text reflects a sense of disappointment that, by adopting modern, mainstream American habits (of work, dress, grooming, and so on), indigenous people have lost their intrinsic nobility.[89]

Mem not only views her first movie in the company of a largely Native American audience, but she also learns about the benefits of motion-picture spectatorship by observing the people around her. To some extent, the Yuma audience is paradigmatic for Hughes. The preceding descriptions of the town make clear how dreary its members lives are; they are shown to be in particular need of motion pictures' uplifting brand of vicarious romance. Moreover, the supposedly primitive mental level of this public makes it a good test case for the universal accessibility of the medium; Mem understands something crucial when she observes that *even this* crowd can easily follow the film.[90] In this new, unfamiliar public sphere, Mem further finds herself surrounded by a group of people who seem especially disposed toward erotic temptation; she sees the "Indians" in the theater "spoon[ing] in the dim light."[91]

But Mem quickly realizes that, as much as the theater's darkness permits a certain degree of romantic contact, the young couples' presence there means that they are necessarily not "wandering . . . along the gloomy river banks or left to the mercy of their own devices in the dark of their wretched homes."[92] Had only Mem enjoyed this kind of access to the film theater in her own hometown, the novel suggests, she might have avoided her tragic fate. As far as these initial reflections go, Mem is aligned with the Native American audience. At this point in the narrative, she too is totally out of step with modern "civilization" and is herself stigmatized as someone devoid of social respectability. But the larger purpose of the scene is to lay the foundation for Mem's precipitous leap into fully modern personhood. She is ultimately a privileged observer in this space, who is able to look critically at a group people who are engaged with modern technology and culture but not fully of it. The impact of Mem's experience is dependent entirely on the assumption that the indigenous spectators' presence in the theater is, as Philip Deloria would put it, "anomalous."[93]

Moreover, *Souls for Sale* is careful to distinguish Mem from the members of this racially stigmatized crowd, indicating that her position in the theater is physically separate from theirs. Mem pays "'two bits' to sit with the aristocrats, while the Greasers, Hopis, and Navajos went in the other door for ten cents."[94] Conflating socioeconomic and racial rhetoric, this odd passage leaves unclear the basis of this separation. By emphasizing Mem's *choice* to pay a higher ticket price and sit with more affluent clientele, the passage seems to portray a socioeconomic distinction. And yet all the patrons mentioned who pay the lower price are stigmatized as nonwhite others; the text lumps together Mexican Americans (identified by the slur "Greasers") with members of distinct Native American groups (identified by what seem like randomly chosen tribal names, details meant to supply a veneer of "local color"). Further, the mention of the separate entrance leading to a separate tier of seats suggests a racially segregated admissions policy.[95]

In any event, Hughes allows Mem to watch the film while watching the nonwhite crowd watching the film from a putatively safe distance. This distance cancels out the earlier sense of similarity or kinship that the text has established between her and the nonwhite people of Yuma. And the move is a significant one, given the novel's persistent rhetoric of racial and national universalism around motion-picture spectatorship. Consider the narrator's rhapsody on the second page of the novel: the "boy and girl who embraced before one camera," Hughes writes, are "later observed by coolies in Shantung, by the Bisharin of Egypt, and the sundry peoples of Somaliland, Chilkoot, Jedda, and Alexandropol—where not?"[96] With the Yuma theater scene, the novel reassures the presumptively white reader that cinema's project of binding together a "shining multitude" need to not disturb actually existing social barriers and status hierarchies within the United States.

Propaganda and Morale Boosting

By "consecrat[ing]" herself to the task of developing her own "magnetic" bond with her public, Mem becomes an apostle of personality's emerging cult, a living advertisement for the benefits of self-cultivation.[97] Mem ultimately follows in her father's footsteps, spreading, however, the gospel of the soul's freedom from privation and repression. Like the moon in the passage describing Mem's ironic fall, her glowing star image communicates in a "lexicon" of pure desire, offering an antidote to the dreary spirit of "subtraction and cancellation" that has, evidently, blighted Americans' lives since the end of the war. What bearing, if any, should Hughes's wartime career as a military censor have on our understanding of his later defense of cinema against the "subtraction and cancellation" of censorship? How might his contribution to the theory and practice of suppressing "hostile propaganda" inform our reading of his account of cinema as the spiritual antithesis to prohibitions on expression?

Hughes, it must be stressed, was by no means a reluctant censor, arguing in *Propaganda in Its Military and Legal Aspects* (1918) that the danger of enemy propaganda had generally been underestimated since the Unites States' entry into World War I. Representing the Military Intelligence Branch's legal opinion, Hughes's brief construes propaganda in an extremely broad fashion in order to assist the Department of Justice in prosecuting cases of subversion under the Espionage Act of 1917.[98] Hughes's attempt to characterize the acute military threat posed by propaganda depends, in the first place, on the wide application of the term to a range of situations in civil life. He begins *Propaganda in Its Military and Legal Aspects* by claiming that "propaganda" already has a "legal status"—it "comes within reach of the law"—"though under other names."[99] Ranging from a cry of "Fire!" in a crowded theater, to the use of "innuendo" to cause a run on a bank, to a fraudulent debt-collection scheme, Hughes's examples of "civil propaganda" are all cases of speech that, either by design or by mere recklessness, cause measurable harm to the "public and private welfare."[100]

If, under normal circumstances, speech carries such obvious material "power," then the "size of armies and the complexities of modern warfare" turns this sort of "propaganda," in times of war, into a "weapon"—one whose difference from a bullet or gas canister is ultimately superficial.[101] Hence Hughes aims to expand the range of offenses punishable under the Espionage Act well beyond spying in the conventional sense of gathering and conveying information about military maneuvers to the enemy. The dissemination of any kind of information or representation that might serve to "disabl[e]" the United States' military campaign or those of its allies—even by merely sapping "morale" or disturbing the manufacture of munitions—is propaganda, defined as "an act and method of war."[102]

For the reader of *Souls for Sale*, Hughes's argument here cannot but come across ironically in that it offers a succinct, persuasive version of the rationale for the "reform" of cinema through the imposition of stronger censorship policies. Certainly, the would-be reformers represented by the fictional Rev. Steddon see Hollywood movies as a form of "civil propaganda" by Hughes's own definition. By spreading a kind of "misinformation" about what constitutes appropriate and inappropriate moral conduct, they lead young people to make detrimental choices (such as having sex before marriage), causing harm to the "public and private welfare." As Hughes's narrator puts it, ventriloquizing these charges, the cinema is "the corrupter of our young men and women—the school of crime"—and, as such, its products should be subject to some kind of legal authority.[103] The danger posed by cinema, further, depends on the medium's unique expressive power and broad reach, a point that Hughes's military intelligence brief stresses. Indeed, Hughes acknowledges that it is precisely the rise of cinema and other forms of mass communication that has made propaganda such a potent weapon of modern warfare.[104]

In this context, Hughes's own creative usage of the term "propaganda" helps to crystallize the objections leveled by his ideological opponents. Although he does not explicitly make the connection, his treatment of these opponents indicates that was well aware of the underlying irony.[105] It appears that Hughes employs two primary strategies to contain this irony in *Souls for Sale*. The first is simple and straightforward: he turns the tables by characterizing the anti-Hollywood forces as the *true* propagandists. In an extended commentary on the Arbuckle case, Hughes uses language that harkens back to his description of "civil propaganda": "garbled" versions of the story of Virginia Rappe's death begin to circulate and are used by "the enemies of the free film" ("editors, politicians, reformers, preachers, clubwomen") to enflame "national wrath" against the film industry and, in turn, generate support for censorship laws.[106]

As in the case of Hughes's person who yells "Fire!" in a crowded theater, these "propagandists" use misleading public speech to create a panic. Their goal is to whip the public into a "lynching mood," such that it will not be pacified until the "whole art" is made to suffer—notwithstanding Arbuckle's innocence in the eyes of the law and the tenuous connection between that particular affair and the industry at large.[107] The rumors and innuendo about Arbuckle (as a representative of Hollywood debauchery) lead to an "avalanche" of condemnation, which does not settle until it destroys reputations and careers, damaging the industry's credit with potential investors.[108] Not surprisingly, Hughes devotes large sections of *Souls for Sale* to counteracting this anticinema "propaganda," portraying Hollywood as a sober factory town, populated by earnest, hardworking young people who get to bed early and enjoy the salutary diversions that the Southern California climate affords.

Hughes's second strategy for dealing with this irony is more complex and counterintuitive, relating directly to his broad belief in the socially beneficial nature of the cinematic medium. In order to lend credence to this belief, Hughes implicitly portrays the products of the Hollywood studios as, in a sense, immune to any charge of propagandistic intent. These films, in Hughes's rendering, do not espouse specific messages. Moreover, they do not lay claim to being true or to promoting the moral good. Thus Hughes establishes a paradox: Hollywood films do good precisely because they do not aim to do any such thing. Such a paradoxical stance is consistent with Hughes's (and Griffith's) disdain for "doing good" and "saving souls," but it also bears the stamp of his experiences during World War I, working as a censor in collaboration with George Creel's patriotic public-relations outfit, the CPI.[109]

As Hughes's *Propaganda in Its Military and Legal Aspects* makes clear, effect, rather than intention, is the decisive consideration in identifying and prosecuting propaganda, especially in cases that concern dissident speech among American citizens (as opposed to the speech of foreign enemies). Whereas, under normal circumstances, the intentions or aims of a person distributing some kind of representation (like a film or a book) would be relevant to a legal judgment of their actions, the need to promote the success of the U.S. military effort trumps all other considerations during wartime.[110] The enforcement of the Espionage Act demands military intelligence officials and judges to determine the effect of speech—in fact, the *probable* effect of speech—on the emotional and psychological state of troops and civilians, understood in utilitarian terms, as a measure of the nation's ability to achieve its military objectives.[111] Hughes makes this reasoning clear in his section on cinema and propaganda, where he discusses the controversy around of Robert Goldstein's Revolutionary War film, *The Spirit of '76* (Continental Producing Co., 1917), applauding the suppression of the film in no uncertain terms.[112]

In November 1917, Goldstein was indicted for violating the Espionage Act after he reinserted scenes ordered cut by municipal censors into a print of *The Spirit of '76* being exhibited in Los Angeles.[113] This footage detailed atrocities committed by British troops—"a British soldier was represented as impaling a baby on a bayonet and whirling it around his head; [an]other as shooting women, dragging American girls away by the hair"—and had already been banned by Chicago authorities (possibly at the urging of the Department of Justice).[114] By allowing the film to be screened with this footage included, Goldstein knowingly flouted the wishes of both local and federal authorities, drawing the particular ire of Judge Benjamin Bledsoe (U.S. District Court for the Southern District of California), who wrote the initial warrant for the film's seizure and heard Goldstein's case.[115]

Judge Bledsoe wrote a long and impassioned ruling against Goldstein's early motion for the return of seized property, which Hughes reprints in full, in order to illustrate the proper "spirit" in which the film must be taken.[116] In his ruling, Judge Bledsoe distinguishes sharply between "ordinary times" and the present situation of "national emergency."[117] Although *The Spirit of '76* might ordinarily be considered a "harmless" piece of entertainment, or even an overtly patriotic work (given its admittedly "inspiring" rendering of historical scenes like Paul Revere's ride), it must be treated as "treasonable," Judge Bledsoe argues, because of those few scenes that have the potential to "incite hatred of England and England's soldiers."[118] The judge likewise dismisses the evident historical accuracy as grounds for allowing it to be shown to the public. "History is history, and fact is fact," he concedes.[119] Yet the need for the "greatest amount of devotion to the common cause, the greatest amount of efficiency, and the greatest amount of disposition to further the ultimate success of American arms" requires that "no man . . . be permitted, by deliberate act, or even unthinkingly, to do that which will any way detract from the [nation's military] efforts."[120]

Expressing admiration for Judge Bledsoe's courage and resolve, Hughes makes clear that he sees any speech or representation that might harm morale, solidarity, efficiency, sympathy for the nation's allies, and so on as "hostile propaganda"—irrespective of its producer's motives. In fact, the proper "legal recognition of the power of hostile propaganda" depends, for Hughes, on the rejection of any appeal to motive or intent as mitigating factors in the punishment of objectionable speech.[121] The power of hostile propaganda achieves proper legal recognition only with the passage in May 1918 of a series of amendments to the original Espionage Act (typically referred to as the Sedition Act), which drastically expanded the earlier legislation's definition of subversive behavior (in title 1, section 3) to include the "utter[ing], print[ing], writ[ing], or publish[ing] of any disloyal, profane, scurrilous, or abusive language" about the United States government or military forces.[122]

In Hughes's view, the new legislation, which began as a bill introduced by Senator Lee Overman (Democrat, North Carolina), finally succeeded in meeting the exigencies of the wartime state of emergency, explicitly criminalizing hostile propaganda. Reprinting twenty-five small-print pages of excerpts from the *Congressional Record*, Hughes calls the Senate's debate of the Overman Bill "one of the great encounters of theory with theory in the history of human liberty."[123] Hughes deems such "liberal quotation" necessary, first of all, because of the attention paid by the bill's backers to the threat of harmful propaganda—a term they use explicitly and repeatedly—circulating in the United States.[124] But second and more important, he wants to highlight the initial threat to the Overman Bill posed by Senator Joseph France's (Republican, Maryland) proposed amendment. The France Amendment, in Hughes's view, represented a misguided "theory" of free speech that would have "nullif[ied]" the force of the Bill, offering the would-be propagandist a legal "cloak of protection."[125]

Intended as an explicit guarantee that the Overman Bill would not abrogate the constitutionally guaranteed right of freedom of speech, France's amendment consisted of a short clause appended to the original text: "Provided, however, that nothing in this act shall be construed as limiting the liberty or impairing the right of any individual to publish or speak what is true, with good motives and for justifiable ends."[126] The bulk of Hughes's excerpts from the debate transcripts consist of objections raised by the senators as well as by the Department of Justice and Military Intelligence Branch, whose opinions against the France Amendment had been read into the record. Through these excerpts, Hughes intends for the reader to surmise, first, that the France Amendment would have made prosecutors' jobs practically impossible, miring them in "academic" and "insoluble" questions about what may be counted as "true," "good," or "justifiable," and, second, that it would have effectively legalized hostile propaganda.[127]

As the Department of Justice opinion makes clear, an individual's belief in the truth, goodness, and justifiability of her or his speech is a defining—if not the defining—feature of hostile propaganda of the most obstinate sort confronting the U.S. government during World War I. Overt expressions of support for the German military, especially those with German sources, are simple enough to identify and prosecute (and, arguably, not liable to be receive a sympathetic hearing from the majority of Americans, anyway). Forms of speech or representation with more elusive goals and origins, however, demand a more comprehensive antisedition law.[128] For instance, the opinion explains, Christian pacifists believe themselves to be driven "by the highest possible motive . . . the purely religious motive"; even if one suspected such individuals as operating under false pretenses, their ulterior motives would be impossible to prove.[129] Further, a pamphlet produced by a Christian group might rely heavily on biblical quotations and glosses, which "are generally true or at least cannot be shown to be untrue."[130] In another striking example, this brief discusses the case of African Americans "engaged in the promotion of greater equality of treatment of [members of their group]": African American civic leaders may oppose military service on the grounds that the nation fails to protect African Americans "from lynchings and various social and political discriminations."[131] Such "statements of fact" about the plight of African Americans, the writer concedes, "are frequently true"—and, as expressions of the desire for "better conditions," serve understandable ends—and yet they too must to be treated as a form of hostile propaganda.[132]

From the military censor's perspective, the France Amendment's adjectives ("true," "good," and "justifiable") are not merely descriptive, marking the parameters of the kind of speech protected by the Constitution—as Sen. France himself held.[133] Rather, they are specious labels that will inevitably be used to pass off treasonous propaganda. In this moment, Hughes comes to view justifications for speech/representation that appeal to motive or intent in skeptical terms, as indicative of the potential to do harm to the national cause. (Note that I am focusing for the moment just on "good motives" and "justifiable ends," setting aside the question of "truth" until the next section of the chapter.)

This skepticism persists to some degree in Hughes's thinking about cinema, even as his return to a full-time civilian career as a writer and filmmaker ostensibly places him on the opposite side—as the target of censorship rather than the censor. To make this connection is not to insist on a procrustean consistency in Hughes's thinking. Certainly, Hughes believed that matters of free speech needed to be evaluated differently in times of war and in "ordinary times," and he was no doubt capable of seeing the question of censorship in complex terms, accepting some forms of it while rejecting others. The point here is that Hughes draws terms and concepts from his legal theory of propaganda into his fictional representation of the controversy over film censorship in the early 1920s.

Notably, *Souls for Sale* does not seek to defend the movies against censorship on free speech grounds; it resists justifying movies in terms of the specific motivations or intentions of their producers (which, the novel seems to concede, may or may not be noble). As if recognizing the weakness of such an argument, *Souls for Sale* refuses to stake its defense of the medium—as developed by the Hollywood industry up to that point—on filmmakers' own belief in the truth, goodness, or justifiability of what they do. The novel prefers instead to judge whether cinema is a "good" or a "bad" phenomenon—in terms of the medium's *effect* on the functioning of society. In Hughes's eyes, cinema (again, defined for him by the films produced by the Hollywood studios) cannot be judged as "hostile propaganda," as champions of the medium's reform would have it, because its primary impact is to raise the morale of the nation (if not the entire world), "warming . . . dreary lives."[134] Even in this context, Hughes seems to treat the question of effect as much simpler to judge, less fraught with philosophical complexity and the possibility for deception than the question of intention.

In any event, Hughes believes the "enemies of the free film" to have a kind of monopoly on moral intentionality. Refusing to contest this monopoly, Hughes is able to defend cinema without having to attribute to it those qualities that he believes to indicate propagandistic intent.[135] Further, he is able to pass off his own public-relations efforts on behalf of the medium as a simple campaign of truth telling, of counteracting the vicious lies propagated by Rev. Steddon's real-world counterparts. In this way, Hughes is able to oppose calls for film censorship while maintaining his posture as an enemy of harmful propaganda, portraying the postwar era as an extension of the wartime state of emergency. "The late war of the nations," Hughes writes in a passage cited briefly earlier, "was followed in America, as elsewhere by a recrudescence of the eternal war between enforced morality and liberty."[136] The revival of this "eternal" metaphysical strife—which is a version of Griffith's "struggle between love and intolerance throughout the ages"—necessitates that the forces of "liberty," including cinema, be vigilant against the efforts of moralists to *demoralize* the public.

Not surprisingly, this bit of narrative appears in the context of one of the novel's many blistering indictments of "moralists" or "zealots," one that portrays such ostensibly benevolent figures as more insidious than out-and-out "despots."[137] Much as the opponents of the France Amendment sought to characterize the special, destabilizing threat posed by well-intentioned domestic antiwar groups, Hughes highlights the moralists' "altruistic cruelty"—the cloak of pure motives that makes it difficult to detect their true project of dictating to "the public" what is "supposed to be good for it."[138] Affirming the public's ability to make this determination for itself, Hughes points to the simple fact of cinema's massive popularity, that it "draws crowds."[139] Lifting spirits and providing a necessary diversion, movies do good at a structural level, without seeking to define norms of conduct or advocate political positions, like a sermon or a tract. They simply dramatize the desires, conflicts, and "symbols" that have preoccupied artists since the era of the Greek epic.[140] In their universally intelligible dramatization of these things, the movies supply the members of modern crowds with a "lexicon" that binds them together, without, however, having said anything in particular.

Hughes, like Lee and Walter Lippmann before him, sees social cohesion (his focus is primarily on the American nation) as the ultimate goal of reform; this objective displaces the moralistic style of earlier Progressive reform campaigns. As a participant in the larger campaign, spearheaded by Creel's CPI, to stoke patriotic consensus during the war, Hughes had observed a useful model for thinking about the socially unifying effects of cinema during peacetime. He came to see that, in both situations, the enhancement of "morale" is crucial. In this regard, his defense of cinema as a form of beneficial propaganda (propaganda that, because indubitably beneficial, is spared this label) recalls the psychologist Granville Stanley Hall's elevation of morale to the status of "the supreme standard of life and conduct."[141] Striking Nietzschean and Bergsonian postures, Hall argues that social institutions need to focus on stimulating the "mysterious developmental urge" in human beings, the "will-to-live" or "*élan vital*" that drives all kinds of historical progress; by contrast, the focus on "right and wrong, honor, and superhumanity" could only lead human beings "astray."[142]

Writing in 1920, Hall saw the recent world war as having "reveal[ed]" the "bankruptcy" of morality as a "supreme standard."[143] For Hall, the war was useful in "mak[ing] intelligent people think and talk about morale"; he hoped to translate the military discussion of how to build and sustain "this intangible, spiritual virtue" into the civilian context.[144] And like Lee, Lippmann (in his early phase), and H. G. Wells, Hall believed, somewhat counterintuitively, that these concepts of morale could be repurposed for the building of a "synthesis . . . of the great peoples of the earth."[145] In other words, Hall believed that the narrowly patriotic component of wartime morale could be removed and that it could be given an international or inter-"racial" scope.[146]

Focused on pleasure, stimulation, and personal fulfillment, Hughes's vision of morale is comparatively prosaic, lacking, for instance, Hall's obsession with bellicose masculinity and his cryptoeugenic ideals of physical hygiene. And yet the two writers adhere to shared logic, whereby moral judgment becomes an obstacle to the necessary and salutary increase of vital energies, the intangible forces that bind people together. In the fashion of late Progressive political thought, morale becomes "the one and true religion of the present and the future"—the theology of "God . . . conceived as immanent . . . and not as *ab extra* and transcendent."[147] For both, World War I both reveals the absurdity of all checks on morale and provides important lessons in how it might be propagated. One of these lessons is that cinema occupies an exalted position within the new religion of morale building.[148]

Lies for the Truth's Sake

Whereas Hughes thoroughly rejects claims of "good motives," his stance on how movies relate to the "true"—the third key attribute at issue in the France Amendment—is decidedly more contradictory. Not surprisingly, Hughes validates film as a source of basic truths about the world, thus juxtaposing them to traditional religious teachings (or even received wisdom generally), which, in his view, continually spread lies. While claiming to speak "the Truth with a capital T," people like Rev. Steddon offer a naïve, oversimplified account of how social relations work and have worked over the course of history. Quite to the opposite, movies, at their best, capture life's frustrations and struggles, offering viewers immediately recognizable "allegor[ies]" of their own experiences; they are simply more "real."[149]

At the same time, *Souls for Sale* takes great pains to emphasize that popular moving pictures, as a form of dramatic fiction, are, in the most basic sense, "lies," invented stories in which actors impersonate people other than themselves. Portraying the fictiveness of film as a virtue, the novel makes its case (discussed earlier) for the social benefit of the movies as a supplier of vicarious emotional experiences—"escape valves" for the beleaguered audience. While Hughes at times portrays this relief as a matter of simple distraction or diversion, he also develops a more elaborate theory of "aesthetics" as a form of "anæsthetics."[150] For Hughes, the underlying awareness that what is being viewed on screen is simulated has a buffering effect, allowing the film spectator to pass through all kinds of experiences, including difficult or traumatic ones. She or he acquires the knowledge that such experiences tend to impart without, however, suffering any lasting emotional damage. For example, the film spectator might gain a new sympathy for people who suffer by watching an actor simulate tremendous sadness.[151] The fact that the movies, in this sense, are not real gives them a redemptive power: in their very theatricality, they teach certain truths, but without imparting the scars of actual experience.

Echoing his paradoxical treatment of cinema's good effects, Hughes offers an elaborate refutation of the moralistic adage "a lie never prospers."[152] The novel first illustrates the practical value of lying through the story of Mem's collaboration with Dr. Bretherick. Crafting a fictional "continuity" about her elopement with a traveling salesman, who dies shortly after their marriage, they succeed in delivering Mem from her impossible predicament as an unwed mother-to-be living in a provincial town. Making possible Mem's actual career in film and marking the symbolic beginning of her professional "histrionism," this process illustrates to Mem not only that lies can bring about "true" and "good" outcomes but also that suppressing the raw truth in favor a more pleasant fiction is a form of social "benevolence."[153] Having internalized the doctrine that all falsehoods are sinful, Mem regrets at first having to conceal her affair with Elwood and subsequent pregnancy, and the novel portrays her "forc[ing] herself to be another self" in no uncertain terms as a kindness, the revelation of these details having the potential only to cause her family anguish.[154] Most importantly, Mem's role-playing spares her from having to endure the townspeople's scorn and, over the longer term, a probable life of sadness and economic hardship—a fate that the novel sees as in no way merited by her supposed transgressions. Mem's predicament represents a clear case where lies are more productive than unvarnished facts and function ultimately "for the truth's sake."[155]

Out of this mixture of contradictory sentiments, Hughes arrives at an idiosyncratic conception of film's relationship to truth. He effectively redefines the true as that which is publicly expressed or exhibited, as in a cinematic image. In the scene in which Mem embraces her vocation as an entertainer, Hughes associates Mem's physical flight to Southern California and concomitant embrace of the personal fulfillment ("freedom of the soul") ethos with a larger reformation in American culture—the beginning of a spiritual New Age. In a syntactically convoluted passage, the narrator describes Mem as "joining the vast hegira of humanity from the dark ages of ritual and ceremonial and uniform into the new era of all things good in their place, and concealment of truth the one irretrievable evil."[156] Rejecting enforced norms of conduct, the "new era" takes the "puritanical" obsession with sin and stands it on its head. From this perspective, most actions are assumed to be good, while repression itself, here exemplified by the term "concealment," becomes the sole instance of "evil."

Given his withering critique throughout the novel of people who claim to make such judgments, it is surprising to see Hughes using the terms "good" and "evil" in what appears to be a straightforward way. At the same time, the passage is consistent with his argument elsewhere in the novel that traditional morality rests on a hypocritical denial of basic truths about human experience. For example, religious figures like Rev. Steddon teach that virtue is always rewarded and vice punished, even though they know that this is not the case. But even more significantly, the immediate context makes clear that truth is a very flexible and capacious label for Hughes. What is at issue here is not the publication of particular statements about the nature of reality and so on (one way of defining truth) but the mere exhibition of oneself, both one's body and, via his somewhat forced metaphor, one's soul.

In fact, the larger passage indicates that truth and publication (the opposite of concealment) are being defined in a circular fashion. Whatever is deliberately exhibited is true by virtue of its being exhibited, and whatever has been publicized or advertised acquires the value of truth. The objective for Mem is not to express an idea that is always and in every case true but to establish the truth about herself in and through what she brings to light. In most cases, this means her physical person. The passage about the "hegira," for instance, is prompted by Mem's struggle over whether or not to accept the Southern California fashion of wearing a bathing suit at the beach, revealing her arms and legs to public view. Her embrace of the practice of "publishing her bodily graces to the world" is represented as a moment of liberation and a step toward her career as a film star. It represents her revelation of the truth about herself in a physical sense.[157] This rather vacuous notion of truth, in turn, conditions the book's discourse about the publication of the soul.

The "bundlesome clothes" that Mem struggles to cast off are described in both literal and figurative terms: the long skirts and sleeves mandated by her parents go along with a "yashmak [covering] her demure mind."[158] As Hughes's Orientalist metaphors through the passage (Mem is also described as secluded in a "mental harem") indicate, the covered soul is like the "caged" soul, whereas a "naked" soul would, implicitly, be free. Extending Lee's ideal of self-realization through expression, Hughes effectively identifies truth with the unconcealed, evoking the desire for "brutal" or "terrible honesty" proclaimed by many American writers of the "postwar generation."[159]

It is crucial to add that Hughes's notion of truth as exhibition allows for, or even demands, a degree of selectivity on the part of the individual. Being a kind of performance, such self-publishing involves fantasy and embellishment as well as judicious censorship. The individual is beholden only to what feels like her or his authentic self. She or he is free to produce an ideal image in order to please the crowd and to disown whatever is ugly or unpleasant in her or his life. For instance, Mem is never compelled to reveal her affair with Elwood nor the fact that she has been pregnant and suffered a miscarriage. These details of her past life happily vanish as she constructs the persona of Remember Steddon, the actress. The adoring letters that she receives from her fans indicate that they have come to "know" her through the embellished, if not invented film star biography—much like the "glowing tributes" she reads when she purchases her first film magazines on the train ride to Arizona.[160] These lavishly illustrated tributes, the novel indicates, focus on the glamorous but solidly respectable "domestic" lives of stars.[161] And even though such reporting includes only those details that make the star seem attractive, desirable, and compelling of attention ("magnetic"), the novel treats them as essentially true. In Mem's case, such profiles better reflect her essential self than would any thorough account of her actual young adulthood, which was largely shaped by circumstances beyond her control.

Hughes's equation of truth with what is publicly expressed in the form of a carefully crafted advertising campaign partakes of the ideology of public relations; this field had been revolutionized during World War I by his friend and fellow Missouri native, George Creel.[162] A journalist who had written an influential book in support of Wilson's reelection, Creel was appointed in 1917 to head a so-called Committee on Public Information. The CPI was charged with "mobiliz[ing] the mental forces of America" in support of the military campaign, with "the production and dissemination of as widely as possible of the truth about America's participation in the war."[163] Under Creel's leadership, the CPI acted as what historian Alan Axelrod has called a "clearing-house" for "coordinat[ing] the activities of Military Intelligence and Naval Intelligence" with other branches of the government, including the Justice Department.[164] Under this arrangement, Hughes was likely to have collaborated with Creel, his office contributing to the CPI-led campaign to stimulate and focus what Creel called the "*war-will*" of the American people and their allies.[165]

A detailed account of the CPI's activities during the war lies well beyond the scope of this chapter, as does an adequate exploration of the historical linkages between the emerging public relations industry and the American cinema of the 1920s. My goal here is simply to demonstrate that the rhetoric that Creel uses to frame the CPI's project provides the ideological context necessary to understand Hughes's equation of "truth" and "publishing" in *Souls for Sale*. In his personal account, *How We Advertised America* (1920), Creel details the CPI's efforts to disseminate a "gospel of Americanism" at home and abroad to propagate faith in the nation and its ideals (or perhaps in an idealized representation of the nation). The quasi-religious zeal that supported this public information campaign enables Creel to portray the CPI as on the side of "*the open and the positive*" and opposed to "*concealment and suppression*."[166] In mounting this campaign of openness, Creel sought to harness the vast communicative resources of the cinema in multiple ways. The CPI commissioned film stars to appear at Liberty Bond drives; organized the "Four Minute Men" (a network of thousands of paid and volunteer speakers who roused movie-theater audiences during the changeover of film reels); and established a Division of Films, which oversaw the production of pro-American films for domestic and foreign distribution.[167]

From his perspective, the CPI was an enactment of the American values of democracy and free speech, an institution that, as he succinctly put it, stood for "*expression*, not *suppression*."[168] The historical reality behind Creel's claim that the CPI absolutely opposed censorship is, of course, complex. His own historical account emphasizes the committee's negotiation of "voluntary" self-censorship by newspaper editors around the country, while leaving out important details about how the enforcement of the Espionage Act factored into the larger program of government control of the flow of "information" about the war.[169] Creel's conviction of the justness of the American cause enables him to treat censorship as an enemy prerogative, just as he does propaganda. Even though Creel is well aware that the term, in its neutral sense, applies accurately to the CPI's methods and goals, he reserves it for the harmful lies emanating from Germany—the sorts of representations detailed in Hughes's *Propaganda* brief.[170]

Thus Creel is able to portray the CPI as being motivated by the ideal of "absolute frankness" and as using only a "simple, straightforward presentation of facts" to impress upon the domestic and global publics the "truth" about the United States (especially its reasons for fighting).[171] And he does this while being quite explicit that such "truth" could only be a carefully crafted message, broadcast with the exclusive goal of stimulating and maintaining morale, or "war-will." Creel will, on a single page, assert this dedication to plain fact while romanticizing the CPI's work as "a vast enterprise in salesmanship, the world's greatest adventure in advertising."[172]

Hughes's representation of the film star as a paradigm of modern self-fashioning depends on this same slippage. The film star embodies the adventure of selling oneself to the public, developing and disseminating a self-image that is deemed to be true, even as this image is manifestly crafted with the goal of pleasing an audience. The revisions, omissions, and embellishments that make this image possible do not, therefore, compromise the truth of the image. Rather the effort that the star makes (working with the studio publicity machinery) to sell her image, constantly exhibiting it in a variety of media, comes to guarantee its authenticity. Hughes's title, *Souls for Sale*, plays ironically on the idea of the Faustian bargain, affirming the idea of society as a marketplace where the individual enters in the form of human merchandise and is, in fact, duty-bound to advertise her- or himself to all possible buyers.[173] Ultimately, Hughes's championing of the film star is a version of Elbert Hubbard's gospel of publicity: to refuse to advertise oneself is to be effectively dead; modern life happens in the public sphere where one's "services and commodities" are made available for purchase.[174]

Rhetorically, *Souls for Sale* constructs this public sphere as universally inclusive, detecting in it the basis of an emerging modern form of community. With its narrative of a young woman rescued by the apparatus of film stardom, who then reciprocates by trying to spiritually liberate her audience, the novel envisions the new society as being defined by unequivocally positive traits like "expression" and "frankness." And yet the novel's own episodes makes clear that preexisting standards of social value dictate which people are able to bring their "services and commodities" to market. Epidermal whiteness is a prerequisite for an individual's being able to turn her or his body into spiritual merchandise, the sort of self-advertising image that Hughes, like Hubbard and the rest of public relations industry, so reveres. By contrast, nonwhite people remain in a state of ostensible concealment, cut off from the networks of communication that Hughes fetishizes. Moreover, the magnetic bonds that form around this image are, fundamentally, based on the aesthetic enjoyment of the white female body, which has been subjected to a process of scrupulous editing. The notion of a new public sphere defined by totally liberated expression is dependent on what are, for all intents and purposes, mechanisms of a priori censorship, mechanisms designed to guarantee that the images circulating within it will be viewed as generally propagating social faith and boosting morale.

5 "Little Grains of Sand"

POSITIVE THINKING AND CORPORATE FORM IN DOUGLAS FAIRBANKS'S *THE THIEF OF BAGDAD*

"Pictures are like music," he declared. "They speak a universal language. Great industry—just in its infancy—before long films will pass from one country to another—internationalism. Why not? Love, hate, grief, ambition, laughter—they belong to one race as much as another—all peoples understand them. It's hard to hate people after you know them. Pictures will let us know each other. They'll break down the hard national lines that now make for war and suspicion."

—Douglas Fairbanks, quoted in George Creel, "A 'Close-Up' of Douglas Fairbanks"[1]

Douglas Fairbanks is an interesting and approved figure, interesting because of the merit and energy of his enterprises, approved in general by the motion picture world, approved in a special way by the author of this book because he is not "incorporated." He has had an individual career as an actor and producer, when even the best movies had a department-store atmosphere and the technical methods of a "Board of Control." Movies, like skyscraper-architecture, at best have a suggestion of the factory.

—Vachel Lindsay, *The Progress and Poetry of the Movies*[2]

George Creel begins his 1916 *Everybody's Magazine* profile of Douglas Fairbanks by gushing about the film star's "indomitable optimism" and habitual "cheerfulness."[3] Always smiling, Fairbanks, or "Doug," as he was customarily called, seems to radiate "courage," "energy," and "buoyant resolve," providing a living advertisement for the personality traits that Creel finds lacking in most modern Americans.[4] Writing just a few months before the United States' entry into World War I, Creel indulges in a brief lark about a state-funded propaganda office charged with countering the national malady of low morale: the "Bureau of Grins," which I discussed in my introduction.[5] According to Creel, simply by flashing his trademark grin around American cities, Fairbanks could make the nation even more prosperous economically: "If the wealth of the United States increased $41,000,000,000 during the last three, peevish, whining years, think what would happen if we learned the art of joyousness and gained the strength that comes from good humor and optimism!"[6] With "the Bureau of Grins," Creel foreshadows his soon-to-be-formed Committee on Public Information (CPI), taking its basic concept a step further. Like the CPI, the bureau is a propaganda apparatus charged with "mobliz[ing] the mental forces of America." Unlike its real-world counterpart, however, it is not constrained by the need to disseminate any specific of "information" at all, nor limited in its operation to times of war.[7]

Creel's imaginary bureau would militate against the perpetual threats to national prosperity and unity posed by irritability and complaint simply by making morale maximally visible. Constructing Fairbanks's smiling visage in these terms, Creel anticipates his friend and associate Rupert Hughes's brief on behalf of the film star in *Souls for Sale*. The star's face has the quality of sunlight, radiating an energy on the members of the audience that automatically dispels negativity (the idea of "don't," or, in the case of the "Doug" Fairbanks persona, "can't") and emancipates the resources of the soul. Creel's advice to the government also takes cues from Gerald Stanley Lee's work. It shares Lee's characteristically earnest but hyperbolic tone as well as his prophetic pretense of dreaming up a completely new, progressive social agency—even as it essentially describes the operations of existing mass culture. Since, as the profile emphasizes, Fairbanks was one of the most visible people living in the United States, his countenance appearing on screens around the country (and, increasingly, the world), the bureau he envisions would be entirely redundant, and yet the supposed morale deficit that prompts Creel's call remains.

While the general features of the Fairbanks persona highlighted in the magazine profile are visible across the star's films in the late 1910s and early 1920s, *The Thief of Bagdad* (Douglas Fairbanks Pictures, 1924) most forcefully illustrates the specific constellation of sociopolitical motifs that Creel encapsulates with his fictitious Bureau of Grins. In fact, the climactic sequence of this film reads self-reflexively, like a staging—albeit in "exotic," "Oriental" trappings—of the American film star assuming his appointed role as crowd-man, assembling and presiding over a mass whose jubilation seems to reflect his own contagious courage, strength, and optimism.[8] Moreover, the emergence of this mass—an army that triumphs over its opponent without ever using its weapons—carries utopian and internationalist connotations.

The Thief of Bagdad ends with Fairbanks's character, Ahmed (the eponymous thief), returning to Bagdad to liberate the Caliph's palace and the surrounding city from its occupation by Mongol invaders. Having undergone a series of redemptive trials in the desert, Ahmed returns transformed, possessing magical tools, such as a box filled with grains of sand that turn into soldiers when cast to the ground. After demanding entrance to the palace gate, Ahmed begins generating an enormous army, several soldiers at a time. The film illustrates the process through a series of impressive trick shots, in which men in white helmets and robes, carrying white lances with flowing banners attached, appear to emerge out of puffs of smoke. The film then offers a dizzying montage, meant to illustrate the awe-inspiring spectacle witnessed by a Mongol guard positioned on a high turret; we see three successive overhead shots in which the camera pans swiftly to left, sweeping across a mass of soldiers that appears to number in the thousands.

As a result of the sheer scale of the cast and the editing pattern, the crowd appears to have no beginning or end. This is Vachel Lindsay's "sea of humanity" writ large, an undulating mosaic of barely discernable parts: white dots indicating helmets and shields, flags and banners flapping, as if in a strong breeze. Although the closer, ground-level shots show many of the men shaking their weapons menacingly in the direction of the palace gates at Ahmed's command, the overhead shots suggest a festive crowd. Indeed, the fighting that the viewer anticipates

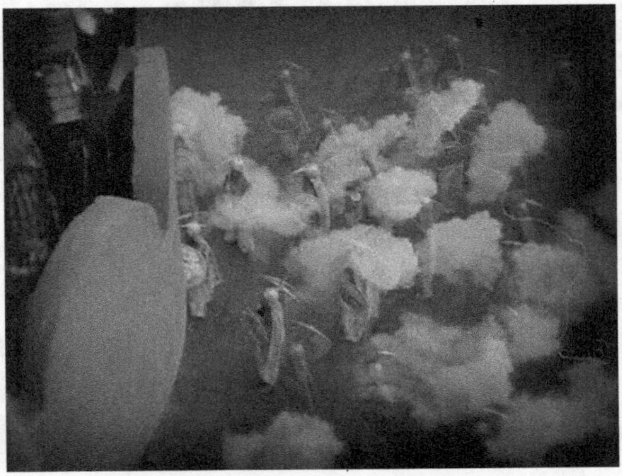

Figure 5.1. Grains of sand turned into soldiers in *The Thief of Bagdad* (Douglas Fairbanks Pictures, 1924).

never takes place. Overawed by the sheer size of the "magic army"—"a hundred thousand strong," in the estimation of the Mongol Prince's counselor—the occupying troops simply flee in terror.

Interpreting the conclusion of *The Thief of Bagdad* as a hieroglyphic of American regeneration, Lindsay uses the paradoxical phrase "conflict without conflict" to describe the army's victory. Although Lindsay actually overstates the amount of fighting represented on screen, his initial characterization recalls Lee's idea of "peace as a better way of fighting": peace as sublated imperial conquest, the quasi-military victory of peace over violence itself. By "symbol[izing]" rather than "show[ing]" the conquest, the film's conflictless conflict ushers in a completely new regime of peace and harmony, indicated by the "magnificent" spectacle of the "vast" conquering army clad in shimmering white.[9] The flight of the opposing army simply frees the would-be invaders to stage a parade or pageant. Riding on horseback, Ahmed leads a triumphant march through the gate and along the narrow streets of Bagdad, his men being engulfed by the cheering residents.

By the end of the sequence, the army itself has assumed its intended role as an audience gathered to watch Ahmed's triumphant exit from

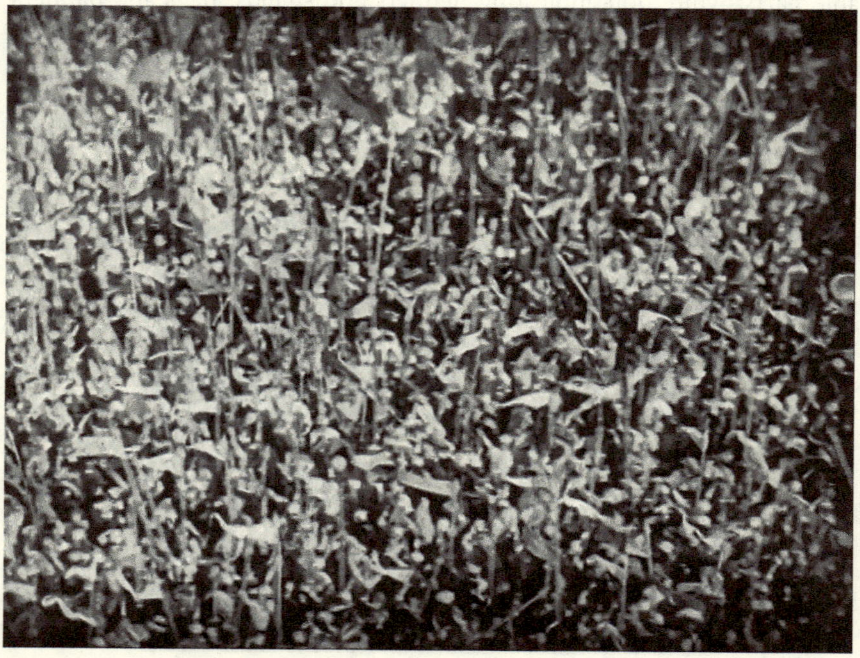

Figure 5.2. The celebratory crowd in *The Thief of Bagdad* (Douglas Fairbanks Pictures, 1924).

the palace. In what is clearly a self-conscious display of the "Doug" persona, Ahmed flies above the army on a magic carpet, saluting and being saluted by the clapping, flag-waving throng—his fans. Freed from the clutches of the Mongol Prince, the Princess of Bagdad (Julanne Johnson) sits at his feet. Finally, before the two fly off toward the horizon, we see Ahmed and the Princess on their carpet superimposed (in a process shot) on top the panorama of the sea of humanity shown previously. Removing any doubt about the essentially nonviolent, festive character of this assemblage, the repetition of this bit of footage reveals the star as crowd-man, giving a distinct, legible face to the abstracted collective body from which he seems to physically emanate. His grin in these shots offers a lesson in what Creel calls "the art of joyousness"; his followers appear suffused with "buoyant resolve."

Taking into account the climax's constellation of themes, the magic sand plot device assumes an unexpectedly wide—if likely unintended—range of resonances. First of all, in *Making Life Worth While* (1917), the second of the two positive-thinking manuals published under the star's name, Fairbanks uses the image of grains of sand to describe a unified corporate body.[10] Fairbanks opens the book by enthusiastically quoting a

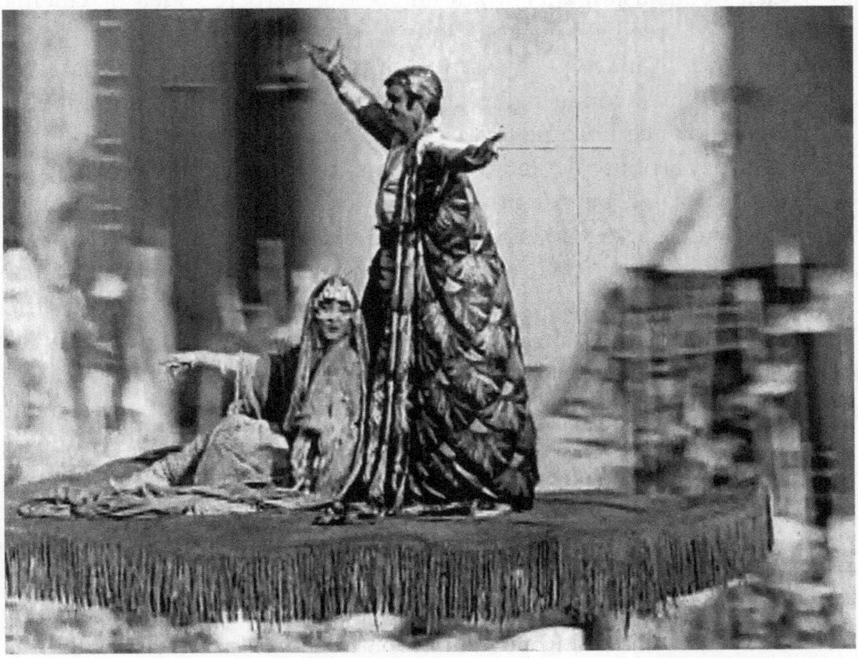

Figure 5.3. The magic carpet in *The Thief of Bagdad* (Douglas Fairbanks Pictures, 1924).

"poem" that his grandmother taught him to recite as a child: "*Little drops of water, / Little grains of sand. / Maketh the mighty ocean / And a pleasant land.*"[11] Echoing Lee and Lindsay's use of the rhetorical commonplace of the crowd as ocean, Fairbanks states that the goal of the book will be to explain how small units, joining together, may "accomplish" great things; the film's climactic "conflict without conflict" literalizes the sand-land side of the metaphor.[12] Ahmed's conjuring an army from sand also resonates with another usage of the term that is crucial to Fairbanks's first book. Early in *Laugh and Live* (1917), Fairbanks equates individual success with the possession of "sand," meaning grit—"the courage of [one's] convictions."[13]

Following Creel's presentation of the film star as an inspirational leader, it makes sense then that the conquering army at the end of the film is Ahmed-Fairbanks's "sand" personified. The crowd manifests his courage, optimism, and vitality—his ability, according the precepts of mental science, to bring into material existence what he desires. From this perspective, Ahmed's magic sand expresses his newfound ability to shape reality according to his will—surely his quest to become a "prince" rather than a "thief" is all about the power of positive thinking—and points to the theme of mind over matter. In Lindsay's reading, *The Thief of Bagdad*'s conclusion allegorizes Hugo Münsterberg's idea of cinema as a means of freeing "our consciousness" from the restrictions of the "outer world."[14] Indeed, as Ahmed dramatically sheds material and physical restraints, conjuring an army out of nothing and taking flight, the film's audience becomes part of the cheering corporate body that witnesses, pays tribute to, and (ideally) mimics his accomplishments.

But if the crowd, being a projection of the leader figure's imagination, also shares his qualities and abilities, then the relationship of the "magic army" within the film to the actual audience becomes quite complicated. However much members of the audience may desire to be a part of the glorious unified mass on screen, they are, presumably, not purely the inventions of Fairbanks's mind. And yet, as the analysis of "sand" imagery suggests, the film equates the purposeful unity of the human aggregate with its correspondence to the positive energy that the inspired leader (the would-be head of the Bureau of Grins) scatters throughout the world. From this standpoint, the crowd on screen connotes "sand" in other, archaic senses of the term not used by Fairbanks: a message that is sent out, or the messenger dispatched to carry it.[15]

The members of the mass on screen are the crowd-man's spiritual envoys. To use another important trope from positive-thinking literature, they are human channels through which the crowd-man's message may be broadcast into the world without being in any way changed or distorted. Rather than symbolizing the unification of disparate individuals and groups, the apparently utopian scenes at the end of *The Thief of Bagdad* could be seen as showing a *replacement* of what is heterogeneous (in physical and intellectual terms) by what is unified, because it resembles and even emanates from a single person. This single person, the Fairbanks hero, possesses particular markers of race, gender, and class identity that the film deems universally representative, reinforcing his dominant position. The film's conclusion, then, allegorizes the conquering or overcoming of difference at a social level. It symbolically purges from the scene those supposed sources of disunity that cause so much anxiety in the reports, examined in this chapter, on the film's production and in Fairbanks's motivational writings: extras working for low pay who seem to lack the imagination to realize the producers' grand vision for the epic crowd film as well as members of racial minority groups who seem to embody the "inertia" or "laziness" against which the "strenuous," economically successful white male must constantly struggle.

Both in its diegetic narrative and in the publicity narrative that circulated around its production, *The Thief of Bagdad* represents the apotheosis of the utopian-universalist defense of cinema in silent-era Hollywood. Fairbanks's performance of the star-as-visionary-leader role neatly folds the (white) corporate ideal into a spiritualist outlook that encompasses both a theory of film's social function and a broader philosophy of successful conduct. Styling his set after the Fordist factory, Fairbanks channels the most modern methods of image production into creating an artifact that is archaic and, in Ben Singer's terms, "anti-modern," a mystical, middlebrow allegory about what it takes to attain success and happiness.

Doug, Incorporated

In this chapter's second epigraph, Lindsay approves of Douglas Fairbanks's "career as an actor and producer" because it has been "individual" rather than "incorporated." According to Lindsay's reasoning, to be "incorporated" is both to succumb to fiscal imperatives in making production decisions and to lose distinct personhood.[16] Operating independently of a corporate "board," Fairbanks has been able to make (aesthetically "pure" and spiritually valid) films conforming to his singular artistic vision.[17] Likewise, Fairbanks has kept his own persona authentic: he is "not a copyrighted character, not an advertisement, not a formula."[18] Lindsay, thus, stakes his admiration for Fairbanks's body of work (the films themselves as well as the star's own public image) on his sense that they contain no trace of Hollywood's predominant, factory method of production.

But the production history of *The Thief of Bagdad*, the very film that provides the occasion for these remarks, demonstrates that Fairbanks himself would have rejected Lindsay's rigid binary of individuality and incorporation, seeing artistry and commerce as fully compatible. *The Thief of Bagdad*'s production shows Fairbanks reveling in his newfound, impresario role—the off-camera persona he began to cultivate when he formed his own production company, Douglas Fairbanks Pictures, and shifted his artistic focus to historical costume epics with *The Mark of Zorro* (1920) and *Robin Hood* (1922). This arrangement certainly gave Fairbanks a greater degree of autonomy than he would have had as an actor under contract to one of the major studios, but it also put him at the center of a substantial corporation, moving "armies of workmen" around a production facility of unprecedented scale.[19] To highlight this role, Fairbanks deliberately staged his studio as a factory, using promotional techniques that had been pioneered by his mutual admirer, Henry Ford.

Following the cues provided by Fairbanks and his collaborators, *The Thief of Bagdad*'s production was represented in the trade and general presses as a marvel of cosmopolitan labor, a manufacturing plant where architecture, machines, and human bodies were smoothly and efficiently orchestrated. Carrying its own dramatic marker, the "Bagdad" lot was available to be consumed as an image of the Fairbanks brand, "Doug," incorporated. The functioning of this plant appeared to illustrate the harmony between Fairbanks as individual creator and his immense workforce, the latter serving to channel his vision and to bring it into material existence. Presiding over this corporate body, Fairbanks sought to enhance the crowd-man aspect of his (already highly trademarked and advertised) star persona, aligning his work with an important tradition of visualizing mass production in utopian terms.

In production photographs of *The Thief of Bagdad*'s vast, imposing set, one detail stands out: a large sign reading "Bagdad" in white block letters, the oversized *B* and *D* framing the others, looms above the construction.[20] The sign sits atop an ironwork tower that rises above the highest section of the set for the exterior of the Caliph's palace. Likely a part of the structural backing for the high walls, the tower has what appears to be a camera platform extending from its side. With "invisible" metal supports that allow the stylized letters to appear to stand freely, the "Bagdad" insignia recalls the signage used by urban merchants during this period, marking the location of their businesses and advertising them to passersby. Along the same lines, it also resembles (albeit on a much smaller scale) the iconic Hollywoodland housing-development sign, which happens to have been erected the same year that *The Thief of Bagdad* went into production.[21]

Although one contemporary historian refers to the "Bagdad" sign as a "neon sign," it seems unlikely that it was electrified.[22] Judging simply by the sign's design, it could have employed neon tubing—like the contemporary sign on the roof of the Roosevelt Hotel on Hollywood Boulevard—or have been otherwise illuminated at night. Yet in the absence of any definitive evidence in surviving photographs or written accounts from the period, "neon sign" sounds apocryphal, having a ring of 1920s Hollywood boosterism about it. Whether or not the "Bagdad" sign did light up, it is a decidedly odd trace of *The Thief of Bagdad*'s production, simply because, while being physically connected to a film set, it was not intended to be filmed.

The sign could not appear in the frame of the finished film without disrupting the mimetic illusion of the story. As a material artifact of 1920s commercial culture, it belongs to a time and place distinct from the fictional setting of the film—"Bagdad, dream city of the ancient east," in the words of one of the opening intertitles. And whereas it is permissible for an intertitle to announce a setting directly to the viewer, the sign's appearance in a shot of the palace would violate the rules of classical-era silent film, according to which overt narrational devices must be excluded from the diegesis.[23]

According to biographer Jeffrey Vance, Fairbanks, the star and ostensible codirector of the film, "ordered the construction of the large 'Bagdad' sign . . . in order to dissuade [other] producers from stealing shots of his set."[24] Although the concern over "stolen" footage was, no doubt, a reasonable one, this stated rationale does not adequately account for the sign's existence, nor for its distinctive appearance. Based on the evidence afforded by the finished film, the single sign (elevated as it is) seems not to have precluded the producers from shooting the palace set from a variety of vantage points. And as the production stills suggest, it would have been difficult, with or without the sign, to generate usable footage from extremely long and aerial shots. At such distances, other unwelcome objects, from scaffolding, to camera rigs, to nearby streets and homes—not to mention the other sets on the lot—tend to disrupt the view. Likewise, one wonders why, if the purpose of the sign was to mark company property, it did not read something more blandly informative like "Fairbanks Pictures" (the name of the company producing the film), "*The Thief of the Bagdad*" (the title of the film), or, assuming that cost was a factor in the decision, something shorter, like "Doug."[25]

Whereas these options seem more practical, the choice of "Bagdad" is not a little whimsical. Appropriating the name of a real place, the sign attributes that place's popular-cultural associations with "Oriental" mystery and fantasy to a location in Southern California. In this way, the "Bagdad" sign also reflects the film industry's own efforts during this period to brand and market its physical plants.[26] Suggesting the collapse of geographic distance and temporal difference, it participates in the rhetorical construction of Hollywood as a (non)place that can stand in for any place: where the fantastic is conjured into material existence, where the ancient sometimes sits uncannily alongside the modern, and where an observer might glimpse the full range of human types—"sans caste," as one of the earliest notices on this production put it.[27] More precisely, the sign spells out an imaginary linkage between a particular part of Southern California, the capitols of great civilizations of antiquity, and the unreal cities of Americans' collective dreams, anticipating Lindsay's impassioned celebration of *The Thief of Bagdad* as an allegory of motion-picture magic.[28] Fairbanks Pictures' "Bagdad" advertises Hollywood as the "dream city" of modernity, taking up the mantle borne by D. W. Griffith's enormous Babylon set, which just over a year after the release of *Intolerance*, had fallen into ruin and been dismantled.[29]

Fusing the real and the unreal in multiple ways, the sign trademarks the production, establishing it as a place that asks to be looked at, if not visited and patronized in the manner of a commercial establishment

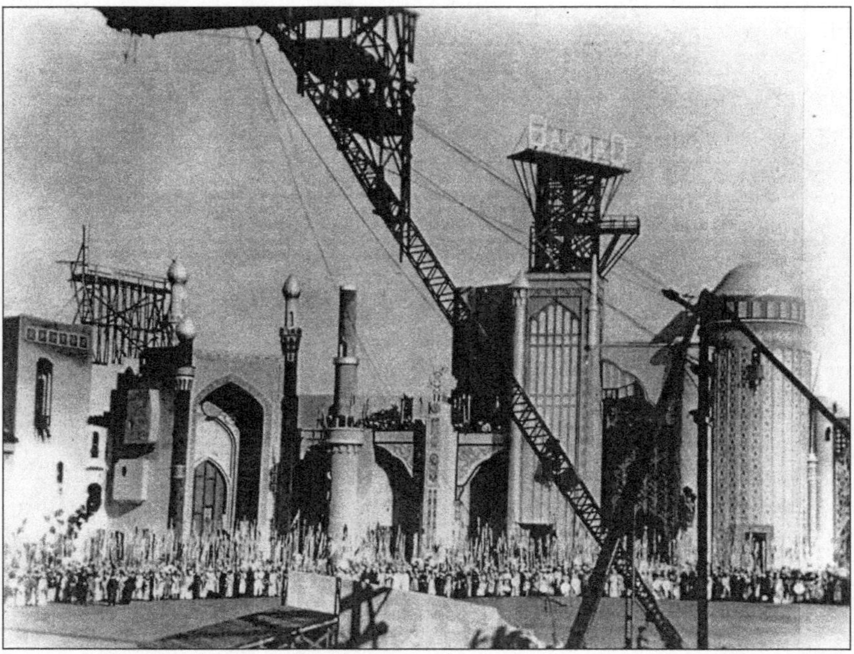

Figure 5.4. The film set marked by the "Bagdad" sign. Courtesy of the Academy of Motion Picture Arts and Sciences.

(like a restaurant, hotel, or theater). Even as Fairbanks may have been concerned about other producers training their cameras on his "Bagdad," the erection of the sign has the obvious effect of directing attention to the production lot, situated as it was in a sparsely populated, semirural section of Los Angeles. The sign identifies the set as a landmark and an attraction, either for crowds of interested "sightseers" or for people living outside of the Los Angeles area who might have seen photographs accompanying newspaper and magazine reports of the production.[30] As had been the case for earlier epic crowd films, *The Thief of Bagdad*'s sets would be a focal point of film fan magazines' coverage of the production, serving to illustrate the producers' monumental ambition and expenditure of resources.

For example, the two-page spread in the rotogravure section of the May 1924 *Photoplay* features several pictures of the palace set, the "Bagdad" sign appearing prominently in two of them but going unmentioned in the adjacent captions. Beginning with the title "How Doug Made 'The Thief of Bagdad,'" the text of this rotogravure feature treats Fairbanks as the creative force behind the film and as its de facto director, to the point of completely obscuring the work of his collaborators—including art director William Cameron Menzies and costume designer Mitchell Leisen, whose vital contributions are so evident in the photos. In *Photoplay*'s account, an early version of the now-dominant Fairbanks "actor as auteur" trope, "Bagdad" belongs to "Doug himself": the costumed star holds the iconic director's megaphone in one photograph and, in another, gestures and shouts instructions from behind the camera.[31]

In the accompanying text, *Photoplay* is concerned even more specifically with the star-auteur's relationship to the many diverse groups of people involved in the production, especially the cast of "4,000 extras" hired to shoot the film's concluding crowd scenes. According to one breathless caption, "Doug frequently assumed the director's platform and himself took charge of what was undoubtedly the most cosmopolitan company ever assembled. He gathered dancers from Java, China, Japan and other parts of the Orient; chemists from Europe and bookworms from universities for his research work; character actors from all over the world for his 'types'; Nubian slaves, Persian magic workers; artists of many countries. And for a year and two months he worked with them, suggesting, instructing, supervising directing, and playing the star role himself."[32] Contemporary newspaper reports from around the country echoed *Photoplay*'s rhetoric of superlative "cosmopolitanism" highlighting both the sheer number of extras cast and the multiplicity of national and racial groups represented therein. An early report in the Oakland *Post-Enquirer* stated, "Douglas Fairbanks broke all records for extra people this week when he used 3348 extras in one scene for 'The Thief of Bagdad,'" while an item from the Silver Springs, New York *Signal* highlighted the "thousands of supernumaries [*sic*]" hired for the production, noting, "The cast supporting Mr. Fairbanks in 'The Thief of Bagdad' includes Thespian representatives of some seventeen different nations."[33]

The Norwich, Connecticut *Bulletin*'s report, also published in September 1924, elaborated on this same theme, connecting the production's cosmopolitanism to that of Los Angeles itself; the set, in this rendering, acts like a miniature of the larger city, which is itself described as a microcosm. "During the making of Douglas Fairbanks' The Thief of Bagdad," the *Bulletin* writes, "more nationalities were employed as actors than in any picture ever before produced. All of the old races and a few of the Caucasians had to be represented: Chinese, Nubians, East Indians, Persians, Syrians, Arabians, Turks, Jews, and many others. In Los Angeles the foreign quarters are larger in proportion to population than in any other city in the country."[34] Throughout this press coverage, the prevailing sense of fascination, elicited by the unprecedented blending of "foreign" populations, is accompanied by an underlying concern over the management of such a large labor force. Especially in those articles that focus on the technological side of the production, the implicit question arises of how to coordinate and visually capture the movements of a group of more than three thousand individuals. A pair of stories from late 1923 asserted, "Aerial photography is to be used for the first time in a big photo-spectacle. Doug. Fairbanks will shoot of the final scene of The Thief of Bagdad from an airplane."[35]

In both text and image, the *Photoplay* report highlights the "ninety-foot boom, operated by a derrick and hoist" and containing a "director's platform which could be swung over any part of the set."[36] Positioned in front of the palace wall exterior, this ironwork crane was used to photograph the final sequence's overhead shots and provided the anchoring structure for the "magic carpet" on which Ahmed and the Princess appear to fly, high above the crowd below.[37] The focal point of Fairbanks's "instructing, supervising, [and] directing" seems to be the coordination of the hordes of extras, divided and grouped into separate "companies," each identified by a letter. His task is to orchestrate bodily movements in relation to built space and to the sophisticated machinery designed to produce the film's distinctive visual effects. In these images and reports of successful production, Fairbanks emerges as a master of crowd psychology and a figure of international communication, enacting his ideals about cinema within the very space of the film lot.

By treating the studio lot as an assemblage of smoothly interacting bodies, structures, and machines, these reports serve to frame *The Thief*

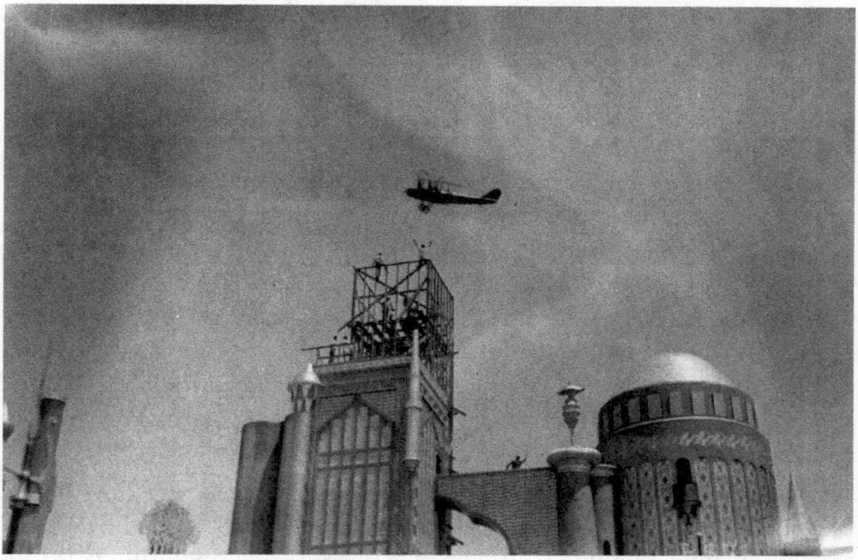

Figure 5.5. Aerial photography in *The Thief of Bagdad* (Douglas Fairbanks Pictures, 1924). Courtesy of the Academy of Motion Picture Arts and Sciences.

of Bagdad's set as a factory for producing a spectacle that is also a spectacle in its own right. In still photographs like the ones reproduced here, where large crowds of extras are pleasingly arrayed behind the camera crane and in front of the palace facade, the film's prospective viewer is treated to an ideal image of unity, one that carries aesthetic, social, and even spiritual implications. Such production stills are, from this perspective, photographs of workers at the factory gate, comparable to the iconic photograph of the Ford Motor Company's Highland Park fronted by a veritable sea of workers. As in the Ford Company photograph, the corporate trademark hovering above the film set marks the invisible but inescapable presence of the creative mind—"Bagdad" as Fairbanks's idea, if not his name—that has brought into existence and continues to guide the factory or plant.[38]

The Highland Park plant photograph comes from a 1915 pamphlet, *Ford Factory Facts*, produced by the company as a way of publicizing its cutting-edge manufacturing practices and its efforts to educate and improve the health of its largely foreign-born workforce.[39] Giving readers unable to visit "the Detroit area" the opportunity to wonder at the factory's remarkable efficiency, centralization, and scale, the pamphlet offers detailed descriptions of the smoothly functioning apparatus of production.[40] Drawing thousands of visitors every day, Ford's Highland

Park plant and, later on, the River Rouge Complex, its still-larger successor, would become major tourist destinations, with journalists portraying the Ford operation as a national monument, a quasi-natural wonder (on par with Niagara Falls), and a religious shrine rolled into one.[41]

In constructing his "Bagdad," Fairbanks adopts the role of industrialist as "inspired millionaire" perfected by Ford, generating advanced publicity for his film while exemplifying the wonders of the film industry at large. He further stages the labor of production—albeit labor of a more temporary kind, taking place on a much smaller scale—as itself an advertisement for definite social goals. The Fairbanks Pictures strategy seems to have been to appropriate the particular appearance of utopian energy that marks what, during this period, Lee called Ford's "organic factories": to open the film plant to visual attention, revealing its workers in harmony with one another and with their visionary leader.[42]

With its voluminous commentary on Ford as an "inspired millionaire" and on his cars as "advertisements" for peace, Lee's work in the 1910s is crucial for understanding Fairbanks's project. At one point in *We* (1916), Lee strikes the stock pose of the awed visitor to Highland Park, recalling the feeling he had when "look[ing] at" the factory and, even more acutely, when witnessing the "faces of the men pouring out" of it. Breaking into a string of poetic lines built around a Whitmanian anaphora, Lee describes the workers' faces as pictures of "peace [as] a sublime energy."[43] Ford's genius, for Lee, is to make peace "transparent," to reveal it to all—to make it visible and knowable or to identify it as an object (an "it") to be exhibited.[44] And this advertising function is ultimately more significant than the factory's physical products.

Lee was not alone in taking such a mystical view of Ford. Consider the account of a visit to the River Rouge Complex given by William Stidger, a Methodist Episcopal minister then based in Detroit, in his 1923 hagiography, *Henry Ford: The Man and His Motives*. Offering a detailed narrative of his elevator ride to the top of the plant's towering blast furnace, accompanied by a Ford executive, Stidger describes a feeling of sublime awe, as the full extent of the facility comes into view.[45] This all-encompassing view ("as though we were hovering over the great plant in an airplane") enables Stidger and his guide to see the operation not as simply "industry" but as authentic "romance," a "miracle" even.[46] What Stidger finds most "fascinat[ing]," however, from his "high height" is the appearance of "the human beings."[47] He watches as the "whistle to change shifts" sounds, cataloguing the cosmopolitan makeup of the emergent crowd, just as reporters visiting *The Thief of Bagdad* set would do roughly a year later: "Out they tumbled, black and white, European and Oriental, men from every corner of the earth, brawny sons of

Ireland, ingenious Poles, Russians with fierce mustaches, smooth-faced Englishmen and multitudes of native Americans."[48] The enumeration of national identities (and their supposedly indicative physical and intellectual traits) reads as a utopian gesture in Stidger's profile, which, tellingly, begins and ends with paeans to Ford's "international mind"—his ability to understand production on a worldwide scale.

According to the concept of the "world picture," this totalizing economic vision necessarily furthers the utopian perfection of social relations.[49] Because Ford can *see* the whole, he is able to conceptualize unity in a more abstract sense. As Stidger states at the very end of his narrative, Ford is "a man with a world-vision not only of industry but of brotherhood."[50] Stidger reiterates Ford's ethical theory, which rests on the same concept of strife as a solvable problem of communication that had, by the early 1920s, become the central, internationalist ideology disseminated by the film industry and its defenders. Like Fairbanks himself, in this account, Ford espouses the idea that if "nations would honestly sit down and get to knowing each other . . . that would do away with all war."[51] Discussing Ford's theories in such flattering terms, Stidger, not surprisingly, ignores what Greg Grandin has described as the paranoid, racist side of Ford's thinking about the "international mind," focusing instead on its utopian, egalitarian side.

On the one hand, the archpacifist Ford viewed nations and national boundaries as outmoded, supported an empowered League of Nations, and theorized about "world government."[52] On the other hand, Ford was a virulent anti-Semite who held a paranoid fear of the "International Jew." In Ford's fevered imagination, Jews were rootless, cosmopolitan figures who sought economic monopolies while introducing corrupting influences into American culture (like the "sensuous" dances of the Jazz Age). Through his *Dearborn Independent* newspaper, Ford mounted a nearly decade-long publicity campaign aimed at bringing to light the "worldwide Jewish conspiracy" threatening American society.[53] As I will show later, Fairbanks's internationalism had its own (albeit different) biases and contradictions. Setting these aside for the moment, it is clear that, for both Ford and Fairbanks—on a strictly ideal, theoretical level—hatred and strife can be permanently abolished through mutual understanding, and the vast, cosmopolitan manufacturing plant seems to foster such harmonious relationships at a microcosmic level.

More important, the plant, when opened to the public gaze through photographs, films, printed accounts, and guided tours, makes utopian internationalism visible on a wider scale. Ford's perspective ("world-vision") can be adopted by anyone, albeit temporarily, and according to the idea of gnostic revelation that seems to saturate the New

Thought–inflected writing of this period, to see the thing is automatically to know it. Whatever kinds of interactions might be taking place among the diverse workers at the plant, from this spiritualist point of view, their becoming visible is more significant still. Ford's role in making *understanding* visible through the very workings of his corporation, down to the factories themselves, seems, then, to place him in a unique cultural role, which combines educator, dramatic impresario, and publicist. It is this role that Fairbanks seizes as the "international mind" behind *The Thief of Bagdad*.

Crowd Psychology and the Factory Gate

The production stills of the extra cast gathered underneath the "Bagdad" sign bring to mind the tradition of the "factory gate" film (ca. 1895–1903). Beginning, as Tom Gunning explains, "with the film(s) of the workers of the Lumière Company leaving their factory in Lyon," factory gate films reflected the early cinema's role as a medium for capturing and viewing ephemeral, everyday phenomena—especially emergent modern phenomena like the urban crowd.[54] Looking at the work of the English company Mitchell and Kenyon—who recorded workers in front of worksites around the country and then exhibited them in the same towns—Gunning is especially interested in the pleasures of mass self-recognition afforded by these films. Citing Lindsay's 1915 description of the modern mass "peer[ing] into Mirror Screen" and beholding its face, Gunning argues that the factory gate film's pleasures are indicative of early cinema's "unfulfilled" utopian "promise."[55]

In the staging and shooting *The Thief of Bagdad*'s crowd scenes, the basic idea of the factory gate film is expanded to such a large scale that the workers' faces become indistinct, while the work being performed at this particular "plant" seems to be entirely directed toward producing the festive movement of collectivity ("pouring out" at quitting time) that the genre's early examples more spontaneously capture. To put the matter another way, the quality that Lee characterizes as "transparency"—the becoming visible of unifying energies—becomes a deliberate, industrial-scale, aesthetic effect. While the process of creating this effect, of course, requires the participation of thousands of low-wage workers (the extras), it in no way emanates directly from them—as the publicity campaign's rhetoric of Fairbanks the crowd-man directing the masses might suggest. It seems, quite on the contrary, to alienate the workers, positioning the production team's goals as something to be accomplished in spite rather than because of them.

Fairbanks himself simply states the matter in a brief *New York Times* interview that he conducted just after finishing production. To illustrate the "troubles [Fairbanks] had with [his] cosmopolitan cast," the star-auteur offers what he intends as a string of amusing anecdotes about actors or craftspeople on the production feeling slighted and refusing to work; three of the four of these pertain to "Oriental" members of the company.[56] In the lengthiest of such anecdotes, Fairbanks finds himself embroiled in a status competition between the Japanese American actors Sōjin (Kamiyama) and Nambu, who played the Mongol Prince and his counselor, respectively. Each actor wants to earn more money and be treated as the superior artist, so Fairbanks must find a way to channel their jealousy and one-upmanship into productive work. This portion of the interview reads like an extended riff on racial stereotypes, with Fairbanks adopting a paternalistic, colonialist pose. He plays the role of the amused but harried boss struggling to keep his subordinates on task, flattering their inflated egos by making shows of "great deference."[57]

Speaking of "troubles" with the "cosmopolitan cast" and "complications of international temperament," the *Times* piece seems to line up with Fairbanks's own ideal of "internationalism" through communication and understanding. And yet it turns out that Fairbanks is not talking about difficulties of communication across national or racial "lines" at all; the "troubles" he refers to seem intrinsic to the members of one particular "racial" group, people of Asian descent. Their supposed tendency to be "difficult to handle" poses a threat to the production and requires a skillful, white guiding hand. Fairbanks explains that, while he can now laugh at these troubles, they "seemed quite serious" during the actual shooting, "because an hour's time, with the overhead of an organization like ours means hundreds of dollars."[58]

Although Fairbanks's comments in this interview focus on Japanese and Chinese American actors playing substantial parts, the tension between individual "temperament" and the smooth translation of the organization's "overhead" into quality footage apply equally—and perhaps especially—well to the many extras in the cast, regardless of their backgrounds. Some version of this tension, of course, characterizes any film production. But as an article written about the shooting of the final scene indicates, the sheer size of budget and extra cast seems to have exacerbated it in the case of *The Thief of Bagdad*. First published in the Modesto, California *News*, Jack Jungmeyer's article, "$3 per Day Is All They Get for a Million Dollar Movie," focuses on the discrepancy between the phenomenon of the "million-dollar picture" and the experience of the "three-dollar-a-day man," the low-paid extra employed in the making of the concluding crowd scenes.[59]

Although Jungmeyer's headline seems to present the story as an exposé of labor exploitation in the film studios, he is not ultimately interested in the question of whether or not these actors are being fairly compensated for their work. For Jungmeyer, the "three-dollar-a-day man" lacks useful skills and is "recruited from the ranks of the unemployed, or casually employed, from every caste and tongue: the castoff of other industries."[60] The typical extra in his account is a degraded figure in appearance, habits, and sensibility, making her or him the antithesis of the "million-dollar" picture's splendor. The extra, in Jungmeyer's account, wears "rusty, wrinkled clothes" and is unable to think about anything beyond immediate physical needs.[61]

With his "three-dollar-a-day mind," the extra seems, to Jungmeyer, a dull, recalcitrant, and resentful character, a person unable to grasp and share in the grand creative vision of the film's producers, if not completely unsuited for artistic endeavors. Thus Jungmeyer muses at length on the paradoxical fact that the "big special" film crucially depends on this "cinema canaille."[62] Because the "mob" scene is the hallmark of this film genre, the producers must find a way to a conjure a unified and dynamic whole out of these abject individuals, who, only "vaguely underst[anding]" the enterprise in which they are involved, are difficult to direct.[63] "To those of us who see pictures in the making," he writes, "it is something near miraculous to watch thousands of these stolid, unimaginative folk of nebulous identity merged for an hour or two into an impressive mass."[64] Like the reports about the production cited earlier, Jungmeyer's initial phrasing—"every caste and tongue"—appears to signal the range of racial, national, and linguistic backgrounds represented in the extra cast. Yet Jungmeyer is even less detailed in his accounting of "caste and tongue" than were some of the other journalists who visited *The Thief of Bagdad*'s set; unlike some of the other shorter, more general reports, his account of the shooting of the climactic "mob scene" contains no catalog of "types" and, therefore, leaves unanswered some major questions about the demographics of this particular segment of the cast.

Whereas the film's intertitle text often identifies characters by race, ethnicity, or nation (using terms pulled from different period discourses, like "Persian" or "Mongol"), it applies no such markers to Ahmed's soldiers—who are, importantly, the products of his sorcery and lack real histories. Likewise, the presentation of these soldiers as a mass viewed at a distance works against the film's general tendency to highlight skin-color differences—a tendency witnessed, for instance, in the shots of the different groups of slaves and other retainers working in the Princess's residence. Individual soldiers appear on screen only in series of quick long shots that establish Ahmed's use of the magic sand. And even then, the viewer catches brief glimpses of the faces, chests, and arms of these men, underneath their helmets and capes; these glimpses do not appreciably distinguish the soldiers from Fairbanks's Ahmed, with his cosmetically bronzed skin.

A novel adapted from the screenplay and published to accompany *The Thief of Bagdad*'s release describes the soldiers as "an immense army of mounted Moslem fighting-men, men of a dozen races, brandishing their weapons."[65] In addition to dispensing with the horses, the scene in the finished film strips away the religious and racial markers; they are missing from the intertitles and (evidently) the images themselves. The viewer, perhaps, is meant to assume that the soldiers are somehow like Ahmed himself, who is identified, of course, as being from "Bagdad" and to some extent a "Moslem"—insofar as he takes advice from a holy man whom he meets in a mosque. But the centrality of the Fairbanks star image tends to mitigate against the character's Arabic or Islamic identity; the viewer is always aware that this is a white movie star engaging in a masquerade. Meanwhile, the distinguishing visual quality of Ahmed's army is the impression of whiteness produced by the fabric used in its members' costumes and flags—a detail that, as my discussion of the final scene later indicates, carries racial connotations.

All of this leaves the question of the soldiers' racial identity quite open and fluid while also making the issue of who was to play them somewhat inconsequential for the producers; anybody would seem to suffice. Walsh, the film's director, makes this point clear in his memoir, describing how he and Fairbanks resolved the "trouble" of finding sufficient extras to create "the crowd in the palace courtyard."[66] Walsh recalls Fairbanks worrying that the company's "need [for] Oriental types" would outstrip the supply available in Hollywood. Replying that he "know[s] a *few* Syrians"—nowhere near the "couple of thousand" people who would be required—Walsh hits upon the solution of recruiting extras from "Mexican town," "the south-central portion of Los Angeles where Mexican-Americans had established their own barrio."[67] Walsh's rationale for his plan to cast Mexican Americans as "Oriental types" illustrates the fungibility of nonwhite bodies on *The Thief of Bagdad*'s set (particularly in the making of the final "mob scene") and the vague understanding for geographical, historical, and sociocultural difference that coincides with the producers' overt discourse of racial typology. He states simply, "A dark-faced Mexican with a head rag hiding everything except his eyes and nose and mouth will pass for an Arab any time."[68]

Walsh's narrative does not specify what proportion of the extra cast was Mexican American, nor what other social groups (if any) were represented in it. For him and Fairbanks, all that mattered was that "desert-type" faces were available, faces that could "pass for . . . Arab[s]."[69]

And as I have tried to suggest, only a few such faces would have been needed, even as the "Arab" identity in question was to be defined in an implicit rather than explicit fashion. Hence it is perhaps not surprising that Jungmeyer does not make any further mention of racial distinctions beyond his initial general statement about the diversity of people seeking extra work in Hollywood. As for Walsh and Fairbanks, what matters for Jungmeyer is the aesthetic effect produced by thousands of costumed bodies moving in front of the film camera. For Jungmeyer, these multiple social and cultural positions that he alludes to give way to a shared class formation, defined by the lack of power and status. This negative or "nebulous" formation is that of the proletarian "canaille" or "rabble," defined by an antiaesthetic inertia that requires forceful management to be overcome.

Starting with the image of the crowd of thirty-eight hundred people gathering at sunup, Jungmeyer details the process whereby a dirty rabble is "momentarily transfigured . . . to [become] servitors of art," only to return to their original, nearly abject state.[70] Costuming provides the first step in this transformation: their "rusty, wrinkled" clothes concealed "beneath tinseled gauds of the orient," the extra cast is given "wooden spear[s]" and "flapping gonfalon[s]" to carry.[71] Thus transformed in appearance, the performers begin to assume a more dignified posture and bearing, mimicking the confident movements of a veritable army. Under the guidance of Walsh, Fairbanks, and the rest of the production staff, they coalesce into a unified, orderly, and expressive body. Momentarily in tune with the creative desires of its masters—cast metaphorically as "shepherds"—the mass (the flock of "sheep") begins to enjoy its labor, becoming a pleasingly festive spectacle—a pageant of sorts.

But even amid this festive atmosphere, the producers and their underlings (the "collies" in Jungmeyer's shepherding conceit) must exert themselves to keep order, barking the same commands repeatedly as performers tire and become distracted. One "minor technician" laments the performers' inability to keep their costumes clean and properly placed while Doug himself—"keen psychologist" of the crowd—mingles with them, complimenting their work and keeping morale high.[72] In Jungmeyer's account, the crowd is always on the verge of dissolving into "its original units," and he dwells on the moment where it starts to become unproductive.[73]

At the moment when the performers line up "at the pay window" to collect their day's wage, the discrepancy that drives Jungmeyer's account—briefly occluded by the mob's outward "cohesion"—becomes fully evident.[74] Once again, it seems impossible that the "million-dollar picture" could be the fruit of such people's work. He characterizes the absolute alienation between the two parties when he imagines the extras as a hypothetical film audience: "Tomorrow, when they see the picture, if they can raise the price, most of the 3800 will recognize themselves as strangers."[75] Implicitly rejecting Lee's and Lindsay's views of moving pictures as an instrument of mass self-portraiture, Jungmeyer assumes that this particular crowd is so alienated from aesthetic experience as to be unable to see itself in the "impressive mass" onscreen.

The crowd's ideal appearance (unified, dynamic, expressive, possessed of a firm identity) will not register as these spectators' own self-image; they will not, in Lindsay's words, "behold [their] natural face in the glass." In other words, the "transparency" that Ford's admirers describe—and for which Fairbanks seems to have strived in mounting his own film factory—does not register with the members of the extra cast. Representing an undue financial burden already, the ticket to see *The Thief of Bagdad* provides a spectacle of aesthetic transfiguration that is meaningless *for them*. In other words, the utopian experience that Gunning suggests workers might have had in viewing early factory gate films will not be forthcoming in this later example of crowd-based cinema.

We cannot assume, of course, that Fairbanks shared Jungmeyer's view of the "$3-a-day man," or that he would have judged the work of *The Thief of Bagdad*'s extras in a similar way. But as I will show in the remaining sections of this chapter, the basic terms that Jungmeyer uses—that of "stolid," "castoff" humanity being replaced by an inspired, "impressive" mass—prove useful for understanding the film's narrative of transformation. Fairbanks uses similar terms in his own advice manuals about how to succeed or "win" in life, and they are prominent in the larger body of New Thought literature on which he draws. Ahmed's emergence as crowd-man, who wills into existence a new corporate body expressive of his winning power or spirit, enacts a replacement not unlike the one that Jungmeyer describes; this replacement is consistent with the utopian idea of corporate form that is operative in mind-cure philosophy. Ahmed realizes the ability that Fairbanks aspired to on set and that was credited to Ford by his contemporary admirers: the ability to be a "sociologist manufacturer," a person who excels in the business not just of making desirable consumer products but of "assembl[ing] men from whole cloth," as Grandin puts it.[76]

"Master Cells" and "Little Entities"

For writers like Stidger and Lee, the physical operations of the Ford Company seem to emanate directly from the "manufacturer's imagination." When Stidger presses his tour guide as to how much "credit"

Ford himself deserves for the "miracle" that is the River Rouge plant, the executive assures him that Ford acted as the sole "seer": "he visualized this great plant."[77] Not only does the physical structure correspond entirely to Ford's vision, but the workers inhabiting it are, by extension, his creations. Stidger sees the "human beings" coming out of the plant as the final "climax" of the magical transformation occurring inside: "Two products [pour] out of the gates and doors—tractors and well-fed, happy workingmen."[78] These men all somehow depend on Ford for their very existence, lacking definite form until they pass through the machine of his imagination; they make themselves in his factory. In Lee's more esoteric terminology, Ford embodies the first-person plural (he "has the We-vision, the We-spirit, and the We-will") so completely that his workers appear to be extensions of his own self.[79]

Although these two writers approach their tasks from very different perspectives—Stidger attempts to Christianize the unorthodox Ford, while Lee claims him as a New Age prophet—both fixate on what they take to be the metaphysical implications of Ford's enterprise. Stidger is ultimately frustrated by the industrialist's many "eccentricities," from his lack of regular church attendance, to his penchant for dietary and exercise fads, to his belief that absolute evil does not exist, to (most worryingly of all) his belief in reincarnation.[80] As much as Stidger wants to discern biblical sources and "Christian principles" at work in Ford's thought, his record of their conversations continually signals Ford's affinity for an esoteric spirituality that, like Lee's, often evokes Emerson; for example, he talks cryptically about "the unseen" and comparing religion to the harnessing of "electricity."[81]

Some five years after Stidger's book came out, Ford would confirm these affinities by conducting a series of conversations with Emerson's namesake, the middlebrow inspirational writer Ralph Waldo Trine. The book that resulted from these conversations, *The Power That Wins* (1928), clearly establishes Ford's interest in what Steven Watts calls the "powers of positive thought."[82] Crucially, for the purposes of this chapter, it spells out his and Fairbanks's shared appreciation of Trine's work. Trine notes the connection between the two men at the beginning of *The Power That Wins*. He recalls going "to see Douglas Fairbanks in Hollywood, in connection with a moving-picture story of [one of his] book[s]," and having Fairbanks show him a copy of Trine's own foundational mental science text, *In Tune with the Infinite* (1899), which Ford inscribed and sent to Fairbanks in 1914.[83] Ford recalls having sent the book, noting that, around that time, he was in the habit of distributing copies of Trine's books to "friends and associates" like Fairbanks, whom he felt would benefit, as he himself had, from the author's approach to problem solving.[84] With this opening exchange, Trine establishes Ford's familiarity with his own body of work and sets the stage for what will become his effort, over the course of the book, to use Ford to ventriloquize his own familiar positive-thinking doctrine.

Throughout the conversation, which took place during an extended visit to Ford's Detroit headquarters, Trine asks Ford to reflect on how the principles contained in *In Tune with the Infinite* have contributed to the successful management of Ford Motor Company. Ford obliges, disclosing the extent of his interest in esoteric concepts like the principle of "attraction," "thought transference," and the use of the mind to heal the body. When Trine flatters Ford "as the originator of a great plant," who began "twenty-five years ago, with practically nothing," Ford dutifully replies by correcting Trine, using the central concept of Trine's own *In Tune with the Infinite* ("the Spirit of Infinite Life and Power"): "Every man starts with all there is," he notes.[85]

In Ford's estimation, his success has been simply a matter of recognizing his own quasi-divinity. Trine paraphrases the lesson contained in Ford's story: "The moment we fully and vitally realize *who* and *what* we are, we then begin to build our own world even as God builds his."[86] Ford then goes on to elaborate his particular theory of world building, using terms that are cryptic but clearly based in the concepts of mental science. Ostensibly, the two men are discussing the construction of a particular domain, the "great [Ford] plant," But Ford's discourse is so abstract that it becomes impossible to determine his intended frame of reference. To attempt a basic summary, Ford's contention seems to be that the individual must first accept that he is a microcosm of "the All" and that his thought, like God's, is a material force, the cause of real effects in the world.[87] Having thus established himself as a "center," the individual must seek to "attract" the aforementioned "little entities" to whatever enterprise he undertakes. These entities assist the individual in achieving his purpose and are drawn to him simply by the magnetic force of his "concentrated" thought. The "world" that is eventually built up is the individual's original idea or vision given material form by the action of "little entities," who "go out from him—through the channel of his thought—as messengers to bring back what he needs."[88]

Ford's tendency to use anthropomorphic language to describe the "little entities" (he even calls them "little lives" at one point) suggests that he is talking about people. It seems like Ford might have in mind the workers in his plants when he describes the messengers who help him achieve his creative goals. And yet, at one point, he translates "little entities" as "the material of growth and achievement," indicating that this category also includes other kinds of objects, including physical resources (iron ore, for instance) and ideas—all of these things being, in Ford and Trine's shared neoplatonic conception, equally "material."[89] Similarly, Ford settles on "organizations" as his preferred means of characterizing the relationship between the individual and the entities perpetually shuttling toward and away from him.[90] Since the conversation begins with a discussion of Ford's plant, and since Ford talks about the "center" individual as being a "Master Cell . . . that holds [a larger structure of 'little lives'] in order," it is again tempting to assign this term to a corporate context or even to conclude that the he is equating himself with the "great plant" that bears his name. The "Master Cell" he describes sounds as much like a complex of electrically powered machines as it does like a person.

In the end, Ford offers not so much an explanation of how "Divine Power" has fueled the success of his corporate enterprise as a program for individual success through positive thinking, which uses simplified, idealized images of the corporation and the factory as its guiding metaphors. Being "in tune" with the source of all power does not explain mastery in the business world so much as mastery in the business world illustrates what it means to reach that exalted state. In a sense, Ford is taking a point implicit in Trine's philosophy and making it plain: the "power that wins" is really the force of will of the individual who *has won* or *has become powerful* (in the material, social sense). While Trine's *In Tune with the Infinite* maintains the metaphysical pretense that the "infinite power" is a "source"—like a battery, dynamo, or underground well—that is external to the individual, Ford's application of Trine's doctrine dispenses with this fiction, making the individual her- or himself the point of origin of all transformative force.

The attribution of worldly success to the "Divine Power" provides a convenient disclaimer, a facade of humility, even as Ford's account completely dispenses with the conventional Judeo-Christian figure of the single divine creator. In Ford's view, the power to make thought an efficient cause of real phenomena falls primarily to human beings, whose own capacity for self-divinization is limitless and who are charged with saving a creation that seems to be in a perpetual cycle of growth and decay.[91] For Ford, "the universe" remains to be built up by the heroic person who "sees thing clearly in the mind" and then gives it form.[92] From this perspective Ford's work exemplifies a moment of tremendous "progress" through "machinery," whereby human beings are realizing intrinsic (quasi-divine) powers—like telepathy, clairvoyance, interstellar travel, and the ability to access the wisdom of lost civilizations—and, therefore, moving toward the (attainable) state of physical, intellectual, and moral perfection.[93]

To be fair, Ford does portray these divine powers in democratic, egalitarian terms, even rejecting Trine's assertion that some individuals have "extraordinary" vision or "sight"; Ford professes not to believe that he belongs to a select "class" of "seers"—the "inventor(s)," "poet(s)," and "prophet(s)" of the world.[94] In Ford's view, people of this ilk do not have a special, "intuitive 'gift'" but, having learned the lessons of "hard-won experience," are simply able to more efficiently use the powers that all people possess.[95] While Ford's point here is to suggest that anyone can become a "Master Cell," his theory of reincarnation makes the salient distinction between his and Trine's positions seem exceedingly subtle. If the experience in question can be earned and "store[d] up" in past "lives"—meaning that more "experienced" individuals are simply "older souls"—then how does being so endowed with wisdom differ from having a special "gift"?[96] Ultimately, for Ford and Trine alike, some individuals are better able than others to transcend limitations placed on their efforts (by understanding these limitations to be illusory) and to impose their wills on their surroundings.

This moment in *The Power that Win* is, I would argue, paradigmatic of positive-thinking literature and is at the heart of those portions of Fairbanks's inspirational writings that focus on individual success and happiness.[97] Like Trine and Ford, Fairbanks insists that every person has an equal chance of achieving these goals (of "winning," in the standard language of motivational literature) because mental habits are all-determining. One can will oneself not only into a pleasant mood but also into success in worldly endeavors, attracting positive outcomes to oneself simply by thinking positive thoughts.[98] At the same time, Fairbanks's version of mental science is distinguished from more familiar versions like Trine's by the great importance it places on "physical training" and bodily fitness.[99]

Arguing that hygiene of mind and body ideally coincide, Fairbanks emphasizes the ways in which bodily movements—from simple laughter to running and jumping—engender positive states of mind. He stretches this idea to the point of asserting that physical action and the enhanced "pep" afforded by regular exercise are a prerequisite for "real thinking."[100] Downplaying its more exotic, spiritualist elements, Fairbanks makes mind-cure philosophy square with his rough-and-tumble "Doug" persona—that of the actor whose screen parts center on difficult athletic feats and who spends his leisure hours jogging, boxing, and playing racquet sports. His books attempt to reconcile positive thinking with the "physical culture" movement then ascendant in Hollywood and also with the somewhat more antiquated notion of "the strenuous life."[101]

Like his hero Teddy Roosevelt, who coined the phrase, Fairbanks here (as in most of his interviews and writings) laments the loss of the aggressive, white, masculine ethos exemplified by the settlement of American West. In turn, he promotes outdoor activities (like scouting) and team sports (like football) as remedies for the supposed enervation of the American body under modern conditions.[102] Fairbanks effectively substitutes the body—with its prodigious but finite capacity for exertion—for Trine's "source of Infinite Power." For both Fairbanks and Trine, the human mind can will the individual to success, insofar as it is wired, according to the operative electrical metaphors, to an external "energy" supply. In Fairbanks's thought, the mind acts as a "dynamo," storing up "an enormous amount of dormant power," and yet this power seems to originate in the body. In his complicated dynamic, "mind controls [all]," but "*we need pep to think*."[103] "Energy is the natural outpouring of a healthy body," he writes, and since "we all have a certain amount of energy"—an amount that varies depending on physical conditioning—we all have a reasonable expectation of being "successes."[104]

Given the crucial role that the bodily dynamo plays in enabling or constraining the mind's operation, its care and maintenance becomes a quasi-religious duty. As in Roosevelt's predictions of bodily enervation, the individual is always menaced by what Fairbanks calls "the inertia of stagnation," a term that turns a physical state into a moral condition.[105] With the threat of this stagnation forever looming, the individual must remain enthusiastic, remaining constantly in motion and demonstrating her or his hygiene, purity, and "fitness."[106] Fairbanks's own loopy habits of constantly running, leaping, and climbing—as documented in the photographs appearing in these books and as attested to by contemporary profiles and subsequent biographies—becomes, then, a paradigm of what he calls "*mental and bodily morale*."[107] Likewise, he counsels his reader to seek out various forms of struggle, especially "physical combat," as proving grounds for "*initiative and self-reliance*"—that is, the victory over stagnation and inertia.[108]

Having posited close, causal links between the physical and the mental, Fairbanks is able to assert that outward appearances are totally trustworthy markers of inner states. "Cleanliness" of body and clothing reliably indicates a "wholesome" mental state, whereas suspicion falls on a person with a disheveled appearance.[109] Any outward sign of a lack of care for the body—not bathing, not being "dressed . . . agreeable to comfort and grace," not "keeping . . . in trim"—indicates a corresponding lack of self-belief, an inability to subdue the "weaknesses in [one's] character."[110] An unpleasant appearance is not merely an obstacle to success, as period advertising discourse would have it, but a warning sign to those who might help a person achieve her or his goals (like prospective employers). It indicates that the person is not deserving of others' trust because she or he lacks self-confidence and the positive mental "powers" that go with it.[111]

For Fairbanks, any and every failure can be attributed to the lack of self-confidence, the lack of what he calls, using a somewhat arcane bit of American vernacular, "sand." In Fairbanks's usage—when we fail, we must ask ourselves, *"Did we lack the sand?"*—"sand" means "grit," a kind of willed self-belief sustained by courage.[112] As Fairbanks's ideal quality, "sand" is both the precondition of success (happiness, "victory," and so on) and an end in itself. By this logic, he is able to implicitly deny that the self-confident individual is ultimately driven by specific worldly interests, money especially. Making what is a standard move in positive-thinking tracts, Fairbanks assumes that anyone following the method prescribed therein will have "an *honest purpose*," "conceiv[ing] to do something for the good of the world," and offers this disclaimer: "Success is not to be computed in dollars and cents, nor [is] the will to achieve a successful life . . . to be predicated on the mere accumulation of wealth."[113] Fairbanks, like Trine, does not deny the validity of wealth as an indicator or success and certainly does not consider its possession to be morally dangerous. He simply treats wealth as a benefit that accrues automatically to the person possessing adequate "sand" while maintaining the fiction that this person necessarily does not see it as an end in itself.[114]

In other words, wealth acts as one of many goods that the individual who has already achieved success on the level of inner disposition magnetically attracts. In *In Tune with the Infinite*, Trine asserts a "law of prosperity," an extension of mental science's famous "law of attraction": people who live in "oneness" with the "Infinite Power" send out a psychic "energy" into the world that "bring[s] to [themselves] an abundance of all things that it is desirable for [them] to have."[115] By suggesting that these people remain spiritually pure, magnetically attracting "desirable" possessions without *desiring* them in an unduly materialistic way, Fairbanks implicitly downplays his own wealth and possessions, rendering them less significant as examples of his success. Because Fairbanks swaps the physical body for Trine's "Infinite Power" and because he places so much trust in the outward legibility of inner states, he nonetheless makes self-confidence a kind of self-regard: oneness with source of all things becomes oneness with oneself.

This point becomes clear in the final photograph that appears in Fairbanks's second book, *Making Life Worth While*. Captioned "In tune with the Infinite," the photograph shows Fairbanks at medium close-up distance, backed by trees; he wears an open-collar white shirt and clutches his hand to his breast, casting a meditative downward gaze.[116] The caption portrays Fairbanks as totally self-actualized, his having achieved the ideal state envisioned by the great sage Trine.[117] It asks the reader to share in the subject's own narcissistic self-regard, admiring his spiritual state as if it is outwardly visible.

But what does the reader actually *see* here apart from a prosperous person who has access to fine clothes and impeccable grooming? Apart from a person possessed of physical traits (epidermal whiteness, an able body, a conventionally masculine appearance) that are socially valued, therefore, conducive to success in any of the ways that Fairbanks has defined it? Notwithstanding Fairbanks's rhetoric of universal opportunity—the equal chance of success that exists for all—the photograph and, indeed, the advertisement for Fairbanks's star persona happening throughout his books have the effect of establishing for the reader an idea of correspondence, like Lindsay's. It suggests that his particular physical markers and the ideal spiritual state necessarily to go together. Fairbanks is presented as an idol to be worshipped and emulated because of these qualities. Here we see the same basic tension that is at the heart of the Trine-Ford conversation: the text's democratic insistence that anyone can win at life is belied by the repeated demonstration of the hero's victory in a struggle for social superiority—the underlying conditions of which go completely unquestioned. The supposedly occult, esoteric wisdom that these texts make public boils down to the banal advice to try hard no matter what happens—an injunction that serves, more than anything, to cast suspicion on the "losers," those who lack in the desiderata of wealth, fame, and cultural authority.

Scenes of physical combat were a staple of Fairbanks's films in the period during which he published his advice manuals. In his 1916 "Close-Up," Creel offers a giddy catalog of eight such brawls, treating them as evidence of the star's physical prowess; Creel claims that these fictional scenes amount to records of Fairbanks *really* sparring with various hired opponents.[118] As Creel's descriptions highlight, the Fairbanks hero's adversaries in a few of these "scraps" are nonwhite men. He "jiu-jitsued a bunch of Yaqui Indians until they bellowed" in *The Lamb* (Fine Arts, 1915); in *The Mystery of the Leaping Fish* (Triangle, 1916), he had "several duels in the dark with Japanese thugs and opium smugglers."[119] Without a doubt, the scenarios that Creel describes are highly conventional ones, scripted by early classical-era narrative film's genre conventions and racial typologies. At the same time, they reflect Fairbanks's investment in Roosevelt's expansionist "manifest destiny" ideology makes the journey into the "wilderness" (whether the American West or not) a topos in his pre-1920 films; as Gaylyn Studlar has shown, several Fairbanks protagonists from this period undertake "adventurous, dangerous journeys" through "'uncivilized' parts of the United States of in foreign lands."[120]

To be sure, Fairbanks's films (and writings, for that matter) offer something much more benign than Roosevelt's grim rhetoric of "race war." The latter's Social Darwinist conceptions, however, provide the backdrop in the former's thought. Rather than overtly lobbying for imperialist expansion and welcoming evolutionary strife, Fairbanks is inclined to project the perpetual struggle of the individual against the forces of "indolence" onto existing imperial frameworks. Native Americans, Latinos, and people of Asian descent seem relegated to the status of what Fairbanks calls in *Laugh and Live* "the débris of humanity."[121] In the context of the passage where this phrase appears, Fairbanks is referring to gloomy people in thrall to negative energy, who act as a drag on those around them. In his usage, "débris" is another particulate image, which, in contrast with "sand" (what is deliberately sent out into the world), indicates precisely the lack of self-possession and inspiration.[122] At the same time, Fairbanks's description of this human refuse as a permanent subgroup capable of tainting the noble individual by association and "dwelling in the dark corners of life" suggests the ease with which invidious spiritual distinctions might slide into racial ones, the latter serving as a ready-made way of dramatizing the former.

A brief magazine profile published the year of *The Thief of Bagdad*'s release perfectly illustrates this slippage. Engaging in what he presents as a "philosophical" dialogue with the star, the writer Charles Taylor surmises that "the central idea" of Fairbanks's films is the need to "earn" one's "happiness" through dramatic gestures of "free agen[cy]." Taylor proposes and Fairbanks concurs that people should defy "fate" and seek to break "the chains of circumstance," proving themselves to be more than mere "automatons."[123] To show how Fairbanks arrives at this philosophical insight, Taylor offers an anecdote from Fairbanks's youth. He describes a "mournful" young Fairbanks, "bored almost to extinction" by his surroundings: a "calm, respectable Denver—placid Denver, whose pioneer days were in the distant past."[124] Fairbanks eventually escapes boredom by concocting an "adventure" filled "with danger and blood-chilling possibility": he throws a rock through the window of a laundry run by a Chinese immigrant, who then chases after but fails to catch him.[125]

More than simply giving the white youth a "thrill," the attack and chase allows him to symbolically conquer his fear, "Chinamen" being, for him, "uncanny . . . and darkly mysterious" figures, the source of "a deep and abiding fear."[126] In order to illustrate his continued defiance of this fear, the young Fairbanks repeatedly stones the same establishment, an act that Taylor applauds, even as his account portrays the "Chinese laundryman" as "hard-working" and "innocent."[127] It is sufficient, on the one hand, that this man forms part of Fairbanks's boring circumstances (however industrious he is, he comes to embody the peril of "indolence") and, on the other hand, that he is an object of Fairbanks's fear (however unthreatening he is, he belongs to a category of person that is deemed inherently foreign, dark, and mysterious). Thus the rock throwing becomes a dramatic gesture of seizing free agency and independent existence; the target of his aggression becomes "dread fate," behavior rendered automatic by convention and the fear of the unknown.

According to the residual ideology of "the strenuous life," the opportunity for racially charged "adventure" is a white-male birthright, especially within this post-"pioneer" locale; the specter of white settlers' violence toward Native Americans hangs over Taylor's lament about "respectable" Denver. The young Fairbanks requires a nonwhite figure to become the "dark" backdrop that he will smash as a means of individuating himself and proving his manhood. Simply by virtue of his availability to play this role, the "Chinese laundryman" is reduced to "débris," the human counterpart of his shattered glass—and from Taylor's and Fairbanks's perspective, justly so. In turn, Fairbanks is able to illustrate his courage, this time using more destructive projectiles than sand.[128]

For Taylor, the bombardment of the laundry represents the birth of the Fairbanks screen persona. The captions accompanying the stills printed with the article cast the actor's recent roles as versions of the boy who confidently flouts fate: Fairbanks's Robin Hood is "a classic example of the man who made romance and high adventure of his war on the world," while in *The Thief of Bagdad*, he plays "a hero of romance [setting] out to overthrow the tyranny of circumstances."[129] Having explored the full extent to which violent individual struggle shapes the star's persona, the fact that Fairbanks was held up (by writers like Creel) as a promoter of social cohesion starts to appear odd. How are we to situate the utopian-collective aspect of his writing and cinematic oeuvre in relation to this idealization of the man who makes "war on the world"?

As the opening of this chapter illustrates, Fairbanks conceives of collective success in terms of the fusion of small particles into a productive, aesthetically pleasing aggregate. Here again, the word "sand" plays a crucial role. At the outset of *Making Life Worth While*, Fairbanks announces his intention to explain how the "little grains of sand" described in his favorite hymn "accomplish so much."[130] In the following sections, Fairbanks elaborates this idea of collective success or accomplishment, making bold, utopian predictions about the "discover[y]" of "intellect" as a *"world-asset."*[131] Offering very few precise details, Fairbanks begins to envision a process whereby the expansion of mental "power"—"intellects [being] fed up into a higher state"—will usher in a new "age" of human society, a "time . . . when *intellectuality* will rule the universe."[132]

Having overcome all forms of ignorance and superstition, the people of the world, Fairbanks predicts, will be able to communicate reasonably and efficiently with one another, thus avoiding war: "Settlements between nations will be made beside the lamp of reason rather than under the flare of the canon's mouth."[133] Conflating perfected understanding (*"mental fellowship"*) with the end of war, Fairbanks's projections bring to mind his earlier statements about cinema's promotion of global understanding—his version of the broader utopian and internationalist defense of cinema that had come into vogue before World War I.[134] In making these comments, Fairbanks notes that current events make the utopian age he describes seem particularly far off; he concedes that human "mental development" has not reached the point where tragedies such as World War I can be avoided.

But instead of simply lamenting the "great slaughter" and looking forward to its end, Fairbanks strikes a patriotic, bellicose pose. Until the time that humans decide that war is unnecessary, "we are bound," Fairbanks asserts, to *"follow the flag of our cause."*[135] Considering Fairbanks's interest in expansionist nationalism and his general belief in the salutary benefits of "physical combat," it is not surprising to find him talking about World War I in these terms, praising "our boys" as embodiments of a uniquely American "pep" and calling on "everybody," the civilian included, "to do his part" in support of the cause.[136] What is unusual and striking here—even more than just his glossing over the evident contradiction between utopian cooperative mind prophecies and aggressive calls to war—is how Fairbanks attempts to reconcile the Rooseveltian celebration of war as purifying, regenerative adventure with the Wilsonian ideal of the "war that will end war."

Echoing Wilson's rhetoric of eventual peace through an initial military intervention, he describes the United States as "want[ing] peace bad enough to fight for it" and the war as making "the world safe for democracy."[137] And he goes further too, casting the war as a struggle between the forces of vitality and what he calls "degeneracy." Like *Laugh and Live*, *Making Life Worth While* poses the "inertia of stagnation" as the ultimate moral threat—but this time at a collective, social level. At the beginning of the book, Fairbanks offers an etiology of this original sin through an esoteric interpretation of Genesis. He asserts that Cain killed Abel out of "indolence" "because of the shiftless life he led."[138] In this reading, Cain was jealous of Abel's "popularity" to the point of becoming enraged and, at the same time, in poor physical conditions. Lacking in the "stamina with which to control his mind," Abel was led, as if reflexively, to act on his worst thoughts about his brother.[139]

According to this bizarre etiology, the combination of physical fitness and mental control ("physical and mental training") that Fairbanks's self-help books advocate would have kept Cain from ever "set[ting]" the "example of murder . . . before mankind."[140] By the same token, such training, promoting a healthy mind and body, will by itself provide a corrective example, eradicating the "degenerate" strain of human ancestry that originated with Cain. As the book wears on, Fairbanks extrapolates the metaphysical struggle between wholesome, vigorous (worthwhile) life and indolent, degenerate life onto the contemporary world war. Rather than a needless "slaughter," the war becomes, through this maneuver, an opportunity for national and ultimately international "regeneration." The need for all Americans to "jump into the . . . ring" provides a remedy for a collective indolence or shiftlessness that has descended on the nation due to excessive prosperity and ease.[141] Likewise, the manly "pep" of American soldiers provides an example of a people awakened in mind and body and committed to resisting an unconscious drift into degenerate existence.

In these passages, Fairbanks echoes Roosevelt's discourse of "preparedness" in the early years of World War I (prior to the United States' entering the conflict). Preparedness becomes a major imperative in Fairbanks's advice literature; without achieving this state, the individual cannot hope for success in any situation, martial or civilian.[142] Albeit with a greater focus on the training of the physical body, the term functions synonymously with "morale" in the writings of Rupert Hughes and G. S. Hall: it is the "supreme standard of life and conduct" as made visible by the tragedy of the war. With this emphasis on preparedness in place, Fairbanks is able to offer a highly traditional account of the war as an opportunity for purifying collective struggle and even to cast that struggle as combat against "indolence" itself. In his heavily abstracted, almost allegorical rendering of World War I, Germany and its allies are not just representatives of militarism (as they were typically portrayed by American advocates of intervention) but also a "great Octopus of Degeneracy . . . strangling . . . the body politic."[143]

On its face, the idea is absurd; Fairbanks offers no warrant for his interpretation of bloodshed in Europe as divine retribution for the excesses of American prosperity. And there is an obvious logical puzzle in Fairbanks's prescribing a theater of death and destruction as a *remedy* for death and destruction. But his underlying intention is clear: Fairbanks wants to cast the war as part of "the great plan of the universe," whereby the essentially "joy-seeking, peace-loving people of the world"—Americans, needless to say—physically subdue the forces that menace them, offering, in the process, a display of their own health and vigor before the rest of the world.[144] As in Lee's World War I–era writings, although for superficially different reasons, peace becomes a "better way of fighting," heroic bellicosity purged of the spirit of militarism.

In this scenario, the United States' enemies are—somewhat analogously to the Chinese immigrant in Fairbanks's tale of youthful rebellion—less real nations or peoples than anthropomorphized spiritual forces. This convenient fiction absolutely removes any suggestion of "slaughter" or "murder" from the American part in the war. The killing of the enemy, in this case, is the ultimate counterexample to Cain's killing of Abel. For Fairbanks, the war represents in historical terms the beginning of *"the regeneration of mankind"*: a process of violently purging murderous ("degenerate") tendencies from the population.[145] With this sense of the finality of World War I, the closing chapter of *Making Life Worth While* recalls the end of Griffith's *Intolerance* (Griffith Feature Films, 1916). It describes the "War Lord and his hosts" becoming enraged and seeking to punish humanity, with humanity's sheer physical motion, its theatrical display of pep, serving to freeze this ultimate enemy in its tracks.[146] Fairbanks encourages his reader, as Griffith does his viewer, to "tak[e] a larger view" of the great "catastrophe," to see its universal significance. What looks like a destructive flood (something like the biblical deluge) will be seen, ultimately, as a nourishing irrigation of the globe—like Griffith's "mighty river of expressed emotion."[147]

Moreover, as in Lee's critique of standard "peace-talk," peace becomes a sublated form of fighting, and the latter serves the interest of the former, bringing about the "settlements between nations" that Fairbanks associates throughout the book with the release of mental "energy."[148] For both writers, energy is something that can only be expanded and increased, never restrained. Likewise, the visionary leader—Ford's "master cell"—drives this expansion of energy, casting out his "sand," modeling courage and resolve while mobilizing the American masses—"little entities"—around himself. Fairbanks goes a step further than Lee in making military aggression itself a first step toward international unity. He includes the interventionist Wilson in his pantheon of "big men" (alongside Roosevelt and Lloyd George), celebrating his rapid "mobiliz[ing]" of the American military to the point that it *"extends around the world."*[149] The idea of the United States, being expanded into a "globe-girdling" presence—even on a "war basis"—seems, for him, to point toward a future order of peace and integrated humanity.[150]

"A Study in Ivory White"

The Thief of Bagdad is a complex film that purports to illustrate a simple moral, spelled out vividly in the opening and closing scenes. Tinted a vivid blue, these framing scenes are set in an austere desert landscape, where, in Lindsay's somewhat florid description, we see "[a] Mohammedan Holy Man, dressed in moon-white, telling the fairy tale to the little boy at his feet, and pointing up toward the stars and the moon." "The stars fall in line," Lindsay says, "and become a proverb jeweled across the sky—'Happiness Must Be Earned.'"[151] Although "Happiness Must Be Earned" sounds, at first blush, like the most generic of morals, it becomes clear, on further analysis, that the phrasing used in the film belongs to the specific positive-thinking tradition that Fairbanks espouses in his writings. "Happiness" here acts, as it does in Fairbanks's books, as a catchall term combining worldly success or victory and the idea of spiritual harmony with the Infinite.

For its part, "earning" is less about gaining a return through sustained effort than it is about harnessing the divine power of the mind to will an ideal outcome into existence. In this context, what is earned

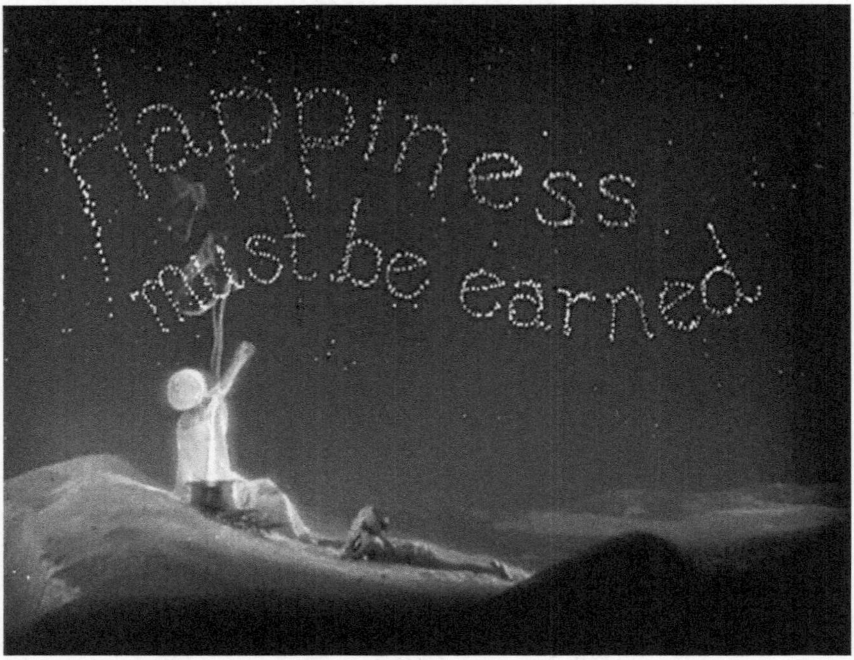

Figure 5.6. The motto offered at the beginning of *The Thief of Bagdad* (Douglas Fairbanks Pictures, 1924).

is the desired thing on which the individual concentrates, attracting it to her- or himself through sheer self-belief. Placing the film in this context, the ultimate moral approximates the somewhat lengthier "message" that William Leach teases out of *The Wonderful Wizard of Oz* (1900), reading the novel in light of L. Frank Baum's commitments to theosophy and other therapeutic beliefs: "As long as one has confidence and realizes that the world is really a very plentiful place full of an overflowing divine energy, one need not . . . struggle or suffer or go through the agonies of growing up or of developing. All one needs, really, is to think positively, to get in touch with one's own 'latent powers' or intrinsic 'royalty' and to over come fear and worry, in order to inherit a kingdom."[152] *The Thief of Bagdad* stands as a parallel attempt to create a modern, mind-cure fairy tale, with Ahmed's transformation from thief to the Princess's worthy suitor representing his recognition of his divine powers.

Following the fairy-tale framing device, the film introduces Ahmed, in the guise of the playful thief. At this point, Ahmed displays some of the characteristic traits of the Fairbanks star persona: he laughs, smiles, and flaunts his physical prowess. Yet he is rather indolent, to use the language of Fairbanks's *Laugh and Live*. He and his partner in crime, the Bird of Evil (Snitz Edwards), support themselves by pilfering jewelry and coins from wealthier neighbors, turning to crime as a way of avoiding honest work. Narrowly avoiding capture, Ahmed takes refuge in a mosque, where he hears a sermon on the virtues of toiling and the need to "earn" happiness. Ahmed scoffs at the lesson, stating in the intertitles that he takes what he wants and that his "reward is <u>here</u>" (i.e., in the material world).

Immediately after this opening sequence establishing Ahmed's character, the film shifts locations to "far eastern Asia," where the Mongol Prince plots to usurp the Caliph's palace, represented by a surprisingly detailed model (a miniature of the film's celebrated "Bagdad" set) that his retainers present to him. Along with the timing of his introduction, the intertitles containing the Mongol Prince's dialogue establish him as a parallel figure to Ahmed: "What I want—I take," he says. Along with other princes from around the film's fictional "East," the Mongol Prince has been summoned to Bagdad to make his case as a suitor to the Caliph's daughter. He aspires to gain control of Bagdad by winning the contest or, failing to do so, by having his retinue mount a surprise siege once inside the palace walls.

In the meantime, Ahmed and his associate infiltrate the palace fortifications themselves, posing as gift bearers. Once inside, Ahmed catches a glimpse of the Princess and becomes distracted from his mission of harvesting more gold and jewels. Ahmed exits the palace empty-handed, save for one of the Princess's slippers. When asked by the Bird of Evil where the "treasure" is, he shows this memento, pointing to his head and heart to indicate that the object of his want has changed. At this point, Ahmed initiates his gradual process of self-reformation, and the film indicates that he will become a rival to and foil for the Mongol Prince. Ahmed rejects the Bird of Evil's recommendation to simply steal the Princess herself from the palace; he decides to present himself as a suitor, entering the procession of princes coming to vie for the Princess's affections. To do this, however, he must first pilfer "princely raiment" from the city's "bazaars."

Whereas the Princess is repulsed by the other suitors, she finds the carefully disguised Ahmed to be "a Prince indeed." She is relieved when, through a series of comedic mishaps, Ahmed is the first to touch the rosebush in the palace courtyard. In doing this, Ahmed unwittingly fulfills the fortune told to the Princess by her trusted attendant and confidant, an unnamed slave character played by Anna May Wong. Despite being chosen by the Princess, Ahmed is overcome by his guilty conscience and considers abandoning his charade, only to be revealed as an impostor. Ahmed repents to the Princess, abjuring his thievery ("What I wanted I took. I wanted to you—I tried to take you") and asserting that true love has killed the "evil in [him]." After Ahmed is apprehended and flogged, the Princess bribes the palace guards into secreting him out of the palace.

As a way of delaying her choice of suitor,-the Princess vows to marry the prince who can secure the "rarest" treasure within a week. In the meantime, Ahmed seeks the counsel of the man in the mosque, seemingly the same figure who appears in the opening and closing shots of the film (Charles Belcher, billed as "the Holy Man"). He tells Ahmed to undertake a sort of pilgrimage through which he can prove himself worthy of the Princess. Although the Holy Man's advice includes some pat advice about "humility," it is really a mind-cure program summed up by the injunction "Make thyself a prince." The gist is that Ahmed will "earn happiness" by having confidence in himself (being "brave," "control[ling his] destiny") and pursuing the "path that leads to treasure beyond [his] dreams." Ahmed then undertakes a quest through a series of remote, magical realms. In each one, he must survive a physical trial (having to slay a monster, for instance) and secure an object to present to the next realm's gatekeeper or to use as a tool or weapon there. In the end, he gains the box of magic sand that produces armies ex nihilo.

Ahmed's multistage quest unfolds in parallel to the treasure hunt undertaken jointly by the Mongol Prince and the princes of Persia

(Mathilde Comont) and India (Noble Johnson). They secure, respectively, a magic apple (which confers the power to heal), a magic carpet (the power to fly), and a magic crystal (the power to see across distances). At this point, it has been revealed that the Princess's trusted slave is one of the Mongol Prince's conspirators. Working on behalf of the Mongol Prince, she poisons the Princess. Observing the Princess's distress in the crystal, the three suitors speed to Bagdad on the carpet and heal her. Arguing that each item is equally rare and has played a crucial role in restoring her health, the Princess again seeks to delay, prompting the Mongol Prince to commence his siege. Ahmed arrives on horseback the following morning, conjuring an army large enough to overawe the Mongol Prince's "twenty thousand troops" and send them fleeing, leading to the scenes of his triumphant entry into the palace walls and the rescue of the Princess discussed in the opening section of this chapter.

In transforming himself from "common thief" to nobleman, Ahmed realizes his "intrinsic 'royalty,'" as Leach puts it, by adhering to Fairbanks's own books' prescriptions. Initially, Ahmed follows the example of his associate, whose defining quality—"inertia, laziness of some sort," as Lindsay's summarizes it—makes him a figure "of evil" in every respect.[153] To escape such indolence, he must embrace the physical combat that Fairbanks celebrates, embarking on a long and arduous journey outside of the city. In other words, he must trade indolence for "the strenuous life," a concept that Lindsay sees as being equally crucial to *The Thief of Bagdad* as to Fairbanks's previous body of work.[154] But again in line with Fairbanks's particular brand of positive-thinking philosophy, Ahmed's active pursuit is combined with an increased belief in the powers of the mind. The Holy Man encourages him to believe in himself and to fixate on his desired object. His new self-belief is rewarded, in turn, with magical abilities: he accumulates tools (the sand box, an "invisibility cloak," and the flying carpet) that allow him to transcend the laws of physical reality and to will desired states into existence.

As much as the repentant Ahmed makes token gestures toward modesty, obedience of law, and moral rectitude, his transformation hinges on the recognition of his quasi-divine abilities, the abilities that mental science literature asserts are universally held. Ahmed does not just prove himself to be noble in spirit but actually attracts to himself an adoring populace, a real kingdom of people who appear to recognize his authentic self—the Fairbanks star image fully revealed. And according to positive-thinking logic, Ahmed is so richly rewarded precisely because he no longer sees material goods or worldly status as ends in themselves; rather, the reformed thief fixates on "the higher world," "past the moon."[155] Lindsay describes Ahmed's transformation as a process of accomplishing a perfect balance between energetic physical action and contemplative repose.

Lindsay's reading reflects, first of all, his attempt to approach the film in strictly "hieroglyphic" terms; he sees *The Thief of Bagdad* as an extended "conversation" between objects with fixed symbolic meanings (such as the moon, which "corresponds" to dreams, beauty, and the eternal).[156] Second, it reflects his projection of the film's moral lesson into a national, patriotic register. Lindsay's attempt to understand the film as a "sermon" to Americans on the need to resist the mindlessly hectic pace and busyness of modernity. In balancing "action" and "light"—the strenuous life and the "mystical soul of man"—Ahmed becomes a walking hieroglyphic of the ideal American.[157] Ahmed's national-hieroglyphic significance emerges, for Lindsay, in the contrasts that the film draws between him and the two most prominently featured prince characters, the Mongol and Persian princes, respectively. As the rhetoric of purity and "moon-white"-ness in the passages already cited indicates, Lindsay's explication of these contrasts is explicitly grounded in a theory of racial essences.

As opposed to Ahmed, who embodies the manly and "Anglo-Saxon" (Lindsay's term) imperative of the strenuous life, the Persian Prince stands as a hieroglyphic of "the eternal Oriental laziness," "a monument to doing nothing at all."[158] For Lindsay, the very physique of the Persian Prince—short, corpulent, and "effeminate"—indicates a racially determined inertia and indolence. This ostensibly grotesque figure of "comic relief" seems only to "eat sweets [and] to sleep."[159] In highlighting the Persian Prince's supposed lack of proper masculine bearing, Lindsay picks up on, while failing to fully recognize, a deliberate facet of the film's gender discourse. To play this feminized male character, Walsh and Fairbanks, in fact, cast a woman, Mathilde Comont, whom, it is also worth noting, was not "Oriental" at all but white and French.[160] Lindsay's "M. Comant, a rotund little fellow who does not look much more than four and a half feet high," thus covers over the film's dual (raced and gendered) cross-casting.[161]

At the same time, Lindsay reads Ahmed in opposition to the thoroughly "sinister" figure of the Mongol Prince, played by a male actor of Japanese descent.[162] Notwithstanding the obvious parallels between him and Ahmed—both covet the Princess and ultimately lay siege to the palace of Bagdad—Ahmed's desire for the Princess as well as his martial exploits are symbolically elevated by his associations with the aesthetic signs of "dream and the eternal things." Again, the underlying basis of this contrast is racial. The Mongol Prince, as Lindsay notes, represents the "Yellow Peril," the phrase employed by early twentieth-century nativists to describe the threat of territorial conquest and sexual violation posed to Western society by the Eastern horde.[163] Although the film's "Bagdad" does not stand in for mid-1920s United States in any simple or straightforward way, with the Mongol Prince character, the production clearly taps into the country's rising xenophobia.

Using a benign facade to gain access to the gated city of Bagdad, the Mongol Prince's soldiers cast off their cloaks to reveal what Lindsay calls "remarkably aggressive and sinister" armor and weapons.[164] Such imagery seems drawn directly from the infiltration narrative propagated by eugenicists and other American opponents of Asian immigration. He is, further, immediately recognizable—through his mannerisms, costuming, and facial hair—as a copy of the Fu Manchu character invented by the British writer Sax Rohmer and featured in a range of Hollywood films from the 1920s and 1930s. Like Fu Manchu, an evil Chinese mastermind bent on world domination, the Mongol Prince is styled to represent "Oriental" decadence, effeminacy, and perversion.[165] Clearly, the prospect of this character's marriage to the Princess suggests a sexual threat to white womanhood.

As a fairy tale that seems at least partly aimed at a children's audience, *The Thief of Bagdad* is careful to keep sexual themes in the background. And yet by highlighting the putatively grotesque qualities of the Mongol and Persian Princes as well as her disgust or fear at the sight all the initial suitors (save Ahmed), the film conveys the idea that a union with any of them would be "unnatural." Like Ahmed, the Princess is nominally an Arab character. In the case of Julanne Johnson, however, the masquerade extends only to costumes; the filmmakers have made no effort to conceal or alter the physical appearance of the white actress who plays the Princess.

Lindsay's reading allows Ahmed to be spared of any stigma of sinister intent (the desire for wealth, "blind lust," or what have you), despite the fact that the character's behavior does not outwardly differ at all from that of his ostensible foil. Echoing the terms of Fairbanks's books and positive-thinking doctrine more broadly, Lindsay stakes this distinction on the purity of Ahmed's motives, the way he tempers his physical vigor with meditative and spiritual energy, properly focused on the "epic" and "eternal."[166] But following the analysis a step further, it is clear that this distinction is entirely predicated on a visual or aesthetic difference. Ahmed seems only to transcend the kind of characterization that Lindsay gives to the Persian and Mongol princes because he is everywhere associated with the imagery of whiteness. While Lindsay treats this imagery as essentially symbolic ("hieroglyphic"), his description of it serves to draw out the racial hierarchies underpinning the film's moral universe.

Ahmed is ultimately a "pure" character because he is not essentially "Oriental"; he lacks the other princes' innate disposition toward laziness and acquisitiveness.

Reading *The Thief of Bagdad* with and against Lindsay, we encounter an allegory of national regeneration—Lindsay, we should note, wished that the film's motto had been "The National Happiness of America Must Be Earned"—rooted equally in spiritualist concepts and in the period's dominant ideologies of race.[167] On a literal level, the liberation of Bagdad from the Mongol siege involves the replacement of the invading "yellow" horde with "an enormous army in white."[168] More figuratively, the arrival of the liberating army suggests the possibility that the populace of Bagdad—the heterogeneous multitudes show in the film's early street scenes—might undergo a process of refinement and improvement similar to Ahmed's. Ahmed's army both casts out the threat of "Asiatic" degradation and represents to the "native" inhabitants the corporate body that they might become.

Hence it is not surprising that Lindsay lingers over the whiteness of this army's regalia (helmets, cloaks, and banners streaming from lances and gonfalons). The combined aesthetic of these details give the transformation or replacement being depicted a complex, hieroglyphic meaning. He reads the film's climax as showing "the well-organized splendor of a growing culture" emerging out of the "cluttered," speed-obsessed, overly commercial reality of contemporary America.[169] Ahmed's army enacts one of the "national rituals" expressive of American "spirit-hungers" that Lindsay felt cinema, at its best, could help establish.[170] Lindsay rhapsodizes at great length about the "silvery sheen" of the film in general and of the final scene in particular; he praises it as a "study in ivory white," a story that seems to be made entirely of "moonlight," "told within" a remarkably "brief range of gray and white" tones.[171]

Lindsay's reading of the film's "study in ivory white" serves to draw out the racial connotations of the film's color imagery, illustrating the implied contrast between the gross materiality of the "Oriental" and the spiritual purity of the "Anglo-Saxon."[172] In following this line of analysis, the point is not, however, to reduce the film's final sequence to a racist-nationalist allegory. The vagaries of the film's setting and internal racial semantics keep scenes like this from mapping simply straightforwardly onto the arguments of 1920s American nativism. The more subtle and apt conclusion to draw is that the film uses conventional racial tropes to explain the idea that strenuous living and positive thinking enable the transcendence of worldly constraints.

As in Fairbanks's childhood anecdote about his lashing out at the Chinese American laundry owner, in *The Thief of Bagdad*, the

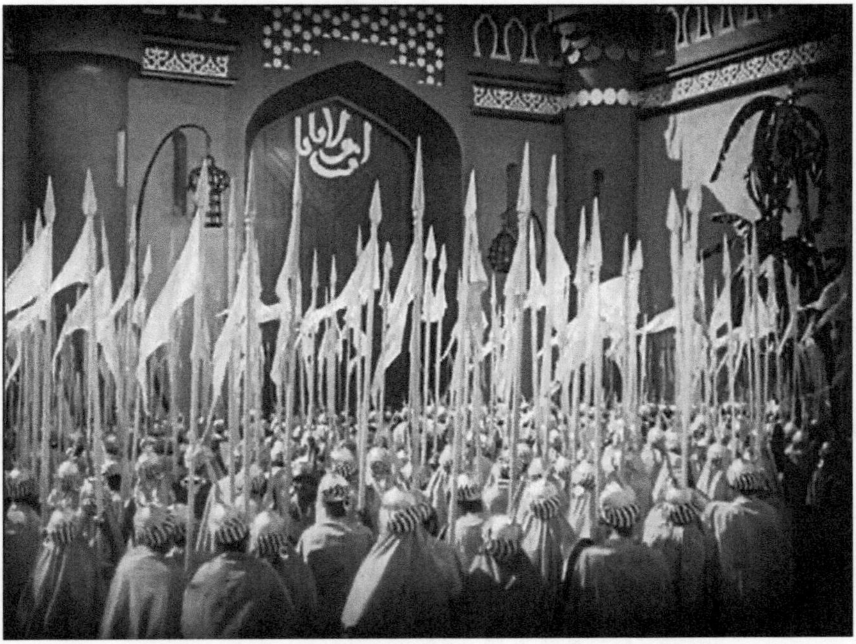

Figure 5.7. The army in white in *The Thief of Bagdad* (Douglas Fairbanks Pictures, 1916).

presence of the "Oriental" menace serves to set off the white protagonist's heroic aspirations. The immorality of the hero's antagonists comes to light in and through their characterization as unassamilable within the social body. Likewise, the imagery of the "Yellow Peril" serves to highlight the Mongol Prince and his army's status as what Fairbanks would call human debris—dwellers in "the dark corners of life." By contrast, the prevalence of "silvery" and "ivory" white tones in the closing crowd panoramas provides a racial gloss for the hero's accomplishment of success and happiness according to the rules of mental science. In these panoramas, the film activates the historical associations of physiognomic whiteness with aesthetic perfection and social dominance to embellish its stated message, "Happiness Must Be Earned."[173]

It is fitting then that the film uses, as Lindsay puts it, a "brief range of gray and white tones" to limn the Fairbanks model of happiness and victory. Invoking racial discourses to dramatically enact the metaphor of the courageous individual casting out his messengers—his "sand"—into the world, this aesthetic strategy provides a point of critical leverage on *The Thief of Bagdad* as well as the spiritualist literature that informs it. The ideal of corporate harmony espoused in this literature is expressed in terms of cosmopolitanism and international understanding. But the notion of mystic union between the crowd-man and the little entities that he draws to himself is, in the end, hostile to difference at a fundamental level. As in Ford's theory of organizations, the persons enlisted in the great leader's project have to be reduced to mere mental projections, their wills made to completely harmonize with his own. This is a philosophy of abstract unity in which the manifest variety (economic, racial, social) that characterizes the material world becomes an obstacle to be overcome, a constraint from which the individual is advised to liberate her- or himself, seeking refuge in a spiritualized existence where everything resembles the quasi-divine self.

Conclusion

UNIVERSAL HISTORY AND THE HISTORICITY OF FILM ENTERTAINMENT

> *Internationalism, or at least the beginnings of friendship between nations and peoples, has been measurably advanced by the universal acceptance of film entertainment. Jealousy, fear, and hatred, born of insularity and ignorance, have been diminished by the spread of the movies. Little by little, all peoples have been unconsciously acquiring knowledge—never before available—of their fellow men of other races and other nationalities, and knowledge must inevitably be followed by understanding and toleration.*
>
> —Benjamin Hampton, *A History of the Movies*[1]

Benjamin Hampton concludes his 1931 tome, *A History of the Movies*, with a reflective summary titled "Today and Tomorrow" that engages in the kind of bold prognostications about cinema's future role in world affairs familiar from earlier utopian-universalist cinema writing. In this conclusion, Hampton stresses film's educational, uplifting effects, recapping arguments made by earlier writers like Will Hays, Edward S. Van Zile, and Terry Ramsaye, whose foundational *A Million and One Nights: A History of the Motion Picture* his history deliberately echoes.[2] He further concludes with a series of statements like the previous epigraph that insist that cinema has previously impacted the world in positive, quantifiable ways, promoting intergroup understanding and, therefore, peace.

Hampton's deployment of these discursive conventions is surprising both in its tense and in its timing. First, Hampton asserts cinema's social benefits as a matter of historical fact: "film entertainment" *has already* "advanced" friendship, understanding, and tolerance—and "measurably" so. Second, Hampton offers these assertions after films with recorded, synchronized sound (which he still calls "talkies") have become the industry standard, rendering "silent" films altogether obsolete. This is to say that the entertainment medium to which Hampton is referring is not the same one that Hays, Van Zile, and Ramsaye confronted. Moreover, the exact manner in which cinema has changed—incorporating spoken national languages into its material body—would appear to invalidate the universal language metaphor, the very basis of the discourse that he employs.

What Hampton does, then, is to reassert his faith in the tenets of the utopian-universalist view of film in the face of evidence that appears very directly and strongly to refute this view. His "Today and Tomorrow" conclusion is contorted by the effort required to reinforce the idea of cinema's intrinsic "internationalism" in the face of his own findings as a historian—both about technological and industrial changes in cinema and about the state of the world in the early 1930s. With respect to this first issue, Hampton shuttles back and forth between two competing narratives: one about the swift global spread of talking pictures—American-produced ones, in particular—the other about the alienating effects of speech in films.

Hampton acknowledges that talking pictures have ushered in a "new phase of mass psychology."[3] "American silent movies," he says, once achieved "universal acceptance" because they invited "foreign" audiences into a "dream world," a space of "perfect illusion" that was both distinct from ordinary reality and utterly convincing.[4] "When the movies began to talk," however, "the novelty of speech coming from the shadow players' lips" punctured the illusion.[5] What had once been a conduit to a fully formed dream world, which allowed viewers to dissociate themselves from "instinctive clan feeling[s]," now aroused their "pride of race and nation."[6] According to this side of the narrative, non-American audiences now felt the "suspicion" that accompanies "the arrival of a stranger" and began to demand "plays in their own languages."[7]

Notwithstanding these admissions, Hampton recuperates the talkies under the utopian-universalist ideology by making a series of striking rhetorical moves. For instance, he asserts that the sheer popularity of films with recorded, synchronized sound illustrates that "all members of the human race are alike"—which is to say that the audience is not fragmented by linguistic differences.[8] He claims—without any apparent warrant—that talkies "will *not* be presented in the hundreds of tongues that now plague mankind."[9] Rather, only about "a dozen or so of the world's principal languages" will feature in talkie production initially and then, over time, the medium of sound film will become a vehicle for promoting "one common tongue"—American English, it goes without saying—for the entire globe.[10] In this way, "talkies will advance the work [of 'internationalism'] begun by the [silent] movies."[11]

Making these predictions, Hampton does not elaborate on the process whereby American English will push aside all other existing "tongues" nor explain why the emergence of this single language as the global dominant would not be perceived by international audiences as a form of cultural imperialism—why it would not continue to elicit feelings of estrangement or arouse nationalist sentiments. Hampton simply finds a way to make the rise of the talking-picture medium consistent with the premise that the very "multiplicity" of national languages is intrinsically a source of evil.[12]

With respect to matters of world history, more broadly, there is an obvious speciousness to what Hampton writes. His "measurably advanced" claim is not accompanied by any supporting evidence that such progress has been made. And needless to say, neither this progress nor film's contribution to it is quantifiable in the first place. More to the point though, when Hampton does look around at what is happening in the United States and Europe—during and in the immediate aftermath of the transition to sound—he finds only distressing signs. Hampton refers at various points to the "world-wide depression of 1930–1931 and the political unrest that prevails in many countries," characterizing these developments as harmful to the international dissemination of Hollywood talkies.[13] In this respect, Hampton's narrative suggests nothing like the triumphant march of internationalism. Instead, the global order that "the spread of the movies" has helped bring into view seems to be in crisis, much like it was during the World War I era.[14]

Here again, Hampton is at pains to reconcile these developments with the narrative of unavoidable, cinema-driven social progress. One of his strategies here is to reframe what plagues humanity—depression and unrest—as illustrations that "the 'brotherhood of man" is no longer "an impracticable dream of idealists" but a "business necessity."[15] In other words, economic interconnectedness means that "war, poverty, disease, and crime" must necessarily "disappear from life."[16] By Hampton's rather fuzzy reasoning, it becomes impossible to discern whence came these contemporary problems. As strong as they seem to be in 1931, the existence of mass media, in general, and sound film, in particular—inevitable "instruments" of unification—mean, for Hampton, that they are always already in retreat. If humanity finds itself still divided—by language, by nation, or by class—even after two and a half decades of cinema history, then what it needs is simply for cinema to penetrate more deeply into all aspects of everyday life.

Reasserting his cinematic faith in the face of contrary evidence, Hampton's *A History of the Movies* neatly illustrates what happens when utopian-universalist defenders of commercial entertainment confront the historicity of their media. Although the transition to sound in Hollywood provides a paradigmatic case of this response, it persists in subsequent, kindred discussions of all kinds of "new media." Typically, the medium's partisan responds by broadly reasserting her or his belief in what John Durham Peters calls "the dream of communication as the communion of souls"; she or he exploits the paradox whereby the very sense of a communication "breakdown" seems to point to the improvement and dissemination of existing communications as necessarily the only solution to the problem at hand.[17]

Rhetorically, these declarations of renewed faith take a very simple form: the writer insistently deploys some mystified and idealized signifier of togetherness, understanding, and unity—the "brotherhood of man" for late-1920s procinema writers or "community" for contemporary internet theorists—in conjunction with references to specific properties of the communications technology being discussed. The linkage of the medium with such notions of communion is part of an effort to disavow what the technology primarily is (a medium of commercial entertainment) and dismiss its more visible or measurable effects—from spreading corporate ideologies and/or the interests of particular media companies to destabilizing existing political culture.

Such a rhetorical strategy serves to keep the medium *on the side of* the dream that Peters describes and *separate from* the corruption of this dream. As the writer confronts the evidence of crisis—and, in turn, registers the historicity of the medium—the narrative of progress and the belief that humanity has no recourse but to go forward down the pathway already outlined are strained. As Hampton's example indicates, we end up with what is obviously marketing jargon: a kind of gauzy mysticism being pasted onto an entertainment commodity that the reader has no trouble recognizing as both decidedly mundane and ambiguous in its functions.

Written in the wake of the 2016 presidential election, Facebook founder Mark Zuckerberg's manifesto, "Building Global Community," is a remarkable contemporary instance of this response. In a section titled "Informed Community," Zuckerberg most directly addresses accusations that Facebook promotes political polarization by trapping users in "filter bubbles" and enabling the dissemination of "fake news."[18] He notes that the very increase in the number of voices in "public discourse" that Facebook allows sometimes threatens to "fragment our shared sense of reality."[19] The challenge here, he argues, is for his company to find ways of "strengthening our common understanding" while "increasing diversity" of ideas.[20] Not surprisingly, Zuckerberg treats phenomena like filter bubbles and fake news as the kinds of "unwanted effects that come with any new medium" rather than as flaws intrinsic to its design or as consequences of its historical undermining of existing institutions (such as "the news industry").[21]

Zuckerberg does not countenance the possibility that Facebook could have socially destructive consequences—even unintended ones—because he treats it as the apotheosis of "social infrastructure," the vague, catchall term he uses throughout the essay to characterize those human inventions that, by leveraging collective power, help build "communities" of ever-increasing size. The conclusion that Facebook is the best means of promoting "informed communities" because it helps people achieve a shared sense of reality (the very thing he begins this section by acknowledging it has served to fragment) is, thus, presupposed by the essay's opening premise: that the entire history of humanity is one of people "learn[ing] to come together in ever greater numbers—from tribes to cities to nations."[22] According to this brief but totalizing narrative of human history, over time, human beings' ability "to build social infrastructure like communities, media and governments to empower us to achieve things we couldn't on our own" has led to the establishment of a single global order.[23]

This order is, for Zuckerberg, the ultimate "community," and yet his writing is motivated by the sense that "now, across the world there are people left behind by globalization, and movements for withdrawing from global connection."[24] Luckily, there is Facebook, which he here presents as neither of these things but rather as simply an agent of measurable progress ("Every year [since its launch] the world got more connected and this was seen as a positive trend") and a harbinger of authentic communion ("Facebook stands for bringing us closer together and building a global community").[25] Thus the dilemma that Zuckerberg poses at the outset—"There are questions about whether we can make a global community that works for everyone, and whether the path ahead is to connect more or reverse course"—is purely rhetorical.[26] More connection can be the only pathway forward—there is no reversing course—and this connection can only be established through the expansive, highly adaptable forms of "social infrastructure" established by Facebook, whose status as a publicly traded company and commercial media platform the essay never acknowledges.

Zuckerberg's essay is significant in this context not only because it illustrates the contemporary persistence of utopian-universalist arguments about media but also because it highlights the crucial role played in these arguments by the genre of universal history. Zuckerberg's condensed historical narrative, previously quoted, seems drawn straight from the pages of popular universal histories, which emerged in the nineteenth century and reached their apogee with the writings of H. G. Wells and Hendrik Van Loon in the early 1920s.[27] Like his predecessors, Zuckerberg reduces human history to a single story of progress, whose prime mover and unquestionable telos is the steady aggregation of human beings into larger and larger corporate bodies. Wells promoted a view of "*history as one whole*," the life of mankind as "one great epic unfolding," illustrating consistent themes from prehistory to the present and a trajectory toward higher forms of social and political unity—culminating in what he described as an incipient "world state."[28]

Compared with Wells—and with the silent-era procinema writers who were influenced by him—Zuckerberg offers a rather vague account of how communication technologies might further the progress of universal history. For Wells, universal history is a brand of historiography with a monumental social function. By synoptically narrating and interpreting the "whole" human epic in compact popular works that draw clear lessons out of past events, Wells hopes to provide modern humanity with a set of common principles that will prompt it to transcend its historical failures. Writing in the immediate aftermath of World War I, Wells is most concerned with providing humanity with a kind of bible of internationalism that would preach against all forms of parochial identification, effectively rendering war obsolete.

Even as Wells places great faith in the idea of books that contain "common knowledge of the general facts of human history," he sees modern mass-communications technologies—cinema, in particular—as superseding print in their power to impart such wisdom.[29] Wells recognized that, by the time of his writing, the cinema had come closer than any other medium to realizing the ideal of a common global audience through its sheer ability to "[put] ideas and arguments swiftly and effectively before people all over the world at the same time such as no one could have dreamt of a hundred years ago," and the later, more historically minded, American procinema writers, like Ramsaye, Van Zile, and Hampton drew inspiration from his arguments.[30]

Whereas earlier procinema writers had stressed the idea that film promoted a generalized knowledge of other peoples—and thus a feeling of intergroup likeness—the writers who took after Wells embraced his idea of cinema as a teacher of historical lessons more specifically. For instance, Van Zile echoed Wells in seeing cinema as doing for the entire human race what knowledge of "past errors" does for individual people: just as the "individual man can . . . pursue a course of safety by aid of the lighthouse of his past," so can cinema act as a tool of "mandatory enlightenment" for humanity as a whole, instructively dramatizing its historical "struggles and failures, triumphs and defeats."[31] In the contemporary guise of internet theory, the utopian universalist media argument eschews such specific pedagogical content, ignoring the deeper past as a guide to future action and adopting a seemingly more simplified view of the inevitability of human progress.[32]

Whereas the synoptic perspective of universal history allows internet theory to forget about the history of technology, sustaining a "fake" sense of the medium's "novelty," American procinema writers during the waning years of the silent-feature era drew on this genre in a variety of ways.[33] With the motion-picture medium having attained a state of technological, aesthetic, and economic maturity, procinema writers became cognizant of its having a history, giving rise to a new genre of historiographical writing about cinema—this as opposed to the strictly speculative or theoretical kind of writing that had been pioneered by Vachel Lindsay. Capitalizing on the popularity of Wells's universal history as well as his portrayal of cinema as the decisive instrument of historical change, the first American film historians begin to tell the story of the medium in terms of this genre's major tropes.[34] Van Zile considers cinema's "significance" against the backdrop of the entire trajectory of human evolution, while Ramsaye begins his study by tracing the urge to make and view movies back to human prehistory, echoing Van Loon's claim in *The Story of Mankind* that "we modern men and women are not 'modern' at all. On the contrary we still belong to the last generation of cave-dwellers."[35]

As Van Loon's statement suggests, universal history approaches the question of progress with some ambivalence. At times, it sees in contemporary conflict evidence of human beings' protracted "infancy" or of their atavistic tendencies—the brittleness of the veneer of "civilization."[36] At other times, the proximity of modern people to their prehistoric ancestors seems to simplify the historian's task of summing up what is needed for humanity to attain full maturity; human beings' afflictions remain primitive and can be overcome by basic changes in behavior. And in all cases, universal history has an apocalyptic imagination in which the catastrophic scope of modern problems (symbolized best by the generalized destructiveness of the world war) paradoxically points the way toward solutions. The recent war is a "cardinal" point in history in which the options for "mankind"—coexisting peacefully or perishing in "the next great war"—come into sharp focus and in which international crisis brings to light the kinds of technological and economic structures that can sustain a salutary international order.[37]

This apocalyptic imagination is pronounced in Van Zile's and Hampton's books, whereas Ramsaye, whose view of culture is populist and primitivist, seems unconcerned with war or with the need for progress. Van Zile, the one writer who directly cites Wells, is dubious about the possibility that human beings can transcend their "savage" predilections.[38] Like Wells, his reflections on cinema are bound up in the preoccupation over whether or not people can, in fact, learn from collective mistakes and mature in the way that individual people do. For his part, Ramsaye celebrates cinema for its comprehensive ability to fulfill primitive human "wishes"—the way it satisfies the (in his view) eternal human desire to experience pleasurable sensations by viewing re-creations of the things that inspire them.[39]

As the preceding discussion of his *A History of the Movies* indicates, Hampton is closer to Van Zile than to Ramsaye in his focus on contemporary world crises. But he shares with both of these writers—and with Wells, for that matter—an essential faith in the power of cinema as a tool of "uplift and enlightenment."[40] He concludes his history by arguing, simply, that modern economics have made the "brotherhood of man" a "business necessity" and that cinema is so imbricated in this circulation of consumer products that it cannot but be the agent of promoting a "knowledge" of common interests.[41] In this regard, Hampton's work illustrates the crucial way in which the narratives and tropes at the heart of the universal history genre serve to shore up the argument in favor of film's instructive and uplifting functions at the end of the silent-feature era.[42]

During the transition to sound, what relation does Hollywood film production and marketing bear to the arguments advanced by a journalist like Hampton, who cooperated with industry leaders to write his history but also had a broader, scholarly agenda in mind? Where and how, if at all, does the belief in cinema's historical-pedagogical function manifest itself on screen? During the transitional period, big-budget historical epics remain a small but significant sector of Hollywood film production despite some of the physical constraints imposed by the new synchronized sound recording apparatus and despite what would appear to be the loss of the universal qualities of film entertainment caused by the appearance of recorded sound.

As Gilles Deleuze has shown, pre–World War II American film has its own "strong and robust conception of universal history": "the American cinema . . . has in common with Soviet cinema the belief in a finality of universal history"—a belief that the "blossoming of the American nation" is tantamount to "the whole of history."[43] This conception, Deleuze explains, is at the heart of silent epics with historical themes, from *Intolerance* (Griffith Feature Films, 1916) to *The Covered Wagon* (Paramount, 1923). During the transitional period, the studios adhere to this conception, celebrating the American nation as what Deleuze calls a "melting pot and fusion of all minorities" through stories that link—whether explicitly or implicitly—scenes of past societies conquering adversity with contemporary American situations.[44]

A film like Warner Bros.' *Noah's Ark* (1928) revives the tradition of multiperiod, parallel narratives established by *Intolerance* and Cecil B. De Mille's first *The Ten Commandments* (Paramount, 1923)—it juxtaposes the story of the flood from Genesis with a World War I morality tale—sermonizing about toleration across national boundaries. A part-talkie that includes some spoken dialogue, *Noah's Ark* both draws attention to the issue of linguistic difference as a source of strife—it references the Tower of Babel in an opening summary of key Old Testament stories—and papers over it, by having characters from a variety of national backgrounds converse in unaccented American English. A still more interesting case study lies in Universal Pictures' 1927 adaptation of Harriet Beecher Stowe's *Uncle Tom's Cabin*—also a part-talkie.[45]

In the narrative of *Uncle Tom's Cabin* and in the marketing discourse around it, the studio articulates a profoundly confident view of motion pictures' ability to act as an instrument of universal-historical knowledge—to provide a synopsis of all times. Despite the fact that the film is derived from an 1852 abolitionist fiction, the studio would insist on the historicity of its story and of its diegetic world, recasting it as a definitive story of the demise of American slavery and, thereby, enlisting the historical popularity of the novel and its various pop-cultural offshoots in service of the studio's assiduously cultivated posture of high-mindedness. As the very name suggests, Universal was the Hollywood studio that first—and most comprehensively—embraced the notion of cinematic universalism in all of its senses. The point is evident across the studio's marketing materials during this period, such as the text of a trade-press advertisement from around 1915, excerpted here:

> Universal pictures speak the Universal language. Universal stories told in pictures need no translation, no interpreter. Regardless of creed, color, race, or nationality, everyone in the universe understands the stories that are told by Universal Pictures.
>
> They tell the history of all peoples, of all times . . . they tell the news of the world in pictures; the stirring events in every country on the civilized globe—not in cold, unspeakable type, but in the universal language of pictures—moving animated pictures that transport one to the very scene, defying time and distance . . .
>
> Beside them the pens of the mightiest master writers of all time are weak and powerless in their human influence. Beside them the sword of the warrior falls to its scabbard from a nervous hand—conscious of a power that touches, reaches, grips, and sways the hearts and minds of all humanity in a realization of the cruelty and uselessness of war.[46]

This ad offers a fairly mundane instance of the conceptual array detailed from beginning to end of this study, running through the gnostic, cultural-democratic, and millennialist claims in short order.

During the 1920s, Universal had increasingly staked its reputation on "super-special" productions, adaptations of hefty nineteenth-century novels, like Victor Hugo's *The Hunchback of Notre Dame* (1923), that were both widely known and regarded as literary monuments. Given the widespread dissemination of the novel's story and characters, through popular stage melodramas, "Tom Shows," and a string of film adaptations stretching back to 1903, *Uncle Tom's Cabin* certainly appeared like an ideal literary vehicle for a Universal Picture. In advertisements and in the pressbook that Universal distributed to potential exhibitors, the studio's marketing department hailed *Uncle Tom's Cabin*'s "universal popularity" and "world-wide interest," calling it "a story that is known to every person in the four corners of the world" and "the most widely translated book in the history of literature" after the Bible.[47] In these descriptions, Stowe's fictional creations are regarded as something close to universal cultural signs, whose exalted status, moreover, reflects the author's historical contribution to enlightening public opinion: her service to the abolitionist cause and to, as these texts tend to put it, the project of humanizing African Americans in the eyes of bigoted white people.

The studio could claim to be furthering Stowe's antiracist legacy in its insistence on casting an African American actor in the titular role, Uncle Tom having been played by white actors in blackface in prior film versions. James B. Lowe's presence on the Universal City Lot was, indeed, offered as support for studio head Carl Laemmle's claim that this production emblematized the "catholicity of motion pictures"—the fact that "Hollywood [was] represented by every state in the Union, every country on the face of the globe."[48] This claim is dubious, on its face since it normalizes the historical exclusion of African Americans from the project of African American screen representation, portraying black actors as supplicants, dependent on the beneficence of white liberals in the industry. But it becomes obviously disingenuous when one considers that the studio assigned all the other major "Negro" roles in the film to white performers.[49]

In attempting to bring Stowe's novel to the screen in the mid-1920s, the studio's main concern was that the film would be rejected by white southern audiences.[50] Universal was well aware that it was taking a huge financial risk, lavishing exorbitant resources on a screen epic that would be virtually impossible to rent to Southern theaters. The fact that the book had been a cause of tension (if not of war) between sections of the country could not be ignored.[51] *Uncle Tom's Cabin* was, historically and actually, a source of exactly the sort of "misunderstanding" that was anathema to the studio. An *Uncle Tom's Cabin* superspecial film could risk exposing the dubious equation of "understanding" (on the level of basic comprehension) and "understanding" (in the deeper, ethical sense of the term) at the heart of procinema ideology. Dredging up abolitionism's contentious past and likely never being seen by a large portion of the American public, such a film could risk de-universalizing Universal Pictures.

The premise of a universally appealing version of *Uncle Tom's Cabin*—a film that would play to large audiences in the North and in the South, thus becoming a site of sectional bonding—is predicated on an a priori limitation. Whereas a main warrant for the utopian rhetoric around the title "Universal Pictures" was, in the first place, the ubiquitous reach of the studio's films, Universal, like all the Hollywood studios during this period, refused to consider African Americans as members of the actual national film audience.[52] In the case of Universal's *Uncle Tom's Cabin*, this refusal is apparent in the dramatic restriction of Tom's character's storyline, one of the film's many sops to the white southern box office. The finished film reduces Uncle Tom to a minor character—this despite the fact that African American newspapers around the country had been covering Lowe's role in the production with great interest, building a strong sense of anticipation around the film's release.[53]

The imperative that the studio embraced once it decided to adapt *Uncle Tom's Cabin* was to refashion this title as a site of total "understanding" in both senses of the term used by utopian-universalist silent cinema discourse and, thus, to "make the picture one to please all creeds and peoples," as Laemmle himself put it.[54] Here we see Laemmle voicing his aspiration to solve the Southern box office problem and, failing that, to at least make a film that was impervious to charges of sectionalist bias. This aspiration manifests itself in a variety of ways in the finished film.

First, in the words of one studio publicity notice, the film posits that the "moral issue of the [slavery] question" has been "settled" since the Civil War, if not before.[55] In one of its many attempts to make Stowe's abolitionist tract palatable to white Southern viewers, Universal's *Uncle Tom's Cabin* begins with the image of a portrait bust of Robert E. Lee. A quotation, attributed to Lee and dated December 27, 1856, is then superimposed on this image: "There are few, I believe, in this enlightened age who will not acknowledge that slavery as an institution is a moral and political evil." This epigraph opens a gap between the ensuing representations of slavery and the "moral and political" *question* of slavery. The viewer can and should, the film implies, enjoy the story to follow without seeing it as taking a stance (or as ever having been involved in taking a stance).

To further portray the question as always already settled, the film will make the action of the novel postdate its publication, such that the narrative's timeline encompasses the years of the war. The film includes a brief montage referencing the Battle of Fort Sumter just before it shifts setting

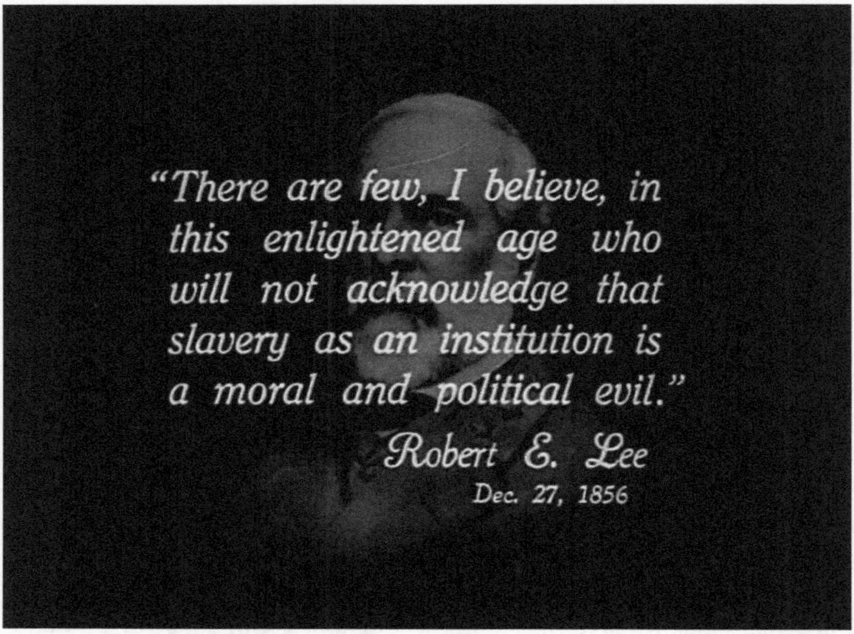

Figure 6.1. Epigraph to *Uncle Tom's Cabin* (Universal Pictures, 1927).

to St. Clare's New Orleans plantation. In the film's climactic scene, Union troops march in, just in time to save Eliza (Margarita Fischer) and Cassie (Eulalie Jensen) from Simon Legree's (George Siegmann) murderous rage.[56] Likewise, the film romanticizes the very institution it posits is intrinsically evil. Representing an early instance of the flourishing of the Hollywood plantation tradition, which would reach its apotheosis with *Gone with the Wind* (Selznick, 1939), *Uncle Tom's Cabin* foregrounds the putatively picturesque elements of slavery. In other words, the film deliberately stages what we might call positive images of slavery, feeding early twentieth-century ideologies of race and slavery back into Stowe's abolitionist narrative.[57]

Moreover, the film aggressively desectionalizes the horrors of slavery, going out of its way to indicate that the characters who perpetrate the suffering of Tom and Eliza are *not* representative of Southerners. In memos and press releases, the film's director, Harry Pollard, a proud Southerner himself, argued that men who caused "the Negro his most cruel suffering" were displaced northern speculators, "not the Southern plantation owners."[58] In a fascinating embellishment, Pollard asserted that Stowe intended the characters of Marks, Haley, Loker, and Legree to represent this villainous class.[59] It is not clear to me that the finished film actually reflects Pollard's insistence on these characters' Northernness;

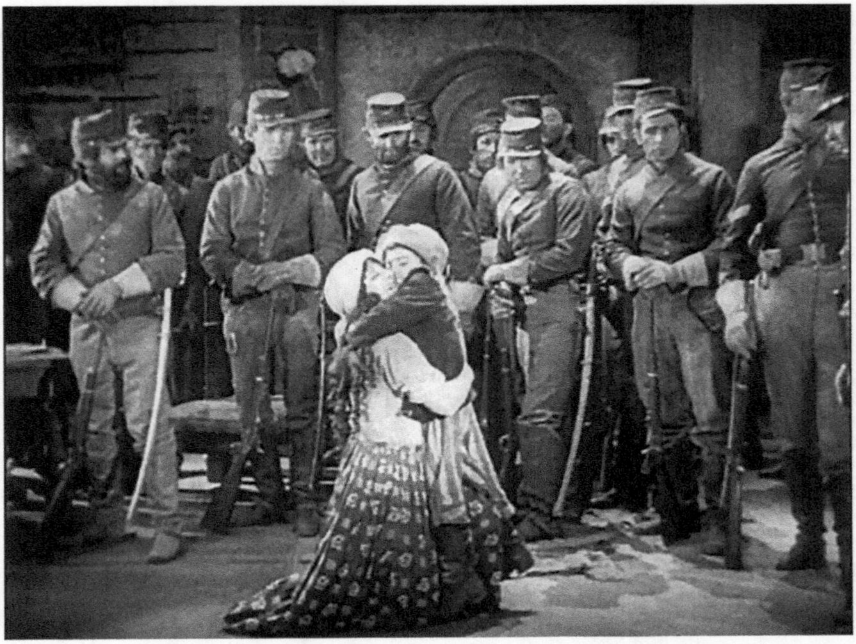

Figure 6.2. Union troops reuniting Eliza (Margarita Fischer) and Harry (Lassie Lou Ahern) in *Uncle Tom's Cabin* (Universal Pictures, 1927).

their geographic origins are certainly never specified in the intertitles. Without doubt, though, the film carefully dissociates slaveholding villainy from any notion of white Southern identity—it opens another gap here.

Finally, the film disconnects the violence directed toward slave characters from its moorings in racial hatred and hierarchy in a number of ways. Eliza, Cassie, George Harris, and Harry are all played by white actors, even as all mention of their ancestry is effaced; side characters even comment, at one point, on Eliza and George's whiteness. On the level of spectacle, then, the film extensively stages slavery as a regime of barbarism carried out by white people against other white people. On the level of language, the erasure of racial epithets from the intertitle text—a move that, to be sure, is consistent with a style of decorum that took hold in the American cinema following the calls for censorship of *The Birth of a Nation* (Griffith Feature Films, 1915)—further renders racism unspeakable. The film confronts the viewer with what might be called "slavery without racism."

By virtue of these representational strategies, any and all viewers are invited to come to the conclusion that the physical and emotional cruelty represented in the film was dreadful and had to be stopped. And

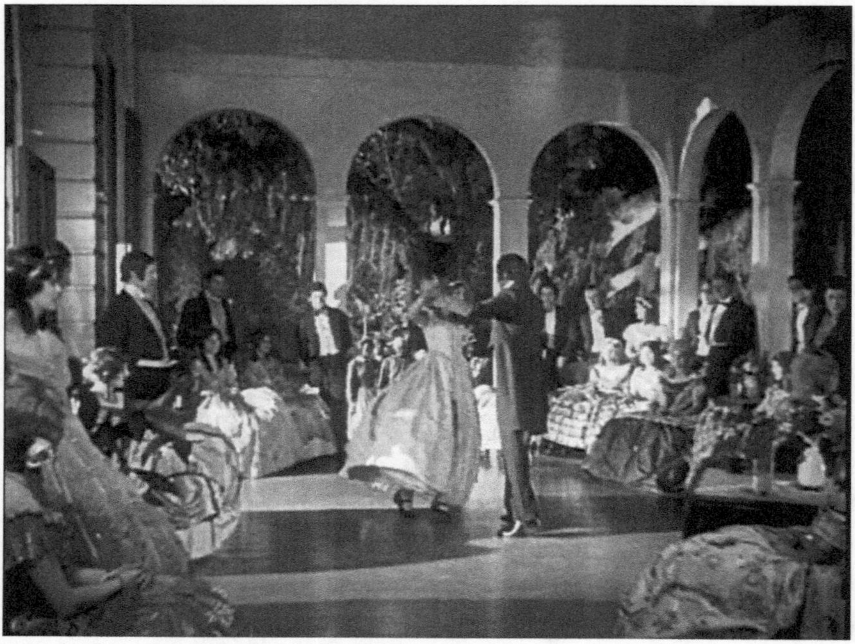

Figure 6.3. The plantation tradition in *Uncle Tom's Cabin* (Universal Pictures, 1927).

yet the portrayal does not appear to offend or indict any white individual or group. In this way, the film is, finally, able to present itself as a site of unity, reaffirming what Pollard had called cinema's role "as a medium for spreading the gospel of tolerance and understanding."[60] What is most fascinating from Laemmle's and Pollard's remarks about the film is that how they co-opted Stowe herself as an advocate for this historically evacuated, logically incoherent notion of universal understanding—as a paragon of communication.

The records of the film's production—press releases as well as memos exchanged between the director and studio head—indicate that the filmmakers, indeed, believed that their version of the story was the true, corrected *Uncle Tom's Cabin*.[61] They repeatedly characterize the author's guiding intention as somehow distinct from the novel's overt polemical stance. That the novel reads to many like anti-Southern "propaganda" was, Pollard argued, simply an effect of Stowe succumbing to the sectionalist "passions" of her era; she truly and authentically wanted, he believed, to produce something that would entertain, move, and educate *all* people.[62] This belief to some extent drove the adaptation process as I have described it: a process of revising *Uncle Tom's Cabin* by introducing gaps and disconnects into the novel's propositions about race, slavery, and moral evil—in order, apparently, to liberate the esoteric "truth" of the text.[63]

It is as if the "mightiest of master writers" like Stowe could have no other political, philosophical, or religious project other than that of promoting understanding of the kind fetishized in silent-era Hollywood—a concept steeped in the New Age, neoplatonic, and late Progressive-Era intellectual currents of that period. At the same time, as the ad previously quoted insists, the communicative force of these writers' pens is so much less than that of the screen. As much as Universal was invested in literary adaptations to solidify its cultural prestige during the silent era, the studio insisted on the superiority of the motion-picture medium. It would take a Universal Picture to recover Stowe's occluded intention, to give her quasi-universal cultural signs the force of a true universal language.

To persuade prospective viewers that their *Uncle Tom's Cabin* was the true one—the novel that Stowe intended to write—Universal repeatedly cited the material "authenticity" of their production, trumpeting the astonishing amount of "research" time that went into designing the film's "sixty-five separate and distinct sets" and the money that was spent to acquire objects from the antebellum period to decorate them.[64] So detailed, elaborate, and accurately furnished are these spaces that, in the studio's characterization, they go beyond being mere sets: "The Shelby mansion was built in duplicate and furnished with real antiques gathered at enormous cost throughout the South."[65] The underlying idea here is that the studio has bypassed the mediations of the text ("cold unspeakable type," in the words of the studio ad), allowing the viewer to communicate directly with lived history.

Of course, this idea of communication depends on the lofty beliefs in currency in the late 1920s about the cinema as the "people's university"—the universal educational medium that "transport[s] one to the very scene [of history], defying time and distance." In making his own specific version of this claim, Laemmle styled the Universal City production facility as a microcosm, an anthology of all places and peoples, across all of human history. In a fashion that recalls the *Ford Factory Facts* pamphlet discussed in the last chapter, his authorized biography rhapsodizes about the land and resources contained within Laemmle's "Jerusalem."[66] Universal City is both a functional "municipality" with its own utilities and police force and a dream factory that hosts a permanent, endlessly reconfigurable "Streets of the World" section, where "you may walk in Monte Carlo, Cairo, Paris, Tokio [*sic*], Madrid, London, Berlin, Constantinople, where you will."[67] With *Uncle Tom's Cabin*, the antebellum American South is added to this roster of historically and geographically significant locales; entering the Laemmle plant in 1927–1928, one could walk onto an authentic plantation composed of a grand mansion, slave cabins, and cotton fields.

In her reflections on mid-1920s cinema writing, which I examined at the start of this book, Agnes Repplier distinguishes two "classes": one that "tells us of the marvels of the mechanism and the dizzy cost of production" and the other that explains "the lofty ideals which animate producers [as well as] the educational value of films."[68] In the studios' promotional campaigns for their historical epics and "big special" films like *Uncle Tom's Cabin*, these two perspectives on the medium converge completely. Detailed accounts of lavish expenditures—like how many barrels of paint, pieces of clothing, amperes of electrical current, and so on were needed to make the film—become evidence of the producers' aspirations to a degree of historical accuracy that not only makes the film the decisive version of the story but also makes it visually overpowering.[69] This listing of production "facts" plays on the idea, as Repplier puts it, that it is immensely "pleasurable" for film fans to contemplate dollar figures in the millions.[70] What is remarkable, though, is how *Uncle Tom's Cabin*'s much-touted two-million-dollar price tag finally becomes the warrant for the sincerity of the producers' claims to spread "the gospel of a tolerance and understanding."

Perhaps better than any other image, the mansion and slave quarters constructed on the Universal lot captures the paradox of the transitional-era historical film, whereby mass history education becomes a mere apology for racism—whereby universalizing language sanctions racism in the name of racial unity or, more precisely, enlists racism in the ostensible cause of overcoming parochialism. Here the plantation becomes consumable as something merely picturesque, even as the discourse around it registers the intrinsic evil of slavery at a highly abstract, deracialized level. African Americans are included in the cast (albeit in a minimal, highly compromised way) in a way that guarantees the production's "catholicity" and recalls Stowe's fundamental humanitarianism—even as the author's abolitionist polemic is transformed into a vehicle for white sectional reunion. All of this, in turn, exemplifies the universal-historical reach of the cinematic medium, highlights its ability to reach all people currently living, and increases its ability to promote social cohesion.

By virtue of the logic of the "Mirror Screen"—that whatever appears in the media spectacle is affirmed and included in the universal whole of society—the reconstructed slave plantation, against all common sense, becomes the staging ground for a pageant meant to symbolize perfected understanding. *Uncle Tom's Cabin* becomes an emblematic instance of cinema as a universal force that allows people to communicate, "regardless of creed, color, race, or nationality," insofar as it forecloses any kind of African American perspective on slavery. In this case, slavery becomes something for white people to relate to in an uplifting way and, thereby, relate to one another with the spirit of "unanism" that Deleuze locates at the heart of the cinematic project of universal history.[71]

The example of *Uncle Tom's Cabin* illustrates where the story that this book has been telling ends up—at least at the climactic point marked by the arrival of recorded sound in the cinema. The spiritual and intellectual imperatives of universal history are reduced to marketing slogans and pasted onto artifacts that are stereotypes, through and through. In this case, the stereotypes take the form of clichés meant to make white people feel innocent. Shrouded in the mysticism of general education about the story of mankind throughout the ages, the film's history, in fact, speaks to much narrower, ideologically determined histories (the plantation tradition's apologia for slavery, the white rebirth of the nation after Reconstruction).

In this way, a huge gap between aspiration and reality opens up around the products of popular entertainment. As Walter Benjamin notes in his essay "Light from Obscurantists," the discourse of their marketing speaks to the "intellectual life of their customers"—addressing a very real need—but in such a way that makes the glittering "details" of what these products purport to teach scattered, impossible to "subsum[e]" into the greater intellectual harmony promised at every point.[72] "Commodities" like these, he writes, "thus drape themselves in the world of knowledge and the human spirit, in order to stand out more alluringly."[73] A "brand-name product that does not hesitate to enlist the whole of world history as a marketing device," a Universal Picture is a fitting metonymy for cinema as a whole, during the era in which the utopian-universalist program holds sway.[74] It is an ambiguous formation in which occultist concepts become "solid business venture[s]" and commodities become sites of spiritual mystery.[75]

Acknowledgments

I am immensely grateful to the institutions, groups, and individuals that have made the research and writing of this book possible. I would like to thank my chairs in the Department of English at the Ohio State University, Debra Moddelmog and Robyn Warhol, for their support of my research endeavors. I composed the bulk of this manuscript while on faculty professional leave from my departmental teaching duties. The College of Arts and Sciences at Ohio State provided me with generous grants to fund travel to international conferences, where I presented earlier versions of this material. I benefited tremendously by being able to share my work in progress with curious and insightful audiences at conferences hosted by the Society for Cinema and Media Studies (2015, 2013, 2012), the Midwest Modern Language Association (2014), the International Society for the Study of Narrative (2012), and the Pacific Ancient and Modern Language Association (2011).

The staffs of several archives and research libraries provided vital assistance in locating and navigating collections of primary sources. I wish to thank the staffs of the Academy of Motion Picture Arts and Sciences' Margaret Herrick Library (especially Faye Thompson and Louise Hilton); the Special Collections at the University of Southern California's Doheny Memorial Library; the Library Special Collections at the University of California, Los Angeles; and the Charles Deering McCormick Library of Special Collections at Northwestern University.

I owe special thanks to a number of colleagues and friends for crucial conversations about the main ideas of this study at early or otherwise formative moments in the writing process: Chad Allen, John Davidson, Ruth Friedman, Jared Gardner, Ron Green, Jesse Schotter, and Julia Stern. Throughout my time at Ohio State, I have been surrounded by brilliant scholars and teachers, both in the Department of English and the Film Studies Program. They continue to mentor, challenge, and provide an outstanding example for me. I wish to thank in particular Adélékè Adéẹ̀kọ́, Tommy Davis, Molly Farrell, Maggie Flinn, Aman Garcha, Harvey Graff, Yana Hashamova, John Hellmann, Beth Hewitt, Lynn Itagaki, Pranav Jani, Erica Levin, Brian McHale, Koritha Mitchell, Linda

Mizejewski, Sean O'Sullivan, Kris Paulsen, Laura Podalsky, Joe Ponce, Dana Renga, Elizabeth Renker, and Andreá Williams.

Since becoming director of film studies, I have been fortunate to work with tremendously talented and dedicated staff. My thanks go out to Kylie Harwell-Sturgill, Mike Polk, Nick Spitulski, and most of all, Matt Swift. Matt truly keeps the program running; he has made it possible for me to bring this book to completion while handling the rigors of academic administration. The broader community of film scholars with which I engage at SCMS and in other intellectual spaces has been a sustaining influence on my work. For all kinds of encouragement—from invitations to join panels, attend conferences, and collaborate on publications to other, more subtle forms of support for my work—I would like to thank especially Jamie Baron, Terri Francis, Cathy Jurca, Arthur Knight, Delia Konzett, Shannon Wong Lerner, Barbara Lupack, Paula Massood, Ellen Scott, and Katherine Spring.

I will be forever indebted to Rutgers University Press for publishing my scholarship. Lisa Banning, Nicole Solano, and the rest of the editorial staff at the press are an absolute pleasure to work with. Under to the guidance of Leslie Mitchner, I have become a much better writer. Leslie's enthusiasm and keen judgment have been tremendous boons to me over the years, and I will miss our conversations in the book fair at SCMS. I wish her all the best in her retirement. I am also grateful to Mark Lynn Anderson, whose own work I greatly admire, for his thorough and astute reading of my manuscript.

The process of revising the manuscript coincided exactly with my getting to know and falling in love with Tatiana Faria. A sharp film critic in her own right, Tatiana has helped me discover new purpose and joy in my work. She continues to inspire me and to make the seemingly impossible appear manageable. I hope to be able to be for her the source of incredible sustenance that she is for me every day and look forward to our many next chapters to come.

Notes

INTRODUCTION

1. Terry Ramsaye, *A Million and One Nights: A History of the Motion Picture*, vol. 2 (New York: Simon and Schuster, 1926), 834.

2. John Durham Peters, *Speaking into the Air: A History of the Idea of Communication* (Chicago: University of Chicago Press, 1999), 1.

3. Peters, 1–2.

4. I adapt the phrase "utopian-universalist" from Michael North's description of the "utopian democratic universalism at the heart" of the belief in the power of visual images to overcome the "arbitrary specificities of the written languages" and, in turn, to "efface the differences between classes and nations." North, *Reading 1922: A Return to the Scene of the Modern* (New York: Oxford University Press, 1999), 155.

5. The era of the silent feature film runs from 1915—the year that saw the release of *The Birth of a Nation* (Griffith Feature Films) and the opening of Universal Pictures' Universal City—through 1928, when Warner Bros. released the first "all-talking" picture. See Richard Koszarski, *An Evening's Entertainment: The Age of the Silent Feature Picture, 1915–1928*, History of the American Cinema, vol. 3 (New York: Charles Scriber's Sons, 1990).

6. Peters, *Speaking into the Air*, 10–11.

7. Peters, 10–11.

8. D. N. Rodowick, *The Virtual Life of Film* (Cambridge, Mass.: Harvard University Press, 2007), 2–24.

9. Michael Hardt and Antonio Negri, *Empire* (Cambridge, Mass.: Harvard University Press, 2000), 189.

10. Hardt and Negri, 3–6.

11. Hardt and Negri, 38.

12. Jabari Asim, *What Obama Means: . . . For Our Culture, Our Politics, Our Future* (New York: William Morrow, 2009), 15–16. Initially, Obama himself, to some extent, embraced the postracial narrative, styling himself as someone who transcended America's major sociocultural divide, due both to his mixed ancestry and to his having come of age after the political tumult of the 1960s (which he saw as the starting point for the contemporary "culture wars"). At the same time, Obama's presence in the Oval Office prompted an immediate conservative backlash that sought to delegitimize not just his presidency but his very claim to Americanness. This reaction simultaneously cited the fact of his

election as confirmation that institutional racism no longer exists in the United States and sought to stake legitimate American identity on whiteness, in ways both covert and overt.

13. Asim, 15–17.

14. Asim, 15–17.

15. Asim, 17.

16. Peters, *Speaking into the Air*, 1.

17. Barack Obama, *What Is Best in America: Speech by President Obama at a Memorial Service for the Victims of the Shooting in Tucson, Arizona* (New York: St. Martin's, 2011), 11.

18. Carlos Lozada, "Please, President Obama. Not Another 'National Conversation,'" *Washington Post*, February 1, 2013,www.washingtonpost.com/opinions/please-president-obama-not-another-national-conversation/2013/02/01/4a7b914c-5e5b-11e2-a389-ee565c81c565_story.html?utm_term=.389a14e671bb.

19. Lozada, 8. To be fair, "conversation" is, for Obama, a legal concept that carries a slightly more precise and complex meaning than the one implied by calls for "national conversation," such as seems operative in the passage cited here. Specifically, he believes that "the law records a long-running conversation"—an ongoing debate about the interpretation of fundamental principles and the resultant compromises struck by legislators—and, therefore, reflects the perpetually unfinished nature of democratic deliberation as well as the constitution's openness to change over time. See Obama, *Dreams from My Father: A Story of Race and Inheritance* (New York: Crown, 2004). See also James T. Kloppenberg, *Reading Obama: Dreams, Hope, and the American Political Tradition* (Princeton: Princeton University Press, 2011), 152–156.

20. Matthew Continetti, "National Conversations Are Worthless," *National Review*, December 13, 2014, http://www.nationalreview.com/article/394583/national-conversations-are-worthless-matthew-continetti?target=author&tid=901092. See also Noah Rothman, "The Conversation about Race That Isn't a Conversation," *Commentary*, February 1, 2015, http://www.nationalreview.com/article/394583/national-conversations-are-worthless-matthew-continetti?target=author&tid=901092.

21. Continetti, "National Conversations."

22. Wesley Morris, "Why Calls for a 'National Conversation' Are Futile," *New York Times Magazine*, August 2, 2016, http://www.nytimes.com/2016/08/07/magazine/why-calls-for-a-national-conversation-are-futile.html. See also Lozada, "Please, President Obama."

23. The obvious difference here is that, for conservatives, this form existed in the past and has simply been corrupted by liberals' nefarious insistence on harping on the sources of division; it simply needs to be recovered. By contrast, for liberals, it has yet to be realized, due to the ways in which the structures of privilege and power neutralize dissenting perspectives on society.

24. Peters, *Speaking into the Air*, 3.

25. Evgeny Morozov, *To Save Everything, Click Here: The Folly of Technological Solutionism* (New York: PublicAffairs, 2013), 17–19.

26. Morozov, 291–293.

27. Mark Zuckerberg, quoted in Morozov, 292.

28. Morozov, 25.

29. Morozov, 352.

30. Morozov, 36.

31. Morozov, 44.

32. Morozov, 45, 292–293. See also North, *Reading*, 16.

33. North, *Reading*, 108–110.

34. Jack London, quoted in Morozov, *To Save Everything*, 293. The quoted line comes from an essay, "The Message of Motion Pictures," which London wrote for the studio publication, *Paramount Magazine*. Reprinted in *Authors on Film*, ed. Harry M. Geduld (Bloomington: Indiana University Press, 1972), 104–107.

35. Agnes Repplier, "The Unconscious Humor of the Movies," *Atlantic Monthly*, November 1925, 603. Repplier was a conservative Catholic writer from Philadelphia whose essays on literature, religion, and politics featured regularly in the *Atlantic Monthly* between the mid-1880s and 1940. See Paul Hansom, "Agnes Repplier," *Dictionary of Literary Biography*, ed. Sharon M. Harris, vol. 221, *American Women Prose Writers, 1870–1920* (Farmington Hills, Mich.: Gale Group, 2000), 305–309.

36. Repplier, 603.

37. Repplier, 603.

38. Repplier, 603. In summarizing this claim, Repplier points to Douglas Fairbanks's statement, "The impression made by the film is greater and deeper than that of any other circulating medium," from "A Huge Responsibility," *Ladies' Home Journal* 41, no. 5 (May 1924): 36, 131, 133. See also Will Hays's succinct statement of the scientific notion: "The quickest way to the brain . . . is through the eye." Hays, quoted in Franklin Gordon, "The Potentialities of Motion Pictures: An Interview with Will H. Hays, Advisor Extraordinary to the Film Industry," *American Hebrew* 116, no. 21 (April 1925): 615. In distinguishing the scientific and aesthetic emphases within this claim, I take a cue from Allan Sekula's analysis of the comparable arguments that had been made about early photographs in the nineteenth century. See Sekula, "The Traffic in Photographs," *Art Journal* 41, no. 1 (1981): 16.

39. See Tom Gunning, "In Your Face: Physiognomy, Photography, and the Gnostic Mission of Early Film," *Modernism/Modernity* 4, no. 1 (1997): 1–29.

40. Repplier, "Unconscious Humor," 605. The phrase "people's university" comes from Louis Weinberg, "Motion Pictures as a Social Force," *Current History* 22, no. 1 (April 1925): 84–92. Utopian procinema writers often equate complete comprehension (of language and history) with perfected human sympathy. Implicit in this view of motion pictures is

the idea that "understanding" (in the cognitive and communicative senses of the word) necessarily begets "understanding" (in the ethical sense).

41. Note also that, in some instances, the cultural democracy claim is made in explicitly internationalist terms—the writer emphasizes the circulation of movies around the world instead of or over and above the leveling of socioeconomic barriers in a domestic context—which allows it to feed much more directly into this third and final claim.

42. Repplier, "Unconscious Humor," 603.

43. My understanding of the slightly earlier iterations of these tropes is indebted to Miriam Hansen's essential *Babel and Babylon: Spectatorship in American Silent Film* (Cambridge, Mass.: Harvard University Press, 1991).

44. See Charlotte Perkins Gilman, "Mind-Stretching: The Mental Area Can Be Made Coterminous with the Universe," *Century Magazine*, December 3, 1925, 217–224. See also Charlotte Perkins Gilman, "Public Library Motion Pictures," *The Annals of the American Academy of Political and Social Science* 128 (November 1926): 143–145. Note that Gilman's essay appears in a special issue of the *Annals* titled *"The Motion Picture in Its Economic and Social Aspects,"* which features several other contributions partaking of one or another of the utopian claims about cinema delineated in this introduction. See, for instance, Ernest L. Crandall, "Possibilities of the Motion Picture in Education," *The Annals of the American Academy of Political and Social Science* 128 (November 1926): 109–115. See also Herbert Francis Sherwood, "Democracy and the Movies," *Bookman* 47 (May 1918): 235–239; Aaron Hardy Ulm, "Once Blind, Now He Teachers Others to See," *American Magazine*, October 1921, 55; Homer Croy, *How Motion Pictures Are Made* (New York: Harper & Brothers, 1918), 351–364; and Marguerite Bertsch, *How to Write for Moving Pictures: A Manual of Instruction and Information* (New York: George H. Doran, 1917), 272–275.

In locating the sources listed here and in the following notes, I have relied heavily on two resources: the microfiche collection *The History of the Cinema, 1895–1940* for book-length works and the Museum of Modern Art/Works Progress Administration venture, *The Film Index: A Bibliography*, especially volume 3, *The Film in Society* (White Plains, N.Y.: Kraus International Publications, 1985), for shorter works in periodicals.

45. See Rupert Hughes, *Souls for Sale* (New York: Harper & Brothers, 1922); Terry Ramsaye, "The Motion Picture," *The Annals of the American Academy of Social and Political Science* 128 (November 1926): 1–19; Ramsaye, "The Prehistory of the Screen," in *A Million and One Nights: A History of the Motion Picture*, vol. 1 (New York: Simon and Schuster, 1926), xxxvii–lxx; Robert Sherwood, *The Best Moving Pictures of 1922–1923* (Boston: Small, Maynard, 1923), viii, x–xi; and Will Hays, "Motion Pictures and Their Censors," *American Review of Reviews* 75 (March 1927): 393–398.

46. Edward S. Van Zile, *That Marvel—the Movie: A Glance at Its Reckless Past, Its Promising Present, and Its Significant Future* (New York: G. P. Putnam's Sons, 1923). Note that the trope of the peoples of the world coming together in and through shared film-viewing experiences was also central to the arguments being made during this time by industry leaders

eager to explain and further promote the dominance of Hollywood films in the global marketplace. See, for instance, Sidney Kent, "The Motion Picture of To-morrow," *The Motion Picture in Its Economic and Social Aspects*, 30–33; and Samuel Goldwyn, *Behind the Screen* (New York: George H. Doran, 1923), 67.

47. Hansen, *Babel and Babylon*, 77.

48. Dana Polan, "The Beginnings of American Film Study," in *Looking Past the Screen: Case Studies in American Film History and Method*, ed. Jon Lewis and Eric Smoodin (Durham, N.C.: Duke University Press, 2007), 44. See also Peter Decherney, *Hollywood and the Culture Elite: How the Movies Became American* (New York: Columbia University Press, 2005), 13–14; and Devin Orgeron, Marsha Orgeron, and Dan Streible, "A History of Learning with the Lights Off," in *Learning with the Lights Off: Educational Film in the United States*, ed. Orgeron, Orgeron, and Streible (Oxford: Oxford University Press, 2012), 22–23.

49. See, for example, Prakash Younger, "Film as Art," in *The Routledge Companion to Film History*, ed. William Guynn (Abingdon, U.K.: Routledge, 2011), 29; Jennifer Peterson, "Educational Films and Early Cinema Audiences," in *A Companion to Early Cinema*, ed. André Gaudreault, Nicolas Dulac, and Santiago Hidalgo (Malden, Mass.: Wiley-Blackwell, 2012), 281; Noël Carroll and Jinhee Choi, "Introduction to Part II," in *Philosophy of Film and Motion Pictures: An Anthology*, ed. Carroll and Choi (Malden, Mass.: Blackwell, 2006), 60; and Kamilla Elliot, "Novels, Films, and the Word/Image Wars," in *A Companion to Literature and Film*, ed. Robert Stam and Alessandra Raengo (Malden, Mass.: Blackwell, 2004), 5.

50. Gilman, "Public," 144.

51. John Amid, *With the Movie Makers* (Boston: Lothrop, Lee & Shepard, 1923), 156–157.

52. Fairbanks, "Huge," 36.

53. Created in the 1880s by Lazar Ludwik Zamenhof, Esperanto is a planned "international language" that borrows grammatical rules, vocabulary, and other basic structures from Romance, Germanic, and Slavic languages. See Pierre Janton, *Esperanto: Language, Literature, and Community*, trans. Humphrey Tonkin, Jane Edwards, and Karen Johnson-Wiener (Albany: Sate University of New York Press, 1993), 23–28, 41–51. As Janton explains, Zamenhof's experience of growing up as a Jew in the multilingual and heavily anti-Semitic milieu of Bialystok (now in Poland, then in the Russian Empire) led him to the conclusion that linguistic diversity was an intrinsic evil. Zamenhof saw languages as tools of national and ethnic self-interest and, thus, a source of discrimination, oppression, and suffering. As a language that was "neutral" with respect to nationality and ethnicity, the dissemination of Esperanto, then, was a project of fostering "universal brotherhood," expressing Zamenhof's "mystical humanism." Janton, 23–33.

The story of Babel appears in Gen. 11:1–9 and tells of a group of people banding together to build a town and brick "tower with its top in the heavens" (Gen. 11:4, Revised Standard Version). Concerned that the group's unity of purpose and "one language" meant that "nothing that they propose to do [would] now be impossible for them," God disperses and imposes linguistic difference on them; the name given to the former site of the tower in Genesis, "Ba'bel," then becomes a metaphor for the confusion of tongues (Gen. 11:5–9, Revised Standard Version). On the history of "Babel" as a trope referring to the "necessity and impossibility of translation," see Hansen, *Babel and Babylon,* 184–185.

54. See Van Zile, *That Marvel,* 10, 16, 138, and passim; and Amid, *With the Movie Makers,* 156. See also, for example, Hughes, *Souls for Sale,* 377; and Gordon, "Potentialities," 615.

55. William A. Brady, "How the Motion Picture Saved the World!," *Photoplay* 15, no. 2 (January 1919): 100. Brady was a producer of theatrical melodramas and a boxing promoter who eventually became involved in film production. During World War I, he was president of the National Association of the Motion Picture Industry and was tapped by President Woodrow Wilson to work with George Creel's Committee on Public Information. By the late 1910s, Wilson had himself come to subscribe to the "universal language" myth of cinema and thus was eager for the Creel committee to harness the powers of the medium (and the opportunities to communicate directly with large audiences afforded by film theaters) in service of promoting "America's plans and purposes" during wartime. See Ken Bloom, "William A. Brady," in *Broadway: Its History, People, and Places* (New York: Routledge, 2012), 78–80; and David Puttnam, *Movies and Money* (New York: Knopf, 1998), 76–79. For more on the relationship between Creel, the Committee on Public Information, and silent-era procinema writing, see this chapter and chapter 4.

56. Sherwood, "Democracy," 235. The prehistoric cave painting analogy seems especially exciting for these writers because it allows them to portray what is perhaps the quintessentially modern medium as satisfying an atavistic desire or need. Recovering this "primitive" impulse in a highly sophisticated form, cinema seems paradoxically to mark a moment of consummation in the history of human culture. As Amid puts it, it is remarkable to think that "the 'new' method [of universal communication] would be the oldest language of all. 'Say it with pictures'" (156). The cave painting analogy receives its most well-known and theoretically sophisticated articulation in Ramsaye's preface to *A Million and One Nights,* vol. 1, xxxvii–lxx. Vachel Lindsay also uses this analogy, while ultimately preferring to compare motion pictures to a later form of pictographic writing, Egyptian hieroglyphics, in his *The Art of the Moving Picture* (New York: Macmillan, 1915), 5, 252–260. For a striking instance of this discourse, see the entry for "Motion Pictures" in the 1918 edition of *The World Book* (vol. 5, pages 3984–3992).

57. North, *Reading,* 155–156 (emphasis added).

58. Walter Lippmann, *Drift and Mastery: An Attempt to Diagnose the Current Unrest* (New York: Mitchell Kennerley, 1914), 283.

59. It is important to note that although Lippmann sees internationally distributed films as harbingers of what he calls "modern communion," he is more interested in motion pictures' ability to circulate and be consumed on a mass scale than he is in the content of actual motion pictures. Lipmann is often dismissive of this content, as when,

elsewhere in this chapter, he adopts the voice of a dedicated schoolteacher lamenting all of the extracurricular influences serving to "miseducat[e]" his pupils. He includes "the movies" on this list. See Lippmann, 278.

60. It must be noted here that during this period, the universal-language metaphor also begins to circulate widely outside of the U.S. context that is the focus of my study. While its most famous European exponent was the theorist Béla Balázs, the trope was also used by filmmakers of such diverse sensibilities as Fritz Lang, F. W. Murnau, and Hans Richter. See Balázs's *Visible Man* (1924), in *Béla Balázs: Early Film Theory*, ed. Erica Carter, trans. Rodney Livingstone (New York: Berghahn Books, 2010), 11–15; Lang, "The Future of the Feature Film in Germany" (1926), in *The Weimar Republic Sourcebook*, ed. Anton Kaes, Martin Jay, and Edward Dimendberg (Berkeley: University of California Press, 1994), 622–623; Jesse Schotter, *Hieroglyphic Modernisms: Writing and New Media in the Twentieth Century* (Edinburgh: Edinburgh University Press, 2018), 39; and Malcolm Turvey, "Dada between Heaven and Hell: Abstraction and Universal Language in the *Rhythm* Films of Hans Richter," *October* 105 (Summer 2003): 19–36. My thanks to Ron Green for bringing Richter's work to my attention. On the use of the universal-language metaphor in Britain during this period, see Andrew Higson, "Cultural Policy and Industrial Practice," in *"Film Europe" and "Film America": Cinema, Commerce and Cultural Exchange, 1920–1939*, ed. Andrew Higson and Richard Maltby (Exeter, U.K.: University of Exeter Press, 1999), 120. In *Fiery Cinema: The Emergence of an Affective Medium in China, 1915–1945* (Minneapolis: University of Minnesota Press, 2015), Weihong Bao examines Chinese intellectuals' use of the universal language metaphor in debates about national film exhibition during the 1940s. See especially her discussion of the poet Xu Chi, who translated Vachel Lindsay's work into Chinese and whose theoretical writings explore what Bao calls the possibility of a "cinematic Esperanto," 288–293. Jason Borge notes that some Latin American avant-garde writers in the early twentieth century held a "utopian vision" of silent film, seeing it as a form of "direct, 'untranslated' communication between artist and audience," in his *Latin American Writers and the Rise of Hollywood Cinema* (New York: Routledge, 2008), 79–80.

61. Weinberg, "Motion Pictures," 92. As Weinberg phrases it, "The whole tendency of history has been toward the perfection of forms for the increasing carrying power of art."

62. Weinberg, 92.

63. Weinberg, 92.

64. Fairbanks, quoted in George Creel, "A 'Close-Up' of Douglas Fairbanks," *Everybody's Magazine*, December 1916, 736.

65. See Gordon, "Potentialities," 615.

66. Sherwood, "Democracy," 238–239.

67. Lillian Gish, "A Universal Language," in *The Theatre and Motion Pictures: A Selection of Articles from the New 14th Edition of the Encyclopaedia Britannica* (New York: Encyclopaedia Britannica, 1933), 33 (emphasis in original).

68. North, *Reading*, 147.

69. Repplier, "Unconscious Humor," 603.

70. North, *Reading*, 155.

71. In addition to the texts cited below, see Hays, "Supervision from Within," in *The Story of the Films*, ed. Joseph P. Kenney (Chicago: A. W. Shaw, 1927), 28–54; and *See and Hear: A Brief History of the Motion Picture and the Development of Sound* (New York: Motion Picture Producers and Distributors of America, 1929), 3–6.

72. Will Hays, "Today and Tomorrow in the Motion Picture Industry," in *The Blue Book of the Screen*, ed. Ruth Wing (Hollywood: Blue Book of the Screen, 1924), 341 (emphasis in original). A quotation (with some discrepancies in wording) appears in Repplier, "Unconscious Humor," 603. *The Blue Book of the Screen* is an important industry publication that also features a contribution by art director Ferdinand Earle, which envisions "the amphitheatre of the screen" encompassing "the whole civilized world," "Screen Renaissance through Motion Painting," *Blue Book*, 345–348. For other instances of this internationalist, millennialist view of cinema, see "I Am the Universal Language," *Photoplay* 15, no. 5 (April 1919): 27; John Herman Randall, "The Motion Picture and Better World Understanding," *National Board of Review Magazine*, June 1928, 4–6; and Lucille Greer, "Picture Potentialities in Relation to World Peace," *The Educational Screen* 9 (March 1929): 71, 90.

73. Hays, quoted in Gordon, "Potentialities," 615, 624. The "distinguished writer" to whom Hays refers is Van Zile. Note that the Gordon-Hays interview appears in a special "Motion Picture Number" of *The American Hebrew*, which features several other pieces characterizing cinema as a utopian-universalist instrument. Among these is Weinberg's "Educational and Social Significance of Motion Pictures," a condensed version of his "Motion Pictures as a Social Force"; see *The American Hebrew* 116, no. 21 (April 1925): 631.

74. See, for example, William C. DeMille, "Bigoted and Bettered Pictures," *Scribner's* 76, no. 3 (September 1924): 231–236; William DeMille, "Film Drama Has 'Infantile Paralysis,'" *Current Opinion* (November 1924): 608, 617; Charles C. Pettijohn, "How the Motion Picture Governs Itself," *The Motion Picture in Its Economic and Social Aspects*, 158–162; and Fairbanks, "Huge," 133. See also Pettijohn's pamphlet, *The Motion Picture—Some Facts about an American Institution with Which Some of Us Are Not So Familiar as Its Importance to Our Lives May Warrant*. This pamphlet lists no publisher or publication date, but judging by the films it mentions as recent releases, it was printed in or around 1925.

75. Sydney S. Cohen, "Contribution of the Screen to Public Welfare," *American Hebrew* 116, no. 21 (April 1925): 618.

76. Cohen, 618.

77. Not only was Cohen a major figure in the exhibition sector of the industry, but his article appears in the same magazine as an interview with Hays. See Gordon, "Potentialities," 615, 624.

78. Cohen, "Contribution," 625. The piece misspells Faure's name as "Elie Leaure," but clearly, Cohen has read and appreciated Faure's *The Art of Cineplastics*, which had recently been translated into English. One of Faure's central theses—which Cohen

wholeheartedly accepts—is that the movies represent a saving form of collective spectacle, which will act as a surrogate religion, enabling modern humanity to overcome its atomized state. See Faure, *The Art of Cineplastics*, trans. Walter Pach (Boston: Four Seas, 1923), 45–46.

79. Cohen, "Contribution," 625. With this last line, Cohen is clearly signaling solidarity with the *American Hebrew*'s primary readership, the "faith [that he] already ha[s]" being Judaism.

80. North, *Reading*, 157. North focuses here on the efforts of Oberholtzer, the influential and widely published head of the Pennsylvania State Board of Censors, a writer who occasionally used the "universal tongue" metaphor to argue *for* the necessity of film censorship. See, for instance, Oberholtzer, *The Morals of the Movie* (Philadelphia: Penn, 1922), 14; and "The Moving-Picture Obiter Dicta of a Censor," *Yale Review* 9 (1920): 620. A 1931 volume meant to summarize the affirmative and negative positions in the censorship debate also indicates the extent to which the metaphor had been used to mark the threat posed by the cinema's cultural ascendancy. See *Selected Articles on the Censorship of the Theater and Motion Pictures*, ed. Lamar T. Beman (New York: H. W. Wilson, 1931), 18, 96.

81. Ruth Vasey, *The World According to Hollywood, 1918–1939* (Madison: University of Wisconsin Press, 1997), 21. As Vasey, Maltby, and Kristin Thompson have shown, the notion of cinema's ubiquitous reach was a source of similar concern for many observers in Great Britain and around Europe. Because the Hollywood studios expanded their share of European markets during and after World War I, many perceived not only a great economic threat to national cinemas but also the erosion of local cultural traditions and sensibilities. As Vasey has shown, in the late 1920s, "the British parliament [passed legislation to increase] the proportion of British-made films to be shown on British cinema screens" as a way of counteracting the perceived Americanization of film audiences throughout the empire. (The idea here was that the ascendancy of American mass culture threatened to displace traditional British imperialism as the dominant authority in the English-speaking world.) See Vasey, *World*, 41–42; and Richard Maltby and Ruth Vasey, "'Temporary American Citizens': Cultural Anxieties and Industrial Strategies in the Americanisation of European Cinema," in *"Film Europe" and "Film America,"* 32–35. Thompson discusses efforts at pan-European cooperation in film production and distribution as strategies for counteracting American control of foreign markets in "The Rise and Fall of Film Europe," in *"Film Europe" and "Film America,"* 56–81.

American films were promoted abroad on the basis of their universal appeal; the idea was that because the United States was a polyglot, classless nation (a "melting pot"), the films' sensibility was inherently democratic and international. To many in Europe, this (utopian) characterization of Hollywood productions read, however, as a rhetorical ruse, a benign covering put on an insidious cultural-imperialist agenda: to promote an intrinsically American culture rooted in consumerism. Indeed, when addressing a domestic audience, industry leaders like Hays promoted film as a showcase for U.S.-made consumer products—the "trade follows the film" idea—and for an ascendant

"American" way of life; as Vasey shows, these leaders had to eschew such rhetoric when speaking in foreign contexts to maintain a facade of ideological neutrality (Vasey, 45).

82. North, *Reading*, 157.

83. See, for example, my discussion of William Sheafe Chase's writings in chapter 1.

84. Lippmann, *Drift*, 277–278.

85. Lippmann, 278–279. It is interesting to note how completely Lippmann's characterization of "modern communion" anticipates Benedict Anderson's theoretical account of nationalism. For Anderson, the modern nation is "an imagined political community" that provides each of its members with "an image of communion" with vast numbers of other fellow members whom she or he is not likely to ever know. Moreover, the nation takes over many of the communally binding functions once associated with traditional religions; it allows the individual to place her or his existence (temporally limited, shaped by chance and contingencies) within a broader horizon of "continuity" and purpose. For Anderson, the nation is the enduring entity in service of which the individual's existence becomes meaningfully connected to a larger sense of necessity or purpose. See Anderson, *Imagined Communities: Reflections on the Origin and Spread of Nationalism*, new ed. (London: Verso, 2006), 6, 10–11.

Lippmann's attempt to envision an imagined community predicated on "devotion to impersonal ends," which is overtly spiritual or religious, matches Anderson's account point by point, save for one crucial departure. Whereas for Anderson, the nation is necessarily a geographically "limited" entity, the "modern communion" that Lippmann espouses is necessarily unlimited. From Anderson's standpoint, Lippmann is attempting to create something logically impossible: international nationalism. It should be noted, further, that this aspect of *Drift and Mastery* reflects the influence of the Fabianism of H. G. Wells and Graham Wallas on Lippmann's thought during this period. (As I show in my unpublished essay, "'Mandatory Enlightenment': American Silent Cinema and the Project of Universal History," Wells's major contributions to utopian-universalist film writing were his espousal of a "world state" and his promotion of the genre of "universal history.") Lippmann quotes Wells at length in the "Modern Communion" chapter and explicitly identifies his hope for a new, world-binding spirit as a substitute for revolutionary socialism. On Lippmann's early attraction to Fabianism, see Charles Forcey, *The Crossroads of Liberalism: Croly, Weyl, Lippmann and the Progressive Era, 1900–1925* (London: Oxford University Press, 1961), 69, 95–96, 100, 117.

86. Lippmann, *Drift and Mastery*, 282–283.

87. Lippmann, 283, 288.

88. Ben Singer, "The Ambimodernity of Early Cinema: Paradoxes and Problems in the Film-and-Modernity Discourse," in *Film 1900: Technology, Perception, Culture*, ed. Annemone Ligensa and Klaus Kreimeier (New Burnet, U.K.: John Libbey, 2009), 45.

89. Singer, 45–46.

90. Singer, 46–47.

91. Singer, 46.

92. Lee Grieveson, *Policing Cinema: Movies and Censorship in Early-Twentieth-Century America* (Berkeley: University of California Press), 4 (emphasis in original).

93. Grieveson, 153.

94. Grieveson, 152.

95. Grieveson, 152–153.

96. Grieveson, 153–154.

97. Grieveson, 210.

98. Grieveson, 210.

99. Mark Garrett Cooper, *Love Rules: Silent Hollywood and the Rise of the Managerial Class* (Minneapolis: University of Minnesota Press, 2003), 3. I am indebted to Mark Lynn Anderson for helping me to articulate this insight.

100. Creel, "Close-Up," 729.

101. Creel, 729.

102. Creel, 736–737.

103. See Douglas Fairbanks, *Laugh and Live* (New York: Britton, 1918), 163–190.

104. Walter Benjamin, "Light from Obscurantists," trans. Rodney Livingstone, in *Selected Writings: Volume 2, 1927–1934*, ed. Michael Jennings, Howard Eiland, and Gary Smith (Cambridge, Mass.: Belknap/Harvard University Press, 1999), 653.

105. Benjamin, 654.

106. Benjamin, 654–655.

107. Benjamin, 654.

108. My thanks again to Mark Lynn Anderson for helping me solidify this point.

109. Singer, "Ambimodernity," 46.

110. Cooper, *Love Rules*, 81.

111. Cooper, 81.

112. Cooper, 80.

113. Cooper, 105.

114. Cooper, 96.

CHAPTER 1 — ENLIGHTENED PUBLIC OPINION

1. Gerald Stanley Lee, *We: A Confession of Faith for the American People during and after the War* (New York: Doubleday, Page, 1916), 128.

2. Gerald Stanley Lee, *Crowds: A Moving-Picture of Democracy* (New York: Doubleday, Page, 1913), 15.

3. Lee, 15 (emphasis in original).

4. Russ Castronovo, *Beautiful Democracy: Aesthetics and Anarchy in a Global Era* (Chicago: University of Chicago Press, 2007), 1–4, 96. See also Gregory W. Bush, *Lord of Attention: Gerald Stanley Lee and the Crowd Metaphor in Modern America* (Amherst: University of Massachusetts Press, 1991), 4–5.

5. Castronovo, *Beautiful Democracy*, 2, 4.

6. Bush, *Lord of Attention*, 77–80.

7. Gustave Le Bon, *The Crowd: A Study of the Popular Mind*, 2nd ed. (New York: Macmillan, 1897), 41. See also Gabriel Tarde, *The Laws of Imitation*, trans. Elsie Clews Parsons (New York: Henry Holt, 1903); and Edward Alsworth Ross, *Social Psychology* (New York: Macmillan, 1908). For more on crowd psychology generally, see also Jeffrey T. Schnapp and Matthew Tiews, "Introduction: A Book of Crowds," in *Crowds*, ed. Schnapp and Tiews (Stanford: Stanford University Press, 2006), ix–x; and Stefan Jonsson, "The Invention of the Masses: The Crowd in French Culture from the Revolution to the Commune," in *Crowds*, ed. Schnapp and Tiews, 73–75. For more on Lee's departure from this tradition, see Castronovo, *Beautiful Democracy*, 93–97; and Bush, *Lord of Attention*, 26–27, 70–72.

8. As Castronovo points out, Lee published an article in the *Atlantic Monthly* in 1901, titled "Making the Crowd Beautiful," 97. One of the five sections of *Crowds* is "Letting the Crowd Be Beautiful."

9. Walter Benjamin, "The Work of Art in the Age of Mechanical Reproduction," in *Illuminations*, ed. Hannah Arendt, trans. Harry Zohn (New York: Schocken, 1968), 241.

10. Bush, *Lord of Attention*, 48–54.

11. Lee, quoted in Bush, 31.

12. Lee, quoted in Bush, 48.

13. Bush, 48.

14. Bush, 48.

15. Lee's construction of these identities anticipates the work of advertising executive turned inspirational writer Bruce Barton. Barton's *The Man Nobody Knows* (New York: Grosset & Dunlap, 1925) portrays Jesus as a charismatic salesman and advertiser whose ability to persuade makes him the "founder of modern business."

16. Lee himself dabbled in writing advertising copy around 1909 to 1910. See Bush, *Lord of Attention*, 124–125, 157.

17. Lee, *Crowds*, 122–123.

18. Bush, *Lord of Attention*, 50, 54.

19. Lee, *Crowds*, 123, 271.

20. Lee, 122.

21. Martin Heidegger, "The Age of the World Picture," in *Off the Beaten Track*, ed. and trans. Julian Young and Kenneth Haynes (Cambridge: Cambridge University Press, 2002), 67–68.

22. On Lee's idea of comprehensive vision as possession, see Bush, *Lord of Attention*, 68.

23. Lee, *Crowds*, 9.

24. Lee, 290.

25. Lee, 271.

26. Lee, 273.

27. Benjamin, "Work of Art," 241. For more on Lee, Benjamin, and the aestethiticization of politics, see my article, "'A Moving-Picture of Democracy': President Obama and African American Film History beyond the Mirror Screen," *Quarterly Review of Film & Video* 30, no. 1 (2013): 12.

28. Lee is fond of descriptions of crowds glimpsed from lofty vantage points. See Lee, *Crowds*, 3–4; and Lee, *We*, 251. See also Bush, *Lord of Attention*, 68. On the role of the "view from above" in the history of crowd representation, see Andrew V. Uroskie, "Far above the Madding Crowd: The Spatial Rhetoric of Mass Representation," in *Crowds*, ed. Schnapp and Tiews, 307–334. On the historical usage of the "oceanic" crowd metaphor in literature and philosophy, see Schnapp, "Mob Porn," in *Crowds*, ed. Schnapp and Tiews, 1–7.

29. On Lee's use of the phrase "composite photograph," see Bush, *Lord of Attention*, 50. See also Lee, *We*, 251.

30. Lee, *Crowds*, 383.

31. Lee, 323. See also Lee, *Crowds*, 460, 551; and Bush, *Lord of Attention*, 130. Lee's language of "composite photographs" and his choice of Wilson as an example suggest that he was familiar with Arthur Mole's "living photographs": panoramic photographs of hundreds or even thousands of subjects arranged into the shape of recognizable people, objects, and religious or military symbols. Mole's best-known work, a portrait of Wilson (1918), is an obvious, literal precursor to Lee's description of the great man's photographed face "as a national film." Whereas Mole's portrait reduces the bodies of the participants to abstract points that graphically render the image of a face, Lee's written description makes Wilson's countenance a kind of magic mirror in which various American faces (and/or the ideas that they are meant to signify) might appear, simultaneously or in succession. On Mole's career, see Louis Kaplan, *American Exposures: Photography and Community in the Twentieth Century* (Minneapolis: University of Minnesota Press, 2005), 1–26. On Mole's work as a precursor to Italian and German fascist photography, see Schnapp, "Mob Porn," 7–12.

32. I want to stress here that Lee's discussion of the human face as a site of revealed, instantaneously legible truth is both physiognomic and gnostic in the senses that Tom Gunning has described in his important essay, "In Your Face: Physiognomy, Photography, and the Gnostic Mission of Early Film," *Modernism/Modernity* 4, no. 1 (1997): 5. Lee's pervasive references to the mechanical reproduction of images illustrate Gunning's point

about the ways in which physiognomy and the "gnostic impulse" had permeated early theoretical discourses about photography and film.

33. Bourne, quoted in Bush, *Lord of Attention*, 49.

34. Lee, *Crowds*, 450–451. See also Bush, 80, 103, 118, 415–416; and Lee, *We*, 107.

35. Lee, *Crowds*, 450. Citing President Calvin Coolidge's 1926 statement that "advertising ministers to the spiritual side of trade," Bush notes that this equation of religious evangelism and the stoking of consumer desires (as two inspirational practices) would become commonplace in 1920s America. See Bush, *Lord of Attention*, 3.

36. Lee, *Crowds*, 450.

37. Lee, 10. This description comes in the context of a call for a new Bible for the "modern world," one of many moments in Lee's writing where he styles himself as a new Isaiah or David, two figures whom he ultimately prefers to Moses—precisely because they lack Moses's associations with prohibitive laws. See Bush, *Lord of Attention*, 56–57.

38. Lee, *Crowds*, 10. Lee had rehearsed this essential dichotomy—the "failure" of the Decalogue's "Thou Shalt Not" versus Moses's sublime crowd leadership—in his *The Shadow Christ* (New York: Century, 1896), 22–35.

39. Lee, *Crowds*, 146–147.

40. Walter Lippmann, *Drift and Mastery: An Attempt to Diagnose the Current Unrest* (New York: Mitchell Kennerley, 1914), 277–278.

41. Lee, quoted in Bush, *Lord of Attention*, 113.

42. Charles Forcey, *The Crossroads of Liberalism: Croly, Weyl, Lippmann and the Progressive Era, 1900–1925* (London: Oxford University Press, 1961), ix–xxv. Forcey, whose timeline is more expansive than that used by some other historians, refers to the 1910–1917 period as the "height" of the Progressive Era.

43. Forcey, xix.

44. Forcey, xviii–xix, xxiii–xxiv.

45. Forcey, x, 11.

46. See Walter Weyl, *The New Democracy* (New York: Macmillan, 1912); and Herbert Croly, *The Promise of American Life* (New York: Macmillan, 1911). See also Forcey, 29–30, 82–83.

47. Forcey, 27.

48. Forcey, 84.

49. Lippmann, *A Preface to Politics* (New York: Mitchell Kennerley, 1913), 21.

50. Forcey, *Crossroads of Liberalism*, 111.

51. Lippmann, *Drift*, xxii.

52. Forcey, *Crossroads of Liberalism*, 36, 49, 112.

53. Forcey, 39–41. The unexamined assumption underlying this representation of elites (business leaders, politicians, and other people who use communication technologies to shape mass attention) is very evident in Lee's writings. His belief that business culture is essentially religious in nature leads him to presume that "crowd-men" will always act disinterestedly, to the benefit of society as a whole. Lee seems not even to consider the possibility that the masses and these elite communicators could have conflicting material interests or that the latter group might create propaganda to serve a particular ideology. The literary critic Van Wyck Brooks first pointed out the assumption of disinterestedness in a shrewd essay on Lee's *Inspired Millionaires* (1908), "Apotheosis of the 'Lowbrow,'" in *America's Coming-of-Age* (New York: B. W. Huebsch, 1915), 133–157.

54. Lippmann, quoted in Forcey, *Crossroads of Liberalism*, 112–116. The last two quoted phrases come from Lippmann, *Preface*, 99, 230.

55. Forcey, *Crossroads of Liberalism*, 101.

56. Forcey, 111. In *Preface*, Lippmann comes to equate "the sterile tyranny of the taboo" with the "use of government [specified by] the ideal of Jefferson." He then defines his own, "totally different" use of government in opposition to that model. See Lippmann, *Preface*, 269.

57. Forcey, *Crossroads of Liberalism*, 111–112.

58. Forcey, 111.

59. Lippmann, *Preface*, 40.

60. Lippmann, 42.

61. Lippmann, 46.

62. Lippmann, 181.

63. Lippmann, 181–182.

64. Lippmann, 180.

65. Croly, *Promise of American Life*, 5, 12.

66. Lippmann, *Drift*, xx.

67. Forcey, *Crossroads of Liberalism*, 84; and Croly, *Promise of American Life*, 357–368.

68. Lippmann, *Drift*, 63–64. On Lippmann's critique of Lee, see Bush, *Lord of Attention*, 142–143. See also Croly's very similar critique of "patriotic prophecies" (which does not mention Lee) in *Promise*, 5.

69. Lippmann, *Drift*, 64.

70. "General process of thought" is Wells's phrase, which Lippmann quotes admiringly in *Preface*, 69.

71. Lippmann, 69.

72. Lippmann, 146.

73. Lippmann, 146.

74. Lippmann, 98–99, 146, 230–231.

75. Lippmann draws the term "myth," meaning a guiding "express[ion of] aspiration," from Georges Sorel, preferring this term in some ways to "opinion" because the former carries irrational, spontaneous connotations. For Lippmann, "myth" refers to "an impulse, not a program, nor a plan"; hence, myths "embody the motor currents of social life." Lippmann, 230.

76. Lippmann, 233–234. It is important to stress that the preceding generalizations about the significance of "public opinion" in Lippmann's work do not apply to his later writing. Adopting a more conservative standpoint, Lippmann's *Public Opinion* (New York: Harcourt, Brace, 1922) construes the eponymous phrase as a social and moral stumbling block. Public opinion comes, ostensibly, to mean "ideology": those deceptions and misperceptions propagated by modern media that hamper democratic citizens' ability to act rationally. See Forcey, *Crossroads of Liberalism*, 297.

77. In a series of essays published in the *Saturday Evening Post* from 1918 to 1919, Lee styled himself as a crusader against censorship of all kinds. See, for instance, "The Glass House World," where Lee advocates for wartime freedom of the press in the United States, calling "the censor spirit . . . a German spirit"; here he describes censorship as a manifestation of the fear that is responsible Germany's fighting the war, equates militarism generally with censorship, and refers to the Kaiser as "the censor." Lee, "The Glass House World," *Saturday Evening Post*, March 8, 1919, 3–4, 70, 73–74, 76. Setting aside the characteristic grandiosity of Lee's pronouncement, the essay clearly endorses the basic philosophy of George Creel's Committee on Public Information (CPI), which portrayed American character as fundamentally averse to censorship and promoted "expression" as a more potent political weapon than "suppression." For more on the CPI's program, see chapter 4. For an indication of the degree to which Lee was regarded as an authoritative anticensorship voice in the context of the debate about film, see Janet Priest, "The Better Photoplay League of America," *Photoplay* 15, no. 6 (June 1919): 79–80.

78. Nancy J. Rosenbloom, "Between Reform and Regulation: The Struggle over Film Censorship in Progressive America, 1909–1922," *Film History* 1, no. 4 (1987): 308.

79. Richard Hofstadter, "Introduction: The Meaning of the Progressive Movement," in *The Progressive Movement, 1900–1915*, ed. Hofstadter (Englewood Cliffs, N.J.: Prentice Hall, 1963), 1.

80. Shelley Stamp, "Moral Coercion, or the National Board of Censorship Ponders the Vice Films," in *Controlling Hollywood: Censorship and Regulation in the Studio Era*, ed. Matthew Bernstein (New Brunswick, N.J.: Rutgers University Press, 1999), 41–42. Founded in 1909, the NBC was renamed the National Board of Review (NBR) in 1916. For simplicity's sake, I will use the acronym NBC consistently in this chapter. On the NBC/NBR, see also Robert Fisher, "Film Censorship and Progressive Reform: The National Board of Censorship of Motion Pictures, 1909–1922," *Journal of Popular Film and Television* 4, no. 2 (1975): 143–156; and Lary May, *Screening Out the Past: The Birth of Mass Culture and the Motion Picture Industry* (Chicago: University of Chicago Press, 1980), 46–47.

81. Stamp, "Moral Coercion," 41.

82. Stamp, 42–43.

83. Stamp, 42.

84. Garth Jowett, "'A Capacity for Evil': The 1915 Supreme Court *Mutual* Decision," in *Controlling Hollywood*, 32, 34.

85. William Sheafe Chase, *Catechism on Motion Pictures in Inter-state Commerce* (New York: New York Civic League, 1922), 9–10.

86. Jowett, "Capacity for Evil," 32–43. Chase objected to motion pictures on the grounds that they were visual spectacles uniquely powerful in their impact on audiences and that they were made strictly with an eye to profit. These were also the primary reasons cited by the United States Supreme Court in its ruling in *Mutual Film Corporation v. Industrial Commission of Ohio* (1915)—a ruling that could also be labeled "Progressive." In a major victory for the procensorship camp, the court judged that motion pictures did not qualify as protected free speech and granted the Ohio censorship board had the right to demand the review of films distributed by the Mutual exchange. See Jowett, 28.

87. Chase, *Catechism*, 57, 116.

88. Chase, quoted in Jowett, "Capacity for Evil," 34.

89. Here I deliberately echo Hofstadter's classic characterization of Progressivism as a reawakening of "moral energies" in response to the rapid "material development" witnessed by the late nineteenth-century United States. See Hofstadter, "Introduction," 1.

90. Chase uses this analogy throughout his *Catechism*; see, for instance, 13, 115. The head Pennsylvania censor, Ellis Paxson Oberholtzer, arguably the most respected voice on the subject (and the authority whom Chase most frequently cites), was also fond of the comparison. See Oberholtzer, *The Morals of the Movie* (Philadelphia: Penn, 1922), 169.

91. On Addams, see May, *Screening*, 48–53; and Miriam Hansen, *Babel and Babylon: Spectatorship in American Silent Film* (Cambridge, Mass.: Harvard University Press, 1991), 65–66. Note that in this highly condensed summary, I am leaving out other self-styled Progressive cinema reform projects, like the Better Photoplay League of America. See Priest, "Better Photoplay," 79–80, 124.

92. Stamp, "Moral Coercion," 41–42.

93. Chase, *Catechism*, 6.

94. The term "agency" comes from Will Hays, "Motion Pictures and Their Censors," *American Review of Reviews* 75 (March 1927): 398.

95. See "Public Opinion as a Moral Censor," *Moving Picture World*, May 11, 1907, 147–148; Elizabeth Wilson, "The Case for the People," *Photoplay* 8, no. 2 (July 1915): 154; "Morals and the Movies," *Nation*, April 20, 1921, 581; and Katherine Fullerton Gerould, "The Nemesis of the Screen," *Saturday Evening Post*, April 8, 1922, 12, 157.

96. See "Morals and the Movies," 581; and Hays, "Motion Pictures," 394.

97. Hays, 393.

98. Lippmann, *Drift*, 283.

99. Hays, "Motion Pictures," 398.

100. In discussing these arguments, it is important to consider the symbolic value of Hays's appointment to head the MPPDA in 1922. As Ruth Vasey explains, Hays was chosen in large part for "his prominent membership in the Presbyterian Church": as a conservative white Protestant, like Chase himself, Hays provided useful cultural cover for Jewish studio heads at a time when anti-Semitism fueled many of the attacks faced by the industry. Vasey, *The World According to Hollywood, 1918–1939* (Madison: University of Wisconsin Press, 1997), 25, 28.

101. Lee's own writings in the immediate postwar period seem to map out this shift. See, for instance, his comments about Mary Pickford and Charlie Chaplin in "The Two-Inch Pipe Line to Europe," *Saturday Evening Post*, April 5, 1919, 127, 131. Chapters 4 and 5 explore the subsequent development of this understanding of the film star.

102. Hays, "Motion Pictures," 398. As the preceding comparisons between Lee and Lippmann should suggest, the eventual position struck by utopian-universalist cinema writers diverges from key tenets of the new liberalism. Obviously, these writers would be opposed in principle to the incorporation of the film industry under federal political control (not that such a thing was even being discussed at the time) and advocate (like Lee does) for corporate entities to be able to operate with total impunity.

103. Hays, 398.

104. May, *Screening*, 60–61. May uses a statement containing the phrase "beyond Babel" (attributed to Griffith by Lillian Gish in her memoir) as the epigraph to his chapter.

105. May, 62, 86. May mainly uses "Victorian" in the popular sense of a reactionary and puritanical style of morality. In this common usage, the term encompasses a constellation of other social attitudes—the cult of true womanhood, a sentimentalized view of domesticity, traditional middle-class identity, individualism and self-reliance, thrift, Protestant religiosity, and so on—some or all of which might, in fact, be shared by the people and institutions that May labels "Victorian." At the same time, May sometimes uses the term "Victorian" to describe the mid- to late nineteenth century as a historical period; thus, some of the people and institutions so labeled (like Griffith) may not be "Victorian" in this other sense. See the first chapter of May, 3–21.

106. May, 62.

107. May, 77–80.

108. I take up this line of argument in chapter 3.

109. Rosenbloom, "Between Reform," 308–309.

110. As I have already suggested, the timeline for considering the relevance of "Progressive" ideas needs to be extended further than the usual boundaries placed on "the Progressive Era" to get beyond this tendency to mark a simplistic historical caesura with the

beginning of World War I. To be fair, May does see Progressivism as experiencing a "temporary revival" during the war (92). Otherwise, though, he would seem to use the standard periodization, which traces back to Richard Hofstadter. In the opening statement to his edited collection of representative texts—itself now more than a half century old—Hofstadter states, "For a long time historians have written of the period roughly between 1900 and 1914 as the Progressive Era, and of its variety of reform agitations, as the Progressive movement" (1). Notwithstanding this statement, the publishers of this collection have rounded the end date up to 1915—seemingly for aesthetic reasons. See Hofstadter, "Introduction," 1.

111. For more on these precursor movements, see William James, *The Varieties of Religious Experience: A Study in Human Nature* (New York: Longmans, Green, 1902), 94–95.

112. James, 188.

113. James, 89.

114. James, 89.

115. James, 11.

116. Fenwicke Holmes, *The Law of Mind in Action: Daily Lessons and Treatments in Mental and Spiritual Science* (New York: Robert M. McBride, 1919), 56.

117. Ralph Waldo Trine, *In Tune with the Infinite* (New York: Collier, 1970), 106.

118. Trine, 105.

119. The neoplatonic influence on Lee's thought at this point is clear. Here he goes beyond the liberal-Progressive embrace of mystical "communion" to countenance the idea that Lippmann dubbed "collective mind." Lippmann himself was ambivalent about the idea of supraindividual cognition. Whereas his positive references to Wells's writing in *Preface* included a tacit embrace of "collective mind," he expressed reservations in *Drift* about the utopian "hope that somehow we shall develop an intelligence larger than the individual," calling it "a *deus ex machina* invented to cover an enormous need." See Lippmann, *Preface*, 180; and *Drift*, 147.

120. Though insufficiently researched, Justine Brown's *Hollywood Utopia* provides an interesting starting point for this inquiry, attempting to draw out connections between Southern California's proponents of theosophy and other "Aquarian" schools of thought (from L. Frank Baum, to Griffith, to the members of the Valentino circle) and the discourse of cinema as restoring humanity to a pre-Babelic state. Justine Brown, *Hollywood Utopia* (Vancouver: New Star Books, 2002). On the Valentino circle, see also Richard Koszarski, *An Evening's Entertainment: The Age of the Silent Feature Picture, 1915–1928*, History of the American Cinema, vol. 3 (New York: Charles Scriber's Sons, 1990), 100.

121. To my mind, the utopian-universalist argument emerging from Lee and Lindsay does finally connect with the region's Aquarian subculture (and with a broader Los Angeles settlement ideology centered on mystical tropes), but only with the screenwriter

Perley Poore Sheehan's tract *Hollywood as a World Center* (Los Angeles: Hollywood Citizen, 1924). In an article that I am currently researching, I will situate Sheehan's book, which has, so far, not received any in-depth treatment by film scholars in relation to the body of material discussed here. The article will show how Sheehan's exceptionally bold claims about cinema's ability to foster "Interracial Brotherhood based on the Common Divinity of Man" partake equally of the beliefs of the Theosophical Society (with which Sheehan and his unacknowledged collaborator, the composer and frustrated film actor Dane Ruhdyar, were involved) and of the "Aryan"-ist racialism of Southern California settlement mythology. For a brief overview of *Hollywood as a World Center*, albeit one that tends to reduce the book to an act of mere industry and city self-promotion, see Koszarski, *Evening's Entertainment*, 100; and *Hollywood on the Hudson: Film and Television in New York from Griffith to Sarnoff* (New Brunswick, N.J.: Rutgers University Press, 2008), 4–5.

122. Lee, *We*, 151.

123. Lee, 158.

124. The title of the chapter I am quoting from here is "The Hardships of Being Done Good to or At."

125. Lee, *We*, 153. In *Inspired Millionaires*, Lee had described socialism in similar terms, as a system appealing only to "scared" people. See Bush, *Lord of Attention*, 103.

CHAPTER 2 — "THE OCCULT ELEMENTS OF MOTION AND LIGHT"

1. *A Dictionary of Correspondences, Representatives, and Significatives, Derived from the Word of the Lord. Extracted from the Writings of Emmanuel Swedenborg* (Boston: Otis Clapp, 1841), 160.

2. Vachel Lindsay, *The Art of the Moving Picture* (New York: Macmillan, 1915), 159–160.

3. Lindsay's *The Art of the Moving Picture* is widely regarded as the first "full length work devoted to serious thought about what film as an art form should be, what it should do, and how it should do it"—the first book of film theory to be published the United States or, indeed, written in English. Glenn Joseph Wolfe, *Vachel Lindsay: The Poet as Film Theorist* (New York: Arno, 1973), 7. See also Laura Marcus, *The Tenth Muse: Writing about Cinema in the Modernist Period* (Oxford: Oxford University Press, 2007), 15. As Marcus notes, Lindsay was a former art student who, by the time he began to write seriously about film, had begun to establish himself as a poet of major stature, aligning himself with the Imagist school and Harriet Monroe's *Poetry* magazine (188).

4. Lindsay, *Art*, 49.

5. Lindsay, 49–50.

6. Lindsay, 50.

7. In her discussion of Lindsay's religious background and beliefs, Ann Massa explains that he came under the sway of Swedenborg "from adolescence onward." Although Lindsay denied being "a literal Swedenborgian," he was, Massa stresses, an avid reader of

Swedenborg's work and made frequent reference to those theories that he found "congenial"—most notably the "science of correspondences"—throughout his poems, fiction, and criticism. Massa, *Vachel Lindsay: Fieldworker for the American Dream* (Bloomington: Indiana University Press, 1970), 52–54.

8. As the chapter's first epigraph illustrates, ancient Egypt was the quintessential "representative" culture for Swedenborg, a fact that accounts for his use of "hieroglyphic" as a generic term for symbols that carry ritual and religious significance—and that explains what Lindsay means when he insists that cinema (and modern American culture more generally) is strongly "Egyptian" in character. Like many of his contemporaries, Swedenborg had a "Cratylitic" view of ancient Egyptian written language, understanding its pictograms to be directly depictive of concepts—and, therefore, likely repositories of esoteric knowledge. See Jesse Schotter, *Hieroglyphic Modernisms: Writing and New Media in the Twentieth Century* (Edinburgh: Edinburgh University Press, 2018), 25–26.

9. Lindsay, *Art*, 172–173. Treating Lindsay's theory of hieroglyphics as a rote instance of the universal language metaphor, film scholars have tended to flatten out the complexities of Lindsay's account—in large part because they have overlooked the influence of Swedenborg on Lindsay's thought. My unpublished essay, "'Spirit-Meanings': Vachel Lindsay's Swedenborgian Hieroglyphics of Film," delves more deeply the tension in Lindsay's film theory between a democratic ideal of accessibility and the elitist assumption of specialized interpretive tools.

10. Lindsay, *Art*, 175.

11. In 1925, Lindsay drafted a manuscript under the working title "The Greatest Movies Now Running," which remained unpublished until 1995, when the film historian Myron Lounsbury edited and published it as *The Progress and Poetry of the Movies* (Lanham, Md.: Scarecrow, 1995). As Lindsay's working title suggests, the book aims principally to apply the theoretical principles articulated in his first book (which had been republished in 1922) to the task of analyzing recently released Hollywood films (historical epics in particular).

12. Lindsay, *Progress*, 183.

13. Lindsay, *Art*, 2, 68.

14. Lindsay was an admirer of admiration for Percy Mackaye's Civic Pageants, large-scale community performances with ritual elements and patriotic themes, which aimed to instill "historical consciousness" in modern Americans. See Massa, *Vachel*, 113.

15. Lindsay, *Art*, 67. See my analysis of Lindsay's "hieroglyphic" reading of *The Birth of a Nation* in "'Spirit-Meanings.'"

16. Lindsay, *Art*, 21, 30, 60.

17. Lindsay, 39. See also Lindsay's later description of the dance scenes from *Monsieur Beaucaire*, which employs the "sea of humanity" trope and reflects on the peculiar

qualities of filmed motion, in *Progress*, 318. There he asserts, "The motion picture is the one art in the world in which the crowd can be the principal actor in scene after scene."

18. Lindsay, *Art*, 50.

19. H. G. Wells was perhaps the foremost proponent of an international political body, holding the "World State" to be the ideal toward which humanity was striving. See, for instance, Wells, *The Outline of History: Being a Plain History of Life and Mankind*, vol. 1 (New York: Macmillan, 1920), v.

20. Lindsay, *Art*, 49.

21. Lindsay's assertion of this scene's effect on its audiences anticipates the important debates about film's viability as an instrument of mass self-portraiture that take place in German cinema theory during the late twenties and early thirties—most notably in the writings of Walter Benjamin and Siegfried Kracauer. Working in this theoretical tradition, Anton Kaes has recently offered a strongly affirmative verdict on the issue, one that, to a surprising extent, evokes Lindsay's idea of the crowd seeing itself seeing—albeit from an explicitly leftist political perspective. Reconstructing the exhibition of Fritz Lang's *Metropolis* (UFA) at the Berlin Zooplast in 1927, Kaes concludes, "Only in the mass medium of film do the masses become visible to themselves—as spectators." See Kaes, "Movies and Masses," in *Crowds*, ed. Jeffrey T. Schnapp and Matthew Tiews (Stanford: Stanford University Press, 2006), 157.

22. Lindsay, *Art*, 65.

23. Gerald Stanley Lee, *Crowds: A Moving-Picture of Democracy* (New York: Doubleday, Page, 1913), 273. For more on the broader influence of Whitman's work on Progressive-Era American intellectuals and artists (Lee, Lindsay, and Griffith included), see Gregory W. Bush, *Lord of Attention: Gerald Stanley Lee and the Crowd Metaphor in Modern America* (Amherst: University of Massachusetts Press, 1991), 24–26; and Miriam Hansen, *Babel and Babylon: Spectatorship in American Silent Film* (Cambridge, Mass.: Harvard University Press, 1991), 195, 345n15.

24. Lindsay, *Art*, 65.

25. Lindsay, 173.

26. It is conceivable that Lindsay got the phrase "Mirror Screen" from Robert Grau's history of cinematic technology, *The Theatre of Science: A Volume of Progress and Achievement in the Motion Picture Industry* (New York: Broadway, 1914), 331–334. There Grau refers to an Indiana-based film exhibitor named F. J. Rembusch, who had been experimenting on a device he calls the "mirror screen": a frosted glass plate meant to provide a better "distribution of light" than the traditional "white wall or sheet."

27. Anne Friedberg, *Window Shopping: Cinema and the Postmodern* (Berkeley: University of California Press, 1993), 65–66.

28. Lindsay, *Progress*, 317.

29. Lindsay, 325–326. On the emergence of plate-glass "show window" and the transformation of store display technology in the late nineteenth and early twentieth centuries, see Friedberg, *Window Shopping*, 65–66, 68; and William R. Leach, *Land of Desire: Merchants, Power, and the Rise of a New American Culture* (New York: Pantheon, 1993), 55–70, 304–305. On the historical associations of display windows and movie screens, see Friedberg, *Window Shopping*, 66; Jane Gaines, "The Queen Christian Tie-Ups: Convergence of Show Window and Screen," *Quarterly Review of Film & Video* 11, no. 1 (1989): 35–60; and Charles Eckert, "The Carole Lombard in the Macy's Window," in *Movies and Mass Culture*, ed. John Belton (New Brunswick, N.J.: Rutgers University Press, 1996), 95–118.

30. Friedberg, *Window Shopping*, 65. Lindsay highlights this connection when he later includes actual mirrors (e.g., in elevators and hotel rooms) among his list of proliferating glass surfaces in *Progress*, 325.

31. "Diamonds now are only diamonds when under glass," Lindsay writes in *Progress*, 326. See also Friedberg, *Window Shopping*, 65–66.

32. Lindsay, *Progress*, 325–326.

33. Lindsay, 317.

34. In a passage that ties directly back to *Art*, Lindsay identifies *Monsieur Beaucaire* as "a picture of crowd splendor" and asserts that the film is "for the most part told by crowds strutting by." See Lindsay, *Art*, 318. This assertion—as well as the poetic reverie on "rhythmic masses" in the film—seems curious, the film's crowd scenes seeming, to this critic's eye at least, relatively brief and small in scale.

35. Lindsay, 317.

36. Fischbeck, quoted in Richard Koszarski, *An Evening's Entertainment: The Age of the Silent Feature Picture, 1915–1928*, History of the American Cinema, vol. 3 (New York: Charles Scriber's Sons, 1990), 151.

37. Lindsay, *Progress*, 326. The terms "transfiguration" and "transfigured" also feature prominently in Lindsay's discussion of specific visual phenomena on screen in *Art*. See, for instance, his description of "furniture transfigured"—inanimate objects made given the appearance of life—in his comments on the "fairy splendor film" (119).

38. See Matt. 17:2–9; Mark 9:2–8; and Luke 9:28–35; I use the King James Version here, as this is the translation with which Lindsay would have been familiar. In my characterization of the transfiguration's key images and themes, I have also relied on John Irwin's helpful summary in *American Hieroglyphics: The Symbol of the Egyptian Hieroglyphics in the American Renaissance* (New Haven: Yale University Press, 1980), 140–141.

39. See "Glorification" and "Transfiguration" in the *Dictionary of Correspondences, Representatives, and Significatives, Derived from the Word of the Lord. Extracted from the Writings of Emmanuel Swedenborg*, 137, 369.

40. Lindsay's rhetoric of transfiguring light recalls the work of his friend, the Jewish American novelist, poet, and editor James Oppenheim, whom Lindsay credited with the idea to explore the "surprising parallelism between Egyptian hieroglyphics and this new silent drama" in *Art*, 4–5. As early as 1911, Oppenheim, who later wrote film scenarios, had used the term "transfigure" to describe the beautifying effects of store window displays and of the film projector's light. In Oppenheim's story "Saturday Night," a young dressmaker attempts to enliven a dull, lonely evening by venturing out of the squalid apartment she shares with her mother onto the Third Avenue (New York) commercial district. The woman imagines herself becoming "one of the Enchanted People" as she mingles with the people on the crowded street: "The lights, the tides of men and women, the sights, the lustrous leather of shoes in the brilliant shop window . . . all these flooded through her until she was transfigured." Later, while viewing her first movies at a nickel theater, the woman feels the room begin to "heave" and "rock," the light of the screen transforming the people inside; she eventually feels herself "absorbed" into the film, "wholly transfigured now and to her own inner eyes a very beauty of womanhood." See Oppenheim, "Saturday Night," in *Pay Envelopes: Tales of the Mill, the Mine, and the City Street* (New York: B. W. Huebsch, 1911), 74, 78, 80–81. Here and in his novel about an aspiring film actress, *The Beloved* (New York: B. W. Huebsch, 1915), Oppenheim, like Lindsay, takes seriously the idea of the nickelodeon as a true "Theater of Democracy" ("Saturday Night," 79). Writing from a working-class or proletarian perspective, Oppenheim tends, nonetheless, to treat the experience of escape afforded by cinema (and commercial culture more generally) somewhat skeptically, using inflated language ironically, to highlight the illusory or fleeting quality of its transcendence.

41. See, for example, Lindsay's lengthy paean to Chapman (a fellow follower of Swedenborg) in *Progress*, 278–282. See also Massa, *Vachel*, 157–162.

42. Lindsay, *Progress*, 326. See also Massa, *Vachel*, 195–201. Note that Lindsay's temperance advocacy was related to his defense of cinema as a socially healthy institution. See his chapter, "The Substitute for the Saloon," in *Art*, 207–216.

43. According to Lounsbury's introduction, his edition preserves the placement of the interpolated poems in Lindsay's original manuscript.

44. Lindsay, *Progress*, 327.

45. Lindsay, 328, 330.

46. Lindsay, 328. See Mary Ann Doane, "The Economy of Desire: The Commodity Form in/of the Cinema," *Quarterly Review of Film & Video* 11, no. 1 (1989): 27.

47. Doane, 30.

48. Doane, 26.

49. Doane, 24–25. Rachel Bowlby, whose work Doane cites, traces the genealogy of "the classical picture of the young girl gazing into the mirror in love with herself" back to late nineteenth century, whose "dominant ideology of feminine subjectivity," she argues, was "perfectly fitted" to the new idea of "the seductive commodity offering to

enhance [one's] womanly attractions." See Bowlby, *Just Looking: Consumer Culture in Dreiser, Gissing, and Zola* (New York: Methuen, 1985), 32. See also Friedberg, *Window Shopping*, 65.

50. Lindsay, *Progress*, 328.

51. Lindsay, 328.

52. Lindsay, 328–329. In the poem, Lindsay uses the phrase "mirror screen" without his customary capital letters.

53. Lindsay, 329.

54. Lindsay, 329.

55. Lindsay, 329.

56. Lindsay, 330. See Edgar Allan Poe, "Ulalume—A Ballad," in *Edgar Allan Poe: Poetry and Tales* (New York: Library of America, 1984), 90.

57. I draw here on Robert S. Ellwood Jr.'s helpful statement that Swedenborgianism—the main influence on this aspect of Lindsay's thought—like its "spiritual progeny . . . Spiritualism, Theosophy, and 'New Thought,'" is focused on the goal of "proper thinking." See Ellwood, *Alternative Altars: Unconventional and Eastern Spirituality in America* (Chicago: University of Chicago Press, 1979), 87.

58. Lindsay, *Art*, 248.

59. Lindsay, *Progress*, 330.

60. Ibid. I use the term "screen idol" to pick up on the 1920s-era usage of the term to describe film stars—whether from a celebratory, ironic, or condemnatory perspective—as objects of worship. See Mark Lynn Anderson, *Twilight of the Idols: Hollywood and the Human Sciences in 1920s America* (Berkeley: University of California Press, 2011), 1–9.

61. "Romance" is Lindsay's term in *Progress*, 334. The racial politics of Lindsay's representation of American colonial settlement—and of Native Americans—are particularly complex and deserve further exploration, beyond what is possible here.

62. Lindsay, 296.

63. See Lindsay's chapter on *The Covered Wagon* in *Progress*, 344–356.

64. Lindsay, 343.

65. Lindsay, 343. See also 290, 303.

66. Lindsay, 297, 343.

67. Lindsay, 340.

68. Lindsay, 340.

69. Lindsay, 235. The phrase "rampant speed-mania" comes from *Art*, 13.

70. Lindsay, *Progress*, 186. See also Lounsbury's comments on Lindsay's fears on pp. 400–401 of this volume.

71. Lindsay, *Progress*, 187, 235. Lindsay describes a hypothetical film viewer who has spent too much time in the theater as suffering from "moving picture nausea" and "photoplay delirium tremens" in *Art*, 201.

72. Lindsay, *Progress*, 186.

73. Lindsay, 235.

74. Lindsay, 235.

75. Lindsay, 235. Notwithstanding his concerns about nervous exhaustion, Lindsay's emphasis on the pace and motion of American life—and his identification of driving with film viewing on that basis—anticipates an important trope in subsequent film criticism. For instance, Terry Ramsaye would later argue that "the hunger for movement is the root of all manner of aspects of our civilization," movies being nothing but a means of satisfying this hunger. See Ramsaye, *A Million and One Nights: A History of the Motion Picture*, vol. 1 (New York: Simon and Schuster, 1926), xlviii. In a somewhat more complex version of this trope, Gilbert Seldes would go on to assert that a film's quality depends on its ability "to move," attributing the worldwide "success of the American movies" to the fact that "America has always been *on the move* and has *kept moving*, its history . . . is a history of transportation." See Seldes, *The Movies Come from America* (New York: Charles Scribner's Sons, 1937), 3 (emphasis in original). Laura Marcus's essential *The Tenth Muse* demonstrates that this equation of film with movement—and with corollary ideas like transport, locomotion, and emotion—was standard in early film theory and in literary representations of cinema during the modernist period, 18–19.

76. Lindsay, *Progress*, 296.

77. See Lindsay, 206, 248, 288, 290. See also P. D. Ouspensky, *Tertium Organum*, trans. Nicholas and Claude Bragdon (New York: Knopf, 1922), 28–29. Ouspensky was a Russian mathematician associated with the mystic G. I. Gurdjieff, whose work was influential among the various communities of Theosophists. According to Peter Washington, Ouspensky saw the fourth dimension as a supratemporal dimension surrounding or encompassing time as experienced in ordinary existence. Washington, *Madame Blavatsky's Baboon: A History of the Mystics, Mediums, and Misfits Who Brought Spiritualism to America* (New York: Schocken Books, 1995), 157–159. American Theosophists appear to have equated Swedenborg's idea of the "spirit world" with the fourth dimension; they saw the latter as simply a twentieth-century (mathematically and scientifically understood) version of the former. See, for example, Claude Bragdon, *A Primer of Higher Space (The Fourth Dimension)* (Rochester, N.Y.: Manas, 1913), 19–20. In theosophy, the terms "spirit world" and "fourth dimension" are also more or less interchangeable with notions like "the astral plane" and the "ether." See C. W. Leadbeater, *The Astral Plane: Its Scenery, Inhabitants, and Phenomena* (London: Theosophical Publishing Society, 1895), 8–9.

In the film studies context, the term is most often associated with the work of Sergei Eisenstein, who used it to theorize an unlocatable dimension of meaning, wherein a montage sequence's visual "overtones" act on the mind and body of the spectator. In his 1929 essay "The Filmic Fourth Dimension," Eisenstein anticipates the objection that he is lapsing into mysticism or occult thinking, quoting Albert Einstein's statement that the physical world is a "fourth-dimensional space-time continuum" to give scientific credibility to his discussion. See Eisenstein, "The Filmic Fourth Dimension," in *Film Form: Essays in Film Theory*, ed. and trans. Jay Leyda (New York: Harcourt, Brace, 1949), 69–70.

78. Lindsay, *Progress*, 239, 297.

79. The text quoted here appears as part of a much longer quotation in Lindsay, 239. See Münsterberg, *The Photoplay: A Psychological Study* (New York: D. Appleton, 1916), 220 (emphasis in original). For other, related discussions, see also Münsterberg, *Photoplay*, 95, 173, 181; and Lindsay, *Progress*, 205–206, 231.

80. Münsterberg, 190, 220 (emphasis in original). For more on Münsterberg's sensibility and on the links between him and Lindsay, see Hansen, *Babel and Babylon*, 138–139.

81. To be fair, Lindsay's sense of common ground with Münsterberg would have been bolstered by the fact that Münsterberg cited his work, however briefly. Münsterberg quotes Lindsay on the concept of "sculpture-in-motion" and then explains the perceptual effect described therein in term of optical science (53). On Münsterberg's neo-Kantian aesthetic philosophy, see Sarah Cooper, *The Soul of Film Theory* (New York: Palgrave Macmillan, 2013), 36–37; and Marcus, *Tenth Muse*, 209.

82. Lindsay, *Progress*, 206.

83. Cooper notes that Münsterberg's theoretical claims about the effects of the "photoplay" are grounded in his concept of "soul." In order to make the "soul" available as an area of legitimate psychological research, Münsterberg had sought, however, to extricate the concept from the occultist fads of the late nineteenth and early twentieth centuries—the very ways of thinking that Lindsay seems to draw on here. See Cooper, *Soul*, 28–33.

84. Fenwicke L. Holmes, *The Law of Mind in Action: Daily Lessons and Treatments in Mental and Spiritual Science* (Robert M. McBride, 1919), 12 (emphasis in original).

85. Lindsay, *Progress*, 279, 343. It is worth noting here that Münsterberg does speak about motion pictures' capacity for "the remolding and upbuilding of the national soul," 233.

86. Lindsay, *Progress*, 288.

87. Lindsay, *Art*, 252–254.

88. Here and throughout the book, I use the currently accepted English spelling, "Baghdad," unless citing the title of the film or historical accounts of it—in which case I use the period variant, "Bagdad."

89. Lindsay, *Progress*, 343.

90. Lindsay, 343.

91. Lee, *Crowds*, 65.

92. Lee, 65.

93. Lee, 65.

94. Lee even lauds "theosophy and Christian Science" as contemporary intellectual movements attesting to the culture's growing awareness of spirit's power over matter. See Lee, 68.

95. Lindsay, *Art*, 249. While "New Jerusalem" is, of course, a conventional and widely used term in Protestant millennialist discourse, it also has a crucial, more specific usage in Swedenborgian theology, where it acts a synonym for "New Church." See Leach, *Land of Desire*, 4.

96. Lindsay, *Art*, 248.

97. Ellwood, *Alternative Altars*, 89.

CHAPTER 3 — "THE MOTION PICTURE IS WAR'S GREATEST ANTIDOTE"

1. Gerald Stanley Lee, *We: A Confession of Faith for the American People during and after the War* (New York: Doubleday, Page, 1916), 120.

2. Robert Edgar Long, *David Wark Griffith: A Brief Sketch of His Career* (New York: D. W. Griffith Service, 1920), 86–87.

3. The film's working title had been *He Who Returned*. Note that although Ince was the head of the studio and the producer of the film, he collaborated with several other directors in making it. See Kevin Brownlow, *The War, the West, and the Wilderness* (New York: Knopf, 1979), 72–73. See also "Ince Completes a World Drama," *Photoplay* 9, no. 6 (May 1916), 32.

4. According to Terry Ramsaye, Wilson's campaign team saw *Civilization* as helping their candidate win reelection in November 1916 by giving "pictorial meaning" to his "slogan 'He Kept Us out of the War.'" Ramsaye, *A Million and One Nights: A History of the Motion Picture*, vol. 2 (New York: Simon and Schuster, 1926), 728. According to Lary May and William Drew, Griffith, who was broadly allied with Wilson's political agenda, sought to influence the election in the president's favor, timing the release of *Intolerance* accordingly. May, *Screening Out the Past: The Birth of Mass Culture and the Motion Picture Industry* (Chicago: University of Chicago Press, 1980), 84; Drew, *D. W. Griffith's* Intolerance*: Its Genesis and Its Vision* (Jefferson, N.C.: McFarland, 1986), 107; and Andrew Kelly, *Cinema and the Great War* (London: Routledge, 1997), 15, 19, 21.

As Drew and Brownlow indicate, the standard critical verdict on both films is that they were box office disappointments because their pacifist messages were ultimately out of step with the times. The argument goes that public support for neutrality was waning by the time they were released and that, once prowar sentiment became dominant, the films were rejected by audiences. Brownlow doubts this argument, pointing to the case of another pacifist film that did big box office business (70). Drew suggests that it conflicts with the narrative about the films' initial impact on the election. He asks, Does it make sense to say that "the pacifist elements that ultimately contributed to [*Intolerance*'s] commercial failure may have been responsible for its initial success" (123)? To resolve this question, what constitutes success or failure would have to be much more clearly defined, while the timing of the presumed dramatic shift in public sentiment would have to be pinpointed.

5. Kelly, *Cinema*, 22.

6. Quotation from the series of intertitles that open *Civilization*, serving as a sort of textual prologue.

7. Quotation from *Intolerance*'s first intertitle.

8. To be clear, *Civilization* never mentions "the Great War"; the conflict in the film is fictional (Wredpryd's enemies are never named), and no particular setting (geographical or in time) is specified. Nonetheless, the references are easy enough to decipher. Scenes depicting trench and submarine warfare give the conflict a contemporary feel, while the King of Wredpryd's "Prussian helmet" clearly aligns him with modern Germany. Brian Taves, *Thomas Ince: Hollywood's Independent Pioneer* (Lexington: University Press of Kentucky, 2014), 98. I disagree with Brownlow's claim that the battle scenes suggested a more antiquated setting, 71.

9. Given the sheer length and complexity of *Intolerance*—which is also, to be fair, the more familiar film—I refrain from offering any kind of plot synopsis here. Perhaps the most succinct general overview of *Intolerance*'s narrative comes in a program distributed during the film's first run at the Liberty Theatre in New York and reprinted in Long, *David Wark Griffith*, 74, 76. The program describes *Intolerance* as "One Theme Told in Four Separate Stories. Paralleling Side by Side" and divides the lengthy list of "principal characters" according to the stories in which they feature, as determined by setting. Characters are said to be "Of the Modern [American] Story," "Of the Judean Story. (27 A. D.)," "Of the Medieval Story. (1572 A. D.)," or "Of the Babylonian Story. (539 B. C.)"; the order of the list follows the sequence in which the stories are first introduced in the film.

The list begins, however, with the category "Of All Ages," containing a single character, "The Woman Who Rocks the Cradle." Apparently encompassing all the other categories, this first item complicates the idea of separate stories "Paralleling Side by Side." "The Woman Who Rocks the Cradle" (Lillian Gish) is not only a character but also a structuring element of the narrative. Under her entry on the dramatis personae, the program reads, "The Rocking Cradle also marks the change from one story to another," and, even before this, makes a vague reference to "A Golden Thread [That] Binds the Four Stories" in the form of "A Fairy Girl . . . Her Hand on the Cradle of Humanity—Eternally Rocking."

10. The term "leitmotif" comes from Christian Metz, *Language and Cinema*, trans. Donna Jean Umiker-Sebeok (The Hague: Mouton, 1974), 109. Although the cradle appears to contain flowers in at least one of the earlier appearances of this motif, the visual emphasis on this detail appears significant here. On the variations in these shots, see Miriam Hansen, *Babel and Babylon: Spectatorship in American Silent Film* (Cambridge, Mass.: Harvard University Press, 1991), 199, 206–207, 211–212.

11. Lee, *We*, 10.

12. Fenwicke L. Holmes, *The Law of Mind in Action: Daily Lessons and Treatments in Mental and Spiritual Science* (New York: Robert M. McBride, 1919), 56 (emphasis in original).

13. Holmes, 56. The rejection of the matter/spirit divide is part and parcel of mental science's monistic view of creation: the human mind is fully participant in the "Divine Will" or "Cosmic Mind," which is, by definition, *creative*.

14. Holmes, 56–57.

15. Lee, *We*, xiii.

16. Lee, 10.

17. Lee, 10.

18. Granville Stanley Hall, *Morale: The Supreme Standard of Life and Conduct* (New York: D. Appleton, 1920), 2–3. I discuss Hall's work further in chapter 4.

19. William James, "A Moral Equivalent for War," quoted in Lippmann, *A Preface to Politics* (New York: Mitchell Kennerley, 1913), 47–49.

20. Lippmann, 47–49. The word "tabooing" is Lippmann's, from *Preface*, 49.

21. Forcey, *Crossroads of Liberalism*, 270–271; and Hofstadter, *The Age of Reform* (New York: Vintage, 1955), 272–282.

22. See Lee, "Superadvertising," *Saturday Evening Post*, September 28, 1918, 3–4, 71, 74, 77.

23. Brownlow, *War*, 144.

24. Lee, *We*, 89.

25. W. Stephen Bush's review of the film in *Motion Picture World* refers to the film as a "sermon": "No stronger appeal on behalf of suffering humanity has ever been made in words or pictures." W. Stephen Bush, "Civilization," *Moving Picture World* June 17, 1916, 2056.

26. Lee, *We*, xiv (emphasis added).

27. I add the qualifier "mind's-eye" perspective here because, although Lee is talking about seeing, his concept of knowing being fundamentally visual, what he ultimately wants the reader to "picture" is finally bigger than anything that could be conceivably be captured in a physical image. See my discussion of Lee in relation to Heidegger's idea of the "world picture" in chapter 1.

28. "Manifest intention" as Hansen's helpful phrase, *Babel and Babylon*, 136.

29. This paradox—and the sense of reversal that occurs at the end of the film—is crucial to my reading of *Intolerance*. Brownlow is correct to state that the film "assault[s]" its audience with three hours of "graphic illustration[s]" of "man's inhumanity to man," in a way that makes a more pessimistic conclusion seem plausible and warranted (77). I argue, however, that there is sufficient textual evidence in the film to reconstruct Griffith's esoteric project of world-picture formation (as spelled out in his published remarks about the film).

30. Lesley Brill, *Crowds, Power, and Transformation in Cinema* (Detroit: Wayne State University Press, 2006), 51.

31. Brill, 50–51. Brill argues that the film's Jesus "not only represents but incorporates humankind," acting "as an inclusive crowd in himself." He sees the film's representation of the "Man of Men" as linked to its positive depictions of the multitudes shown throughout, especially the festive crowds that appear in the film's coda. I appreciate Brill's attention to the film's optimistic coda, which other contemporary critics overlook, and find his emphasis on the utopian view of crowds in the film to be productive. As interesting as Brill's reading is, though, the film does not provide sufficient evidence to substantiate it. In my reading, the Jesus character is displaced by other unifying figures or "containers."

32. Brill, 51.

33. As I stress in this chapter, the film's particular emphasis on the uplift campaigners' opposition to popular amusements (like dancing in saloons) stems from Griffith's rage over efforts by intellectuals, clergy, and other civic leaders to censor or suppress his virulently racist *The Birth of a Nation*. In the wake of the crisis surrounding the exhibition of the earlier film, Griffith conceives of film censors and advocates for limits on cinematic expression as the ultimate agents of "intolerance" and the exemplars of misguided efforts at "uplift"; cinema is, for Griffith, the ultimate (and maybe only viable) tool of social reformation. Griffith's hostility toward censorship proponents is one crucial determinant of the film's broad indictment of Progressive reform movements. In addition to being overdetermined, this indictment, it must be noted, verges on the incoherent. *Intolerance*'s viewer learns little about how the reformers in the film justify their actions publicly or about the exact targets of their campaign. They seem initially to be temperance advocates but eventually establish a foundation that (utterly implausibly) allows them to meddle freely in the individual lives of slum-dwellers; hence their forcible seizure of the Dear One's baby.

34. The reformers, thus, align with the Pharisees in the Judean narrative, the Priest of Bel in the Babylonian narrative, and Catherine de Medici and her allies in the medieval French narrative.

35. Long, *David Wark Griffith*, 77.

36. Long, 77. The phrase "uniter of here and hereafter," which the speaker of the poem offers as a self-description, is totally decontextualized here and in the film. In Long's account, "here and hereafter" gets translated as "present [and] past" and seems to lose its otherworldly dimension. The film, which is certainly interested in the relationship between worldly existence and eternity, preserves this dimension but does not make clear in what precise sense the cradle acts as a "uniter." As I argue in what follows, this quotation serves mainly to introduce a generic idea of uniting into the diegesis, which can then be attached to other moving containers that are introduced later on.

37. Long, 77.

38. See here Hansen's discussion of the symbolism of the "three fates" in some of the cradle shots, in the representation of the "vestal virgins of Uplift," and in Griffith's pamphlet decrying film censorship. Hansen, *Babel and Babylon*, 206–212.

39. Hansen, 183. The film describes Cuneiform as "a universal written language . . . [that] was made to become an unknown cypher on the face of the earth," evoking a tradition of scriptural interpretation that equated Babylon with the Tower of Babel. As Hansen points out, the film's costuming plays up this association, by having Belshazzar and the Priest of Bel wear hats that recall conventional artistic representations of the tower. Through this and various architectural details in the film, the civilization that they oversee (up until the Priest's treasonous collusion with Cyrus) becomes associated with the dream encapsulated in Babel—coming into contact with divinity—which here is figured positively rather than as an instance of human folly.

40. Julian Smith, "A Runaway Match: The Automobile in the American Film, 1909–1920," in *The Automobile and American Culture*, ed. David Lanier Lewis and Laurence Goldstein (Ann Arbor: University of Michigan Press, 1983), 188.

41. Smith, 188.

42. Smith, 188.

43. Smith, 188 (emphasis in original).

44. Smith, 187–188.

45. Smith, 189.

46. It is significant in this connection that the racing car finally succeeds in catching up to and stopping the train: it benefits from the fact that its driver is not restricted to a predetermined track and can improvise routes.

47. Francesco Casetti, *Eye of Modernity: Cinema, Experience, Modernity*, trans. Erin Larkin and Jennifer Pranolo (New York: Columbia University Press, 2008), 118.

48. Hansen, *Babel and Babylon*, 169–170.

49. Casetti, *Eye of Modernity*, 117.

50. Casetti, 117.

51. Casetti, 118.

52. The phrase "golden thread" is from Ramsaye, *Million and One Nights*, 758.

53. Casetti, *Eye of Modernity*, 117.

54. James Doolittle, *The Romance of the Automobile Industry* (New York: Klebold Press, 1916), quoted in Smith, "Runaway Match," 188.

55. Remarkably, there exists an Internet Movie Cars Database (http://www.imcdb.org/movie.php?id=6864), which has proved most helpful in identifying the makes of cars appearing in the film.

56. Vachel Lindsay, *The Progress and Poetry of the Movies*, ed. Myron Lounsbury (Lanham, Md.: Scarecrow, 1995), 235.

57. For more on Lindsay's ideas about speed and on his relationship to Münsterberg's work, refer to the previous chapter.

58. Hugo Münsterberg, *The Photoplay: A Psychological Study* (New York: D. Appleton, 1916), quoted in Casetti, *Eye of Modernity*, 119.

59. This recontainment is crucial because, as Casetti stresses, acceleration, however thrilling, can also be frightening. "Speed . . . has something ambiguous about it," he writes, connoting liberation and pleasure on the one hand and danger and loss of control on the other. As he and Smith point out, the flip side of the utopian discourse around automobiles in the 1920s was a pervasive anxiety about the carnage caused by car wrecks. Thus *Intolerance*'s viewer might initially feel herself headed inexorably toward some type of calamity. It is only the encompassing gaze of the film, the evident "ubiquity" of what Casetti calls the "cinema-eye," that allows the viewer to experience such headlong acceleration without fear: the "film eye is able to deal with speed" because it stays "a step ahead of things," leaving the viewer comfortable in the foreknowledge that he will remain unharmed by whatever is about to happen. See Casetti, *Eye of Modernity*, 118–120. See also Smith, "Runaway Match," 189.

60. Louis Weinberg, "Motion Pictures as a Social Force," *Current History* 22, no. 1 (April 1925): 92.

61. Weinberg, 92.

62. Program reprinted in Long, *David Wark Griffith*, 76.

63. Long, 85. See also Lewis Jacobs, *The Rise of American Film: A Critical History* (New York: Harcourt, Brace, 1939), 192; and Gregory Bush, "Like 'A Drop of Water in the Stream of Life': Images of Mass Man from Griffith to Vidor," *Journal of American Studies* 25, no. 2 (1991): 220. The rhetoric of the "mighty river" recalls Weinberg's idea of "carrying power," that phrase—which he uses a measurement of the historical efficacy of different art forms—seems apt, "carry" being long used to refer specifically to the work that different channels (natural or man-made) do in moving water. See *Oxford English Dictionary*, 2nd ed., s.v. "carry" and "carrying capacity."

64. Jeffrey T. Schnapp, "Mob Porn," in *Crowds*, ed. Schnapp and Matthew Tiews (Stanford: Stanford University Press, 2006), 3–4.

65. Hansen, *Babel and Babylon*, 330n16. The verse cited here is from the King James Version.

66. Brill, *Crowds*, 41.

67. Brill, 41.

68. Long, *David Wark Griffith*, 83.

69. Lee, *We*, xiii. Lest this connection seem forced, note that Lee explicitly identifies the "real war" as the war going on in the minds of the actual war's "spectators." In other words, there is much more at stake for Lee in the internal conflict of civilians trying to decide whether the World War signifies that humanity is essentially bad or good than in the actual life and death of the "few million men [fighting] in Europe."

70. D. W. Griffith, *The Rise and Fall of Free Speech in America* (Los Angeles: self-published, 1916), 1 of 56 unnumbered pages. Melvyn Stokes notes that, in the months following the release of *Birth*, Griffith would style himself as "perhaps the leading publicist for the motion picture industry in the struggle against censorship." Stokes, *D. W. Griffith's* The Birth of a Nation*: A History of "The Most Controversial Film of All Time"* (Oxford: Oxford University Press, 2007), 133. As Stokes's thoroughly researched chapter illustrates, *Birth* came under immediate scrutiny from the National Board of Censorship (NBC) and the National Association for the Advancement of Colored People (NAACP) because of its vicious portrayals of African Americans. Believing that the film would, as the organization's Los Angeles branch put it, "palliate and excuse the lynchings and other deeds of violence committed against the Negro," the NAACP encouraged the NBC to call for the film's outright suppression, or at least for the removal of the most racially prejudicial scenes (quoted in Stokes, 130). Although the NBC was ultimately not supportive of this effort, the NAACP continued to protest showings of the film and—in cities like New York, Boston, and Chicago, where it had large chapters—to lobby local censors in cities to cut certain scenes (such as the infamous "Gus chase" scene). While the success of these efforts was mixed, they prompted a swift counteroffensive from Griffith and his supporters, in which the director began, melodramatically, to style *himself* as the victim of oppression.

71. Long, *David Wark Griffith*, 83.

72. Griffith, *Rise and Fall*, 2 of 56 unnumbered pages.

73. Griffith, 2 of 56 unnumbered pages.

74. Griffith, 2 of 56 unnumbered pages. Recall here Lee's construction of the inducement of boredom as a modern sin, which I discussed in chapter 1. Gregory Bush's work is helpful in contextualizing this discourse: the notion of inspiring the public as a duty of leaders (economic, civic, political) coincides with the rise of public relations as a profession during and after World War I. See his comments on public relations pioneers Edward Bernays and J. Walter Thompson in *Lord of Attention: Gerald Stanley Lee and the Crowd Metaphor in Modern America* (Amherst: University of Massachusetts Press, 1991), 223–224. See also my discussion of Douglas Fairbanks's motivational writings in chapter 5.

75. Griffith, *Rise and Fall*, 2 of 56 unnumbered pages.

76. The first three of these quotations are from remarks attributed to Griffith by Lillian Gish in her memoir, written with Ann Pinchot, *The Movies, Mr. Griffith, and Me* (San Francisco: Mercury House, 1969), 130, 358. The reference to "the millennium" comes in a tribute letter that Gish wrote to Griffith following Griffith's death in 1948.

77. Griffith, "Pictures vs. One-Night Stands," *Independent*, December 11, 1916, 47–48, excerpted in *Focus on D. W. Griffith*, ed. Harry M. Geduld (Englewood Cliffs, N.J.: Prentice-Hall, 1971), 48.

78. Griffith, *Rise and Fall*, 13 of 56 unnumbered pages.

79. Griffith, 19 of 56 unnumbered pages.

80. Hansen, *Babel and Babylon*, 135.

81. Metz, *Language and Cinema*, 95–96, 109–110. Gilles Deleuze's discussion of the film does much the same thing; see *Cinema 1: The Movement-Image*, trans. Hugh Tomlinson and Barbara Habberjam (London: Athlone, 1986), 149.

82. Hansen, *Babel and Babylon*, 135.

83. Hansen, 134, 136. See Metz, *Language and Cinema*, 78.

84. Hansen, *Babel and Babylon*, 140.

85. For example, Julian Johnson's review complained that the effort required to "assimilate the mountainous lore" of the film caused "mental exhaustion" in the viewer; he also preferred the Babylonian section to the others, going so far as to call the modern section "dull, commonplace movie melodrama." Johnson, "The Shadow Screen," *Photoplay* 9, no. 1 (December 1916): 78, 80.

86. Hansen, *Babel and Babylon*, 4.

87. Hansen, 141–144.

88. Hansen, 140.

89. Hansen, 171. Hansen traces this response through early reviews of the film and the example that I use here, Keaton's *The Three Ages* (see 339n22).

90. Long, *David Wark Griffith*, 86.

91. Long, 85–86.

92. Long, 86.

93. Long, 86.

94. Long's anecdote reads like a variation on an image that appeared in a lengthy trade-magazine report on the film, published before its release. One of the many full-page production stills accompanying Henry Stephen Gordon's glowing "The Real Story of 'Intolerance'" shows the walls of Babylon set during the shooting of one of the siege scenes. The caption draws the viewer's attention to an automobile in the photo: "the intrepid Ford, right at home in the domain so soon to be won by Kaiser Cyrus." By calling Cyrus (the leader of the invading army that destroys the Babylonian civilization) "Kaiser," the writer connects him with the German emperor and, thereby, draws a subtle connection between the historical event being re-created in the film and the contemporary World War. Anticipating Long's anecdote, the image and caption humorously frame the obvious anachronism here, making it seem apt rather than inappropriate, pointing toward the film's efforts to evoke transhistorical connections. Gordon, "The Real Story of 'Intolerance,'" *Photoplay* 10, no. 6 (November 1916), 38–39.

95. Hansen, *Babel and Babylon*, 171.

96. J. Edwin Hartill, *Principles of Biblical Hermeneutics* (Grand Rapids, Mich.: Zondervan, 1947), 14, 117. See also John J. Davis, *Biblical Numerology* (Winona Lake, Ind.: Baker Publishing Group, 1968), 122.

97. E. W. Bullinger, *Number in Scripture* (1894; repr., New York: Cosimo, 2005), 2003. Definition of "gematria" comes from Davis, 126.

98. Lee, "The Two-Inch Pipe Line to Europe," *Saturday Evening Post*, April 5, 1919, 131.

99. Lee, 131.

100. Drew, *D. W. Griffith's* Intolerance, 106–107. See also Scott Curtis, "Douglas Fairbanks: Icon of Americanism," in *Flickers of Desire: Movie Stars of the 1910s*, ed. Jennifer Bean (New Brunswick, N.J.: Rutgers University Press, 2011), 237–238.

101. Lee, "Two-Inch," 127, 131.

102. Lee, 131.

103. Lee, "Spineless Leagues and Faceless Nations," *Saturday Evening Post*, March 22, 1919, 151, 155, 159.

104. Lee, 155.

105. Will Hays, "Motion Pictures and Their Censors," *American Review of Reviews* 75 (March 1927): 398.

CHAPTER 4 — "EVERYTHING WOOED EVERYTHING"

1. Hughes, quoted in "Movie Men Favor a Federal Censor," *New York Times*, February 5, 1922, 25, 27. See also "Authors Oppose a Censor," *New York Times*, April 7, 1921, 20; "Brought into Focus," *New York Times*, April 17, 1921, 75; and James O. Kemm, *Rupert Hughes: A Hollywood Legend* (Beverley Hills, Cal.: Pomegranate, 1997), 108–109. Hughes's primary target was Ellis Paxson Oberholtzer, head of the Pennsylvania state censor board and author of *The Morals of the Movie* (Philadelphia: Penn, 1922).

2. Kemm, 108. See also Raymond Moley, *The Hays Office* (Indianapolis: Bobbs-Merrill, 1945), 30–31. On the history of NAMPI, see Richard Koszarski, *An Evening's Entertainment: The Age of the Silent Feature Picture, 1915–1928*, History of the American Cinema, vol. 3 (New York: Charles Scriber's Sons, 1990), 205–206.

3. All following references will be to the hardcover edition of *Souls for Sale* (New York: Harper & Brothers, 1922).

4. On the Arbuckle and Reid affairs and the subsequent redefinition of the film star in terms of scandal in the early 1920s, see Richard deCordova, *Picture Personalities: The Emergence of the Star System* (Urbana: University of Illinois Press, 1990), 117–147. For a bibliography of early 1920s novels about young women succeeding in the Hollywood film industry, see Hilary A. Hallett, *Go West, Young Women! The Rise of Early Hollywood* (Berkeley: University of California Press, 2013), 231n15.

5. Kemm, *Rupert Hughes*, 135. The MPPDA followed NAMPI, the studio system's initial (and failed) attempt at rehabilitating its public image. See Ruth Vasey, *The World According to Hollywood, 1918–1939* (Madison: University of Wisconsin Press, 1997), 30–38.

6. Rupert Hughes, *Souls for Sale* (New York: Harper & Brothers, 1922), 4, 166, 377, 385. I have chosen to focus on the novel rather than the film because the latter lacks the former's utopian-universalist perspective. A fairly conventional melodrama about the rise of a young woman to Hollywood stardom, the *Souls for Sale* film does advertise on behalf of the film industry and Los Angeles at large by portraying the movie colony as a place inhabited by ordinary, sober, hardworking people, who happen to be especially glamorous. It also features the kinds of cameos by famous actors and scenes detailing the moviemaking process familiar from other 1920s star-making films (like King Vidor's *Show People* [MGM, 1928]), as well as MGM's own nonfiction *1925 Studio Tour* short film. At one point, the *Souls for Sale* film does tacitly represent cinema as a globe-spanning medium, though not a universal language: a scene set in Cairo, Egypt (which has no counterpart in the novel), shows a theatrical audience watching an MGM film with simultaneously projected Arabic and French intertitles. Beyond this one moment, however, the film, does not venture into any kind of philosophical reflection on the nature of the medium.

7. While Hughes's fiction and drama had begun to be adapted for the screen as early as 1914, he began working in Hollywood, first as a screenwriter and later as a director, in 1919, following the conclusion of his military service. Kemm, *Rupert Hughes*, 66–67, 94–97. Kevin Brownlow uses the term "tribute" to describe Hughes's program comments, which are reprinted in his *Hollywood: The Pioneers* (New York: Knopf, 1979), 64–65. On Griffith's efforts to preempt the censorship of *Birth*, see Melvyn Stokes, *D. W. Griffith's* The Birth of a Nation*: A History of "The Most Controversial Film of All Time"* (Oxford: Oxford University Press, 2007), 129–170.

8. Hughes, quoted in Brownlow, 64–65.

9. Kemm, *Rupert Hughes*, 93.

10. Hughes, "Brought into Focus," 75. See also Hughes, "Movie Men," 25; and Hughes, *Souls for Sale*, 294. Hughes's novel had also been the subject of a short-lived "censorship" controversy in New York City. Under the headline "Censorship at Its Very Worst," a *Times* editorialist alleged that a patron of one of the public libraries had been told that the institution would not purchase the book for circulation, due, ostensibly, to its graphic depictions of sexual violence by German soldiers against women in occupied Belgium; the director of the New York Public Library promptly denied this allegation and made clear that copies of the novel had been purchased and would be available in its various branches. See Kemm, *Rupert Hughes*, 186–187; "Topics of the Times," *New York Times*, September 3, 1918, 10; and E. H. Anderson, letter to the editor, *New York Times*, September 4, 1918, 10.

Oberholtzer's *The Morals of the Movies* reprints the full text of Pennsylvania's censorship law, passed in 1915. One of "Standards" listed in the law reads, "Prenatal and childbed scenes, and subtitles describing them, will be disapproved" (212). On the Pennsylvania board during this period, see Koszarski, *Evening's Entertainment*, 202.

11. Hughes, "Seeing Things: The Macinery of Miracles," *Pearson's Magazine*, January 1, 1909, 188–197. See also Hughes, "Rupert Hughes Derides 'Proof' of Spiritualists," *Sunday Oregonian*, September 14, 1919, 2; and Kemm, *Rupert Hughes*, 105.

12. Hughes, "No," *New York Times*, October 17, 1920, 26, 33. Hughes's negative piece appeared as part of a forum responding to the question "Will the League Stop Wars?" with Raymond Fosdick arguing the affirmative case in "Yes," *New York Times*, October 17, 1920, 26, 32.

13. Hughes, "No," 26 (emphasis added).

14. Hughes, *Souls*, 1–2.

15. Hughes, 9–10.

16. Hughes, 9–10.

17. Hughes, 9–10.

18. Hughes, 6, 15.

19. Hughes, 15.

20. Hughes, 15.

21. Hughes, 48–49. By opening the novel with the drama of the unmarried couple conceiving a child—and by suggesting that the ignorance of reproductive biology enforced on them by their repressive society is in part to blame—Hughes is clearly thumbing his nose at Oberholtzer. It is interesting to note that the film adaptation of *Souls for Sale* eliminates the relationship between Mem and Elwood as well as the maternity plot; clearly Hughes the screenwriter and director had to concede that he could not deal as frankly with some types of material as could Hughes the novelist. The film version essentially replaces the story of Mem's pregnancy out of wedlock with the story of her marriage to a man who turns out to be a notorious "Bluebeard" named Owen Scudder (Lew Cody). The film begins with Mem (Eleanor Boardman) and Scudder's honeymoon train journey to Los Angeles. During the journey, Mem has an ominous feeling and, taking advantage of a stop, flees from the train. What she must conceal, in this version, is the fact that she has been married; Scudder reemerges once she has become famous and attempts to blackmail her but is eventually caught by the police.

22. Hughes, 91. The quoted passage lists a number of examples of "enforced morality" campaigns. On the economic hardships faced by the studios during the postwar recession, see Hughes, 369–370; and Koszarski, *Evening's Entertainment*, 203–204.

23. Hughes, *Souls*, 6.

24. Hughes, 20.

25. Hughes's move here recalls some of the more eccentric rhetoric that Griffith uses in his "free speech" pamphlet, such as his grim predictions of "functionaries" appointed by politicians to enforce personal "prejudices" and "whims." He imagines a "censor who is vegetarian forcing the people of his city to abstain from meat" and similar scenarios involving the "censorship" of coffee and tobacco. D. W. Griffith, *The Rise and Fall of Free Speech in America* (Los Angeles: self-published, 1916), 55 of 56 unnumbered pages.

26. Hughes, *Souls*, 8.

27. Hughes, 30.

28. Hughes, 8.

29. Hughes, 8.

30. Ralph Waldo Emerson, "Self-Reliance," in *The Essential Writings of Ralph Waldo Emerson*, ed. Brooks Atkinson (New York: Modern Library, 2000), 135.

31. Hughes, *Souls*, 175–176.

32. Hughes, 177.

33. Hughes, 175.

34. Hughes, 178.

35. Hughes, 178, 180.

36. Underlining the themes of patterning and variation, Hughes describes Mem as beginning to perceive the "artistic beauties of the pictures" at a purely abstract level: "She loved sunsets and moon dawns and light on leaves and the textures of fabrics embracing shadows in their folds. She loved the war of gloom and glow. She found the pictures overwhelmingly beautiful to her eyes, kaleidoscopes of leaping masses and lines, symphonic tempests of shape and color" (*Souls*, 178).

37. Gerald Stanley Lee, *We: A Confession of Faith for the American People during and after the War* (New York: Doubleday, Page, 1916), 158.

38. *Intolerance* Program, quoted in Robert Edgar Long, *David Wark Griffith: A Brief Sketch of His Career* (New York: D. W. Griffith Service, 1920), 83.

39. Just after the initial conversation about elopement, Mem and Dr. Bretherick learn that Elwood has been run over by a car and fatally injured. Mem then decides to flee the town alone, hoping to establish a new life for herself (and eventually her child) in the Southwest. She does so in consultation with Dr. Bretherick, who conceives of his and Mem's planning process as a matter of writing a "continuity" for the screen. He likewise counsels her to consider film acting as a means of employment. Mem's way to moving to Los Angeles and attempting a career in the movies is cleared by her eventual miscarriage: one day, shortly after her arrival in the Southwest, Mem goes for a hike, slips, and falls over a cliff; in the process, she injures herself and loses her baby.

40. Hughes, *Souls*, 398.

41. Hughes, 398. This conversation occurs after Mem has returned to her hometown as part of a studio-financed promotional tour for her latest film.

42. Hughes, 17.

43. Hughes, 178.

44. Hughes, 172.

45. Hughes, 172–173.

46. Hughes, 173.

47. Hughes, 172–173.

48. Hughes, 173.

49. Hughes, 173.

50. Hallett's work is helpful in seeing Hughes's positive portrayal of a Los Angeles–specific culture as an instance of "Hollywood Bohemia," one of the two "competing stories about . . . the [film] industry's postwar transformation influenced" American life. The other "story," "The Movie Menace," is, of course, the one promoted by Rev. Steddon. See Hallett, *Go West*, 103.

51. Hughes, *Souls*, 168–169.

52. Hughes, 168–169.

53. Hughes, 319.

54. Hughes, 36.

55. Hughes, 15, 110.

56. Hughes, 2.

57. Eccles. 1:9, King James Version.

58. Hughes, *Souls*, 54.

59. Hughes, 53–54.

60. Hughes, 53–54.

61. Hughes, 54.

62. Hughes, 54. On the novel's collapse of the idea of the copy and the original and on its celebration of impersonal, exchange-based relationships, see Michael North, *Reading 1922: A Return to the Scene of the Modern* (New York: Oxford University Press, 1999), 158–159.

63. Hughes, *Souls*, 54.

64. Lee, *We*, 308.

65. Hughes, *Souls*, 185.

66. Hughes, 35.

67. Hughes, 35.

68. For other uses of invisible communications tropes to describe the workings of cinema, see Hughes, 296.

69. Hughes, 185, 244.

70. Hughes, 35, 405.

71. Hughes, 47, 235.

72. Hughes, 235.

73. Hughes, 235.

74. Hughes, 235.

75. See, for example, William E. Smythe, *The Conquest of Arid America*, rev. ed. (New York: Macmillan, 1911). See also Kevin Starr, *Inventing the Dream: California through the Progressive Era* (New York: Oxford University Press, 1985), 12.

76. Hallet, *Go West*, 218.

77. Hughes, *Souls*, 42–43.

78. Hughes, 196.

79. Hallett, *Go West*, 16, 218. Given the title of Hallett's study (and her general characterization of Hollywood as "frontier"), it is surprising that her discussion of *Souls* is so brief and does not mention the scene in the novel when Dr. Bretherick advises Mem to seek her fortunes in California. He borrows and revises Horace Greely's fabled statement, exhorting her, "Go West, young woman, and go up in the world!" Hughes, *Souls*, 43. The only period usage of the Greely quotation as addressed to a woman that Hallett cites (the source of the title of her book) comes from a 1920 Louella Parson's profile of Josephine Quirk. See Hallett, *Go West*, 99.

80. Laura Mulvey, "Visual Pleasure and Narrative Cinema," in *Film Theory and Criticism*, ed. Leo Braudy and Marshall Cohen, 7th ed. (New York: Oxford University Press, 2009), 715.

81. Hughes, *Souls*, 376.

82. Hughes, 376.

83. Richard Dyer, *White* (London: Routledge, 1997), 2.

84. At one point, Mem encounters Holby on set, "painted like an Indian brave." Hughes, *Souls*, 295. On the history of redface performance in Hollywood, see Michelle Raheja, *Reservation Reelism: Redfacing, Visual Sovereignty, and Representations of Native Americans in Film* (Lincoln: University of Nebraska Press, 2010), 71–72.

85. Hughes, *Souls*, 107. Yuma sits on Quechan tribal land and takes its name from Yuman, the name of the language family to which Quechan belongs (and the name frequently but mistakenly given to the Quechan people). Since 1884, the Quechan Tribe has been based on the Fort Yuma Reservation, which sits to the north of the city on the lower Colorado River and stretches roughly seventy miles west into California. See Jack D. Forbes, *Warriors of the Colorado: The Yumas of the Quechan Nation and Their Neighbors*

(Norman: University of Oklahoma Press, 1965), ix–xi; and Robert L. Bee, "Quechan," in *Handbook of North American Indians*, vol. 10, *Southwest, 1983*, ed. Alfonso Ortiz (Washington, D.C.: Smithsonian Institution, 1983), 86–98.

86. Hughes, *Souls*, 107.

87. Hughes, 109.

88. Hughes, 107.

89. Hughes, 107. Mem's perspective throughout this section of the novel exemplifies the paradox that Renato Rosaldo has labeled "imperialist nostalgia": "Someone deliberately alters a form of life and then regrets that things have not remained as they were prior to their intervention." Renato Rosaldo, *Culture and Truth: The Remaking of Social Analysis* (Boston: Beacon, 1989), 70. Confronted with contemporary American Indians, Mem finds herself trying to locate them in relation to various Romantic racialist clichés that she has internalized, and yet at no point does she recognize her membership in the social group that has, historically, fostered the cultural changes that she seeks to comprehend. As Raheja explains, imperialist nostalgia is "a strategy of ameliorating guilt," which mystifies colonial history, allowing what has been lost to be mourned in a putatively innocent way, 32.

90. Hughes, *Souls*, 109. The passage reads, "The Indians . . . laughed at the low comedy and sighed at the low pathos. They could read the first universal language, and romance was warming their dreary lives."

91. Hughes, 109.

92. Hughes, 109–110.

93. To judge this presence "anomalous" is to reinforce the dominant cultural "expectation" that Indigenous people are alien to the category of modernity. Deloria, *Indians in Unexpected Places* (Lawrence: University Presses of Kansas, 2004), 4–7.

94. Hughes, *Souls*, 109.

95. It seems highly plausible that movie theaters (and other spaces of commercial leisure) in the American Southwest would have maintained racial segregation policies in the early 1920s. I have not, however, located any scholarship that deals specifically with this context. Christopher McKenna's work on "tri-racial segregation" in movie theaters in Robeson County, North Carolina, has been helpful to my thinking about the pertinent questions here but highlights the tremendous regional specificity of segregation practices. See McKenna, "Tri-racial Theaters in Robeson County, North Carolina, 1896–1940," in *Going to the Movies: Hollywood and the Social Experience of Cinema*, ed. Richard Maltby, Melvyn Stokes, and Robert C. Allen (Exeter, U.K.: University of Exeter Press, 2007), 45–59. My thanks to Chad Allen for his guidance in reading this scene in *Souls for Sale*.

96. Hughes, *Souls*, 2. This type of ethnographic catalog is a rhetorical commonplace in the utopian-universalist discourse on cinema. For comparable examples, see John Amid,

With the Movie Makers (Boston: Lothrop, Lee and Shepard, 1923), 156–157; and Will Hays, "Motion Pictures and Their Censors," *American Review of Reviews* 75 (March 1927): 398.

97. Hughes, *Souls*, 244. My language here draws on Warren Susman's classic account of the shift from "character" to "personality" as modern American ideals of "self-fashioning." Susman's most useful definition of personality in this discursive context comes from Henry Laurent's eponymous 1915 manual, *Personality, How to Build It*: "Personality is the quality of being Somebody," meaning the quality of being known or having fame. By contrast, character is a question of moral goodness. Laurent, quoted in Susman, "'Personality' and the Making of Twentieth-Century Culture," in *Culture as History: The Transformation of American Society in the Twentieth Century* (New York: Pantheon Books, 1974), 277.

98. Along with the Trading with the Enemy Act of 1917 and the Sedition Act of 1918, the Espionage Act was a crucial piece of legislation passed by the U.S. Congress following the country's entry into the war, which provided the government with broad authority to control speech and the flow of information about military affairs. Opponents of "outright censorship" like George Creel and Senator Henry Cabot Lodge successfully pushed to remove language (favored by President Woodrow Wilson) covering the activities of the press before the act's passage. Thus the act was widely greeted as "an antispy law, nothing more and nothing less," reserving a space for legitimate political dissent (in the press and elsewhere). Alan Axelrod, *Selling the Great War: The Making of American Propaganda* (New York: Palgrave Macmillan, 2009), 64, 71. And yet the text of the act explicitly prohibited and imposed penalties for an array of different kinds of "false reports or statements"—anything that might be construed as harming the United States' cause or aiding the enemy. Bolstered by subsequent amendments (which, together, would become the Sedition Act of 1918), the act gave the government broad powers censorship, allowing, for instance, the Post Office Department to suppress any "treasonous" material circulating the through the mail. And the Justice Department did prosecute thousands of cases under this law. Axelrod, 98; Robert Mann, "World War I: 'The Poison of Disloyalty,'" in *Wartime Dissent in America: A History and Anthology* (New York: Palgrave Macmillan, 2010), 72–73. Further, as historians like Axelrod have shown, the act "incorporated all of the authority necessary for controlling the news"; the fact that it was "silent on the mechanisms of enforcement . . . actually gave" Creel's CPI tremendous "implied power" (Axelrod, 97). Ostensibly a proponent of "persuasion" over "coercion," Creel established a "voluntary self-censorship" regime, whereby newspaper editors around the country understood that they needed to abide by his office's guidelines on acceptable reporting (Mann, 72; Axelrod, 86). Creel, further, was appointed by Wilson to sit on a censorship board that monitored "all messages that passed between the United States and any foreign country" (Axelrod, 72). These activities illustrate the extent to which Creel's public-relations-based approach—his vision of the CPI as an organization disseminating positive propaganda that would elicit patriotic sentiment—was always supplemented by the kinds of censorship that he overtly disavowed as being contrary to the American ethos.

99. Rupert Hughes, *Propaganda in Its Military and Legal Aspects* (Washington, D.C.: Military Intelligence Branch, Executive Division, General Staff, 1918), 1, https://archive.org/details/cu31924027889868. In 1935, Hughes published a four-part series of articles in the *American Legion Monthly* that reflect in his time military intelligence during World War I. The second installment in the series details Hughes's work on drafting *Propaganda in Its Military and Legal Aspects*. See "Memories of M.I.D. (Part 2)," *American Legion Monthly*, February 1935, 56. I accessed this article and the others from the series cited in this chapter through clippings contained in box 13, folder 20 of the Rupert Hughes Papers, USC Libraries Special Collections.

100. Hughes, *Propaganda*, 1.

101. Hughes, 2–4.

102. Hughes, 2–4.

103. Hughes, *Souls*, 1.

104. Hughes writes, "The motion picture offers [the enemy] a most inviting medium for propaganda. It appeals to a vast public, even to those who cannot read. In the course of a dramatic or melodramatic story, he can carry across to the audience the most dangerous message" (*Propaganda*, 96).

105. In his 1935 reflections, Hughes addresses the initial oddity of his being appointed to this post, given his vocal opposition of censorship. He describes how, despite his general opposition to censorship, he saw the exigency of certain forms of suppression during wartime, while trying, in specific cases, to resist the more excessively (and, in his view, irrationally) suppressive impulses of some of his colleagues. He eventually suggests that he was chosen for the job precisely because it was assumed he would wield his authority only reluctantly. See Hughes, "Memories of M.I.D." (Part 2), 50; and "Memories of M.I.D." (Conclusion), *American Legion Monthly*, April 1935, 22.

106. Hughes, *Souls*, 241–242, 246–248.

107. Hughes, 246–247.

108. Hughes, 247.

109. Hughes details his office's relationship to the CPI in "Memories of M.I.D." (Part 3), *American Legion Monthly*, March 1935, 64–65.

110. Needless to say, an obvious, deliberate intention to do harm (e.g., to weaken morale or provoke mutiny) counts as grounds for determining a representation to be "propaganda." The point here is that other purposes (e.g., to save lives or to promote class consciousness) are considered not to have any mitigating effect.

111. See Hughes, *Propaganda*, 146–147.

112. Goldstein was a costume supplier, who, after working with D. W. Griffith on the production of *The Birth of a Nation*, founded his own production company (Continental) to make historical epics. The film is now presumed lost. See Anthony Slide, *Robert Goldstein and "The Spirit of '76"* (Metuchen, N.J.: Scarecrow, 1993), xiii–xxiii.

113. See Slide, xvii, 91–94; and Hughes, *Propaganda*, 96. See also Axelrod, *Selling*, 156.

114. The quotation comes from Hughes's synopsis in *Propaganda*, 96. On the film's exhibition in Chicago and Los Angeles, see Slide, 56–67, 79–91.

115. The long and complicated story of Goldstein's subsequent trial, which was likely still in process at the time of Hughes's writing, is addressed in detail in Slide's monograph. Suffice it here to say here that Goldstein was eventually convicted and sentenced to serve ten years in federal prison, later had his sentence commuted, and was released after about three years.

116. Hughes, *Propaganda*, 96.

117. Judge Benjamin Bledsoe, quoted in Hughes, 98. The text of the ruling, dated November 30, 1917, also appears in Slide, *Robert Goldstein*, 207–211.

118. Bledsoe, quoted in Hughes, *Propaganda*, 98.

119. Bledsoe, quoted in Hughes, 98.

120. Bledsoe, quoted in Hughes, 97.

121. Hughes, 150.

122. Axelrod, *Selling*, 72.

123. Hughes, *Propaganda*, 150.

124. The senators discuss "propaganda" being spread by a range of "disloyal" parties, from "pan-Germanists" writing in German-language newspapers, to the members of the International Workers of the World and other "Bolshevik" groups, to Christian pacifists. It is worth noting here that, during the blacklist era, Hughes would style himself as "a fervent anticommunist," cofounding the conservative Motion Picture Alliance for the Preservation of American Ideals. See Larry Ceplair and Christopher Trumbo, *Dalton Trumbo: Blacklisted Hollywood Radical* (Lexington: University of Kentucky Press, 2015), 144–145.

125. "Cloak of protection" is a phrase used by Sen. Overman in his rebuttal to Sen. France. See Hughes, *Propaganda*, 164.

126. Hughes, 150.

127. Hughes, 171.

128. Department of Justice memorandum (dated April 25, 1918), reprinted in Hughes, 169.

129. Hughes, 169.

130. Hughes, 169.

131. Hughes, 170. Hughes alludes to these particular "propaganda" threats in his discussion of the circumstances surrounding his drafting of *Propaganda in Military and Legal Aspects*, in "Memories of M.I.D. (Part 2)," 56–57.

132. Hughes, *Propaganda*, 170.

133. See Hughes, 163.

134. I am allowing here for the habitual tendency of social and political groups—in this case, the Hollywood film industry—to reserve the term "propaganda" (with its sinister implications) for their opponents' efforts to persuade the broader public of the veracity of their opinion. The conventional usage of the term "propaganda," of course, allows for one to disavow the term relative to the representation of one's own opinion on the basis that this position is believed to be the truth. For more on the shifting connotations of the term, see note 170.

135. It is tempting to read Hughes's own use of utopian-universalist claims in his novel in light of this reasoning. Hughes may, indeed, not have believed that cinema had such lofty powers, and yet, he cannot be held guilty of propagandizing on behalf of the medium because his sole aim in parroting these claims is to boost morale. Moreover, he is insulated from criticism because the particular belief (authentically held or not) that he espouses—people deserve to be happy—is so general as to be uncontroversial.

136. Hughes, *Souls*, 91.

137. Hughes, 91.

138. Hughes, 90–91.

139. Hughes, 90.

140. Hughes, 92.

141. Granville Stanley Hall, *Morale: The Supreme Standard of Life and Conduct* (New York: D. Appleton, 1920).

142. Hall, 1, 20.

143. Hall, 20.

144. Hall, 22.

145. Hall, 21.

146. Hall, 21.

147. Hall, 2.

148. Note that one of Hall's examples of wartime morale boosting centers on American soldiers' viewing of comedic films starring Charlie Chaplin and Douglas Fairbanks, 72–73.

149. Dr. Bretherick uses the phrase "Truth with a capital T" when criticizing Rev. Steddon's assertion from the pulpit that, in "the good old days," children obeyed their parents. From the doctor's viewpoint, "plain horse sense, some truth with a little t" reveals this to be a dangerous idealization of the past, one belied by an ignominious history of child labor and unrestrained corporal punishment (Hughes, *Souls*, 42). For a critique of received wisdom about marriage, see Hughes, 366. For descriptions of the cinematic "allegory," see Hughes, 185, 319.

The narrator makes this particular contrast between cinema and traditional religion explicit in the figure of the young actor Tom Holby. He describes Tom's "profession [as] the opposite of a preacher's": "He tried to show how people actually did behave, not how they ought to." The passage goes on to lament that the writers of Tom's films compromise his efforts, by always "forc[ing] a moral," thus sustaining the "pretty lie" that "life punishe[s] wickedness and reward[s] virtue" (214).

150. Hughes, 77.

151. See Hughes, 264–268.

152. Hughes, 120. See also Hughes, 4, 22, 205.

153. Hughes, 36–37.

154. Hughes, 38. There is also a sense here that the doctor believes that fabricating an elaborate adventure fantasy will have a therapeutic benefit for Mem. By becoming a spectator to her own imagined future, she may establish psychological distance between herself and her present predicament. See Hughes, 20, 32.

155. Hughes, 120.

156. Hughes, 185.

157. Hughes, 185.

158. Hughes, 185.

159. Ann Douglas, *Terrible Honesty: Mongrel Manhattan in the 1920s* (New York: Farrar, Straus and Giroux, 1995), 31–40. I mean here only to signal a very general affinity between Hughes's work (with its rejection of "hypocrisy" and seeming embrace of the "naked" fact) and the literary ethos that Douglas describes. In Douglas's terms, Hughes, in fact, belongs to the "older generation" of American writers.

160. Hughes, *Souls*, 56, 354–355.

161. Hughes, 57. On the history of the kind of star profiles that Mem reads, see deCordova, *Picture Personalities*, 107–108.

162. On Hughes's relationship with Creel, see Kemm, *Rupert Hughes*, 83, 85, 91. Creel was also briefly associated with Lee, when, in 1908, Progressive author Charles Ferguson recruited the two men to write for his short-lived newspaper, the *Newsbook*. See Gregory W. Bush, *Lord of Attention: Gerald Stanley Lee and the Crowd Metaphor in Modern America* (Amherst: University of Massachusetts Press, 1991), 60–61. It is also worth noting here that in 1916, Creel had profiled the film star Douglas Fairbanks for *Everybody's Magazine*. I discuss this profile in detail in the next chapter.

163. These descriptions come from a speech by Secretary of War Newton D. Baker, which appear as a foreword to Creel's *How We Advertised America: The First Telling of the Amazing Story of the Committee on Public Information that Carried the Gospel of Americanism to Every Corner of the Globe* (New York: Harper and Brothers, 1920), xiii–xiv.

164. Axelrod, *Selling*, 98, 104.

165. Kemm, *Rupert Hughes*, 85; and Creel, *How*, 5 (emphasis in original).

166. Creel, 4 (emphasis in original).

167. See Hallett, *Go West*, 155; Axelrod, *Selling*, 147–152; and Creel, 84–98.

168. The quoted phrase is from Creel's autobiography, *Rebel at Large: Recollections of Fifty Crowded Years* (New York: G. P. Putnam's Sons, 1947), 157 (emphasis in original).

169. Creel, *How*, 16–27; and Axelrod, *Selling*, 97–112. Axelrod argues that while Creel presented the CPI as an "alternative to censorship," it in fact constituted "an alternative form of censorship," 105.

170. Hughes's own usage demonstrates the complexities and contradictions that accrued around the term "propaganda" during this period. While styling himself as the scourge of propaganda in his role as military censor, Hughes also clearly shared a general faith in the emergent field of publicity, as shaped both by Creel himself and by former CPI member Edward Bernays. The author of the founding texts of modern public relations theory, Bernays was well aware that the term "propaganda" had come to carry a "decidedly sinister complexion," especially in the wake of "the late war." Bernays sought to restore the term's "lost" dignity by looking back to its original usage in Roman Catholic Church discourse: "propaganda" in Latin meaning propagating the faith. Stressing this neutral or descriptive definition and withholding judgments of "merit," Bernays contended that the "organized effort" by any party in a democratic society to "disseminate" its ideas on a broad scale was an inherently legitimate act. See Bernays, *Propaganda* (New York: Horace Liveright, 1928), 20–23. On Bernays's role within the CPI, see Axelrod, *Selling*, 115–122.

171. Creel, *How*, 103, 229.

172. Creel, 4.

173. See Hughes, *Souls*, 189.

174. Elbert Hubbard, quoted in William R. Leach, *Land of Desire: Merchants, Power, and the Rise of a New American Culture* (New York: Pantheon, 1993), 42.

CHAPTER 5 — "LITTLE GRAINS OF SAND"

1. George Creel, "A 'Close-Up' of Douglas Fairbanks," *Everybody's Magazine*, December 1916, 737.

2. Vachel Lindsay, *The Progress and Poetry of the Movies*, ed. Myron Lounsbury (Lanham, Md.: Scarecrow, 1995), 165.

3. Creel, "Close-Up," 729.

4. Creel, 729. By the time of Creel's writing, "Doug" had become journalists' standard way of referring to Fairbanks—a marker of the "ordinary guy" associations (plainspokenness, ruggedness, lack of pretense) carried by his star persona. See Alistair Cooke, *Douglas Fairbanks: The Making of a Screen Character* (New York: Museum of Modern Art, 1940), 13; and Scott Curtis, "Douglas Fairbanks: Icon of Americanism," in *Flickers of Desire: Movie*

Stars of the 1910s, ed. Jennifer Bean (New Brunswick, N.J.: Rutgers University Press, 2011), 218–241.

5. Creel, "Close-Up," 729.

6. Creel, 729.

7. The medium of film was ultimately central to the CPI's efforts to explain and promote the United States' war effort both home and abroad. See the chapter "Fighting with Films" in Creel's *How We Advertised America: The First Telling of the Amazing Story of the Committee on Public Information That Carried the Gospel of Americanism to Every Corner of the Globe* (New York: Harper and Brothers, 1920), 273–282.

8. On Lee's concept of the "crowd-man," see chapter 1. Fairbanks's persona as described by Creel and his character in the film fits that description in that both are simultaneously national symbols and figures representing the innate internationalism of the movies, and thus, embodying Lee's inspired leader archetype, Fairbanks, in both settings, seems able to parlay the project of national unification into something global.

9. Lindsay, *Progress*, 250.

10. The Britton Publishing Company of New York published Fairbanks's two inspirational or self-help books, *Laugh and Live* and *Making Life Worth While*, printing and selling selected chapters from the first as individual pamphlets. In 1924, Fairbanks published *Youth Points the Way*, a book of advice first serialized in the Boy Scouts of America publication, *Boy's Life*. According to Fairbanks's biographer, Jeffrey Vance, the books published under Fairbanks's name, as well as his 1917–1918 columns in *Photoplay*, were "ghostwr[itten]" by the actor's longtime friend, Kenneth Davenport, whom Fairbanks "employed . . . as a factotum . . . secretary, [and] confidant." See Jeffrey Vance, with Tony Maietta and Robert Cushman, *Douglas Fairbanks* (Berkeley: University of California Press, 2008), 41–44. See also Curtis, "Douglas Fairbanks," 235.

Although I disagree with Cooke's assertion that the issue of the books' being ghostwritten is "irrelevant," space constraints force me to bracket off the interesting theoretical questions about authorship that they raise. Throughout the chapter, I treat Douglas Fairbanks as the texts' author in the sense that they consistently reflect the ideologies that he circulated in other venues (interviews, his films, and so on) and in the sense that they form a crucial pillar of his efforts to shape his "Doug" star persona during the late teens and early twenties. See Cooke, *Douglas Fairbanks*, 20. As Cooke aptly points out, these texts "generalize the screen activities of 'Doug' into moral precepts for Everyman's workaday practice," in turn helping promote the idea of Fairbanks as "the popular philosopher." Moreover, as Vance's research indicates, the "Doug" persona itself was a sort of corporate product, depending as much on Fairbanks's screen work as on an "effective marketing machine" composed of talented, like-minded advisors and assistants, such as Davenport (44).

11. Douglas Fairbanks, *Making Life Worth While* (New York: Britton, 1917), 15 (emphasis in original). Erik Routley identifies "Little Drops of Water" as a Victorian-era children's

hymn of uncertain origin, citing variant versions of the verse from English and American printed sources, in *A Panorama of Christian Hymnody*, ed. Paul A. Richardson (Chicago: GIA, 2005), 278–279.

12. Fairbanks, *Making*, 15.

13. Fairbanks, *Laugh*, 21.

14. Lindsay, *Progress*, 239. For more on Lindsay's citation and embellishment of Münsterberg's theories of cinematic perception, see chapter 2.

15. Among the obsolete meanings for the noun "sand" in the *Oxford English Dictionary* (online edition) are the following: "The action of sending; that which is sent, a message, present; (God's) dispensation or ordinance" and "A person or body of persons sent on an errand; an embassy; an envoy, messenger."

16. Lindsay, *Progress*, 166–167.

17. Lindsay, 167.

18. Lindsay, 166.

19. Cooke, *Douglas Fairbanks*, 28.

20. Covering a six-and-a-half-acre lot in West Hollywood, *The Thief of Bagdad*'s set reused some of the same structural elements that had supported the (similarly massive) castle walls during the shooting of the earlier Fairbanks costume epic, *Robin Hood*. See Vance, *Douglas Fairbanks*, 166–167.

21. For a detailed history of this sign as well as a discussion of commercial signage in 1920s Los Angeles more broadly, see Leo Braudy's *The Hollywood Sign: Fantasy and Reality of an American Icon* (New Haven: Yale University Press, 2011), 69–90.

22. Robert S. Sennett, *Setting the Scene: The Great Hollywood Art Directors* (New York: Harry N. Abrams, 1994), 43.

23. See David Bordwell, "Classical Hollywood Cinema: Narrational Principles and Procedures," in *Narrative, Apparatus, Ideology: A Film Theory Reader*, ed. Philip Rosen (New York: Columbia University Press, 1986), 22–23.

24. Vance, *Douglas Fairbanks*, 166. For *The Thief of Bagdad*, Fairbanks hired Raoul Walsh, a director whose prior experience was in westerns and gangster films and who, by his own account, felt unsuited initially to the task. In his memoir, Walsh credits Fairbanks with convincing him that he was capable of successfully directing the film and with making crucial decisions during the production. See Walsh, *Each Man in His Time: The Life Story of a Director* (New York: Farrar, Straus and Giroux, 1974), 165. While acknowledging the contributions of Fairbanks's collaborators, Walsh included, Vance treats Fairbanks as the film's ostensible auteur, "the real force both in front of and behind the camera," who "took charge of the difficult scenes"—especially those involving large crowds. See Vance, 155.

25. The closest analogue for this strategy of trademarking a production would seem to be early film companies' (like Edison and Biograph) practice of including visible company

names or logos in interior sets. As the summary in this chapter is meant to indicate, the "Bagdad" sign works in a very different ways than those logos. See Tom Gunning, *D. W. Griffith and the Origins of American Narrative Film: The Early Years at Biograph* (Urbana: University of Illinois Press, 1991), 51.

26. These efforts play out in a range of different venues, from star-fashioning novels (like Hughes's *Souls for Sale* [New York: Harper and Brothers, 1922] and Henry Leon Wilson's *Merton of the Movies* [New York: Grosset and Dunlap, 1922]), to the films based on them, to the genre of the "studio tour" short film. See also Fairbanks, *Youth Points the Way* (New York: D. Appleton, 1924), 38–39.

27. See "Make-Believe Land," *Motion Picture Magazine*, October 1923, 38.

28. According to Myron Lounsbury's editor's introduction to Lindsay's posthumously published second film book, Lindsay "visited the movie capital in late summer of 1924 [and] talked with Douglas Fairbanks on the set of the soon-to-be-completed *The Thief of Bagdad*" (Lindsay, *Progress*, 133). The visit was part of Lindsay's effort to cultivate relationships with powerful figures in the industry, with an eye to promoting his critical writings and spreading his ideas about film aesthetics to people capable of influencing production trends. Although Lindsay was largely frustrated in this effort, he did eventually publish a well-received profile of Fairbanks: "The Great Douglas Fairbanks," *Ladies' Home Journal* 43, no. 8 (August 1926): 12, 114. Lindsay does not mention the "Bagdad" sign, but he would certainly have seen it during his visit to the set.

29. The Babylon set for Griffith's *Intolerance* was the one of the first such structures to have received significant press coverage. See, for instance, "The Walls of Jericho? Or Babylon? Or Nineveh? Or Tyre?," *Photoplay* 9, no. 2 (January 1916): 34–35; and "Griffith's Masterpiece," *Photoplay* 9, no. 6 (May 1916): 52–53. A little more than a year later, the set had decayed and become overgrown with weeds, to the point that the same publication could photograph it with a joking caption; see "Belshazzar Griffith's Babylon—Today," *Photoplay* 12, no. 2 (July 1917): 34. See also Kevin Brownlow, *Hollywood: The Pioneers* (New York: Knopf, 1979), 77.

30. In a caption accompanying one of the production stills, Vance quotes Fairbanks's son, Douglas Fairbanks Jr., as "recall[ing] that portions of the set were 'a source of wonder and curiosity for hordes of sightseers,' for many years after [the production finished]" (Vance, *Douglas Fairbanks*, 166).

31. "How Doug Made 'The Thief of Bagdad,'" *Photoplay* 25, no. 6 (May 1924): 60–61. For an example of "the actor as auteur" trope, see John C. Tibbets and James M. Welsh, *His Majesty the American: The Cinema of Douglas Fairbanks Sr.* (South Brunswick, N.J.: A. S. Barnes, 1977), 143. See also Vance, *Douglas Fairbanks*, 156, 160.

32. "How Doug," 61.

33. *Oakland Post-Enquirer*, December 1923; *Silver Springs Signal*, September 25, 1924. Clippings containing these and all the newspaper stories cited in this chapter are in the publicity file for *The Thief of Bagdad*, Mary Pickford Papers Collection, Margaret Herrick

Library, Academy of Motion Picture Arts and Sciences (hereafter *Thief* publicity file). As is typically the case with material gathered by professional press clipping bureaus, these generally lack page and/or section numbers, as well as, in some cases, headlines or bylines; in each case, I provide what publication information is available.

34. *Norwich Bulletin*, September 1, 1924, *Thief* publicity file. See also "Diverse Types Appear in 'Thief of Bagdad,'" *Los Angeles Express*, December 27, 1924, *Thief* publicity file.

35. *Fresno Bee*, December 8, 1923. See also the notice in the *Omaha World-Herald*, December 23, 1923.

36. "How Doug," 61.

37. On the construction of this rig, see Fairbanks, "Films for the Fifty Million," *Ladies' Home Journal* 41, no. 4 (April 1924): 47; Vance, *Douglas Fairbanks*, 169–170, 173; and Walsh, *Each Man*, 168–169.

38. David Lewis explains that twelve thousand of Highland Park's sixteen thousand workers appear in the photograph, originally taken in 1913, in *The Public Image of Henry Ford* (Detroit: Wayne State University Press, 1976), 54, 161. Widely reprinted in newspapers around the country, the image was described as "'the largest posed photo ever taken, and far and away the most expensive, given the employees' time and loss of production'" (53).

39. *Ford Factory Facts* (Detroit: Ford Motor Company, 1915), 5–6. The "Interesting Figures" section of this marketing brochure is very similar to the lists of personnel and material expended in production, which appear in the souvenir programs distributed by the Hollywood studios upon the release of their "big special" films during the 1920s. I discuss the "Amazing Facts and Figures" section of the "Special Advertising Pictorial" supplement prepared by Universal Pictures for the 1927 release of *Uncle Tom's Cabin* in the conclusion. For another example, see also Famous Players-Lasky Corporation, Souvenir Program for *The Covered Wagon* (1923), 6 of 16 unnumbered pages, Paramount Press Sheets File on *The Covered Wagon*, Margaret Herrick Library, Academy of Motion Picture Arts and Sciences.

40. *Ford*, 6.

41. See David E. Nye, *American Technological Sublime* (Cambridge, Mass.: MIT Press, 1994), 130–131; and Lewis, *Public Image*, 54, 161.

42. Gregory Bush states, "The organic factory, as Lee saw it, was a place that could be 'as spiritual as a church and as educational as a school,' where 'the employees and owners and the public become as members of one body moving and growing in conscious health, and in strength and joy together.'" Bush, *Lord of Attention: Gerald Stanley Lee and the Crowd Metaphor in Modern America* (Amherst: University of Massachusetts Press, 1991), 105.

43. Gerald Stanley Lee, *We: A Confession of Faith for the American People during and after the War* (New York: Doubleday, Page, 1916), 124.

44. Lee, 126.

45. William L. Stidger, *Henry Ford: The Man and His Motives* (New York: George H. Doran, 1923), 111–113.

46. Stidger, 112.

47. Stidger, 112.

48. Stidger, 113, 118. On the demographics of Ford's workforce during this period, see Greg Grandin, *Fordlandia: The Rise and Fall of Henry Ford's Forgotten Jungle City* (New York: Metropolitan Books, 2009), 38. Grandin states that Ford extended his signature "Five Dollar Day" wage plan "to all male employees regardless of skin color," a practice that encouraged African American migration to Detroit. At the same time, Grandin notes, black workers "were generally assigned the hardest jobs and the ones with the least potential for advancement" (38). My thanks to Leslie Mitchner for recommending Grandin's important book to me.

49. On the concept of the world picture, see chapter 1.

50. Stidger, *Henry Ford*, 207.

51. Henry Ford, quoted in Stidger, 207.

52. Grandin, *Fordlandia*, 41, 45.

53. Grandin, 71, 286.

54. Tom Gunning, "Pictures of Crowd Splendor: The Mitchell and Kenyon Factory Gate Films," in *The Lost World of Mitchell and Kenyon: Edwardian Britain on Film*, ed. Vanessa Toulmin, Patrick Russell, and Simon Popple (London: British Film Institute, 2004), 50.

55. Gunning, 57–58. See Vachel Lindsay, *The Art of the Moving Picture* (New York: Macmillan, 1915), 49; and chapter 2 of this study.

56. "Troubles of a Bagdad Thief," sec. 8, *New York Times*, March 2, 1924, 5. The rhetoric here—bouts of complaining and peevishness on set, met by Fairbanks's contagious optimism and morale building—recalls Creel's "Bureau of Grins" passage.

57. "Troubles of a Bagdad Thief," 5.

58. "Troubles of a Bagdad Thief," 5.

59. Jack Jungmeyer, "$3 per Day Is All They Get for a Million Dollar Movie," *Modesto News*, December 13, 1923, *Thief* publicity file. Jungmeyer's story was reprinted (minus his byline) with the title "$3-A-Day Extra Makes Big Films" in the *Kansas City Journal*, April 17, 1924, *Thief* publicity file. The version that appears in the *Kansas City Journal* features a number of likely accidental changes, such as expanding the size of the extra crowd from "3800" (as it is written in the *Modesto News* version) to "thirty-eight thousand strong."

It is important to note the role that wages play here as a marker of the difficulties of communication between boss and employees (and of smooth production in general). Ford's reputation as an "inspired millionaire" and operator of "organic" factories depended largely on his radical decision in 1914 to institute a uniform five-dollar daily wage, a wage above the industry standard. In his patronizing account of Hollywood's "three-dollar-a day men"—performers in "mob scenes" being the lowest-paid group of extras in the Hollywood studios—Jungmeyer suggests workers and labor quality that falls short of the Fordist standard. On the history of Ford's Five Dollar Day, see Grandin, *Fordlandia*, 38–39. On the wages paid to mob scene extras in the 1910s and 1920s, see Anthony Slide, *Hollywood Unknowns: A History of Extras, Bit Players, and Stand-Ins* (Jackson: University Press of Mississippi, 2012), 25, 63–77.

60. Jungmeyer. Throughout Jungmeyer's piece, the extra is always a "man," even though he mentions "men and women" in his initial description of the workers gathered on the outskirts of the film lot at dawn. Since these extras have been hired to play the role of male soldiers (as specified in the story materials), it is reasonable to assume that they were all men. Supporting this assumption is the fact that the initial, relatively close shots of the soldiers magically appearing (where faces are visible) seem to include male actors only. On the other hand, the fact that the panoramic overhead shots show only a sea of bodies with indistinct faces means that any actors regardless of sex (or race) might have been involved. It is worth noting here too that (as my discussion of the film at the end of the chapter will highlight) there are precedents for gendered and raced cross-casting in the film.

61. Jungmeyer.

62. Jungmeyer.

63. Jungmeyer.

64. Jungmeyer.

65. Achmed Abdullah, *The Thief of Bagdad* (New York: A. L. Burt, 1924), 230. Achmed Abdullah was the pen name of Alexander Romanoff, a Crimean-born American writer of Orientalist fantasies. See the Internet Speculative Fiction Database (http://www.isfdb.org/cgi-bin/ea.cgi?Achmed_Abdullah).

66. Walsh, *Each Man*, 164.

67. Walsh, 164 (emphasis in original). Typifying the slipperiness of racial markers in Walsh's account, his choice of the term "Syrian" is peculiar. It may be that the terms "Syrian" and "Arab" were interchangeable in his mind.

68. Walsh, 164. Walsh bolsters this justification by concocting an elaborate anthropological rationale, whereby he adduces that "Mexicans" are "Oriental" by descent: "Many Mexicans, I remembered, had Indian blood, and were not those same Indians reputed to have come across the Bering Strait from Asia." This notion of American-Indian descent through "Asia" broadly speaking is sufficient for Walsh to conclude that Mexican people as a group are virtually Arabs.

69. Walsh, 165. Walsh mentions that United Artists sent "four big buses" into "Mexican town," bearing "placards . . . reading 'Free Ride! See Douglas Fairbanks in person making The Thief of Bagdad!'" He claims, further, that this strategy yielded huge crowds of the kind that Fairbanks enjoyed having around set—a kind of live audience—so many that the casting department easily filled its quota of "desert-type faces" and "turned hundreds [of applicants] away."

70. Jungmeyer.

71. Jungmeyer.

72. Jungmeyer. The description portrays Fairbanks as doing the kind of strategic flattery of subordinates described in "Troubles of a Bagdad Thief," 5.

73. Jungmeyer.

74. Jungmeyer.

75. Jungmeyer.

76. Grandin, *Fordlandia*, 34. The phrase "sociologist manufacturer" is a quotation from a period source in Grandin.

77. Stidger, *Henry Ford*, 110.

78. Stidger, 118.

79. Lee, *We*, 121.

80. Lee, 37, 124–129.

81. Lee, 36, 38, 136. Notwithstanding the many inconsistencies that characterized Ford's publicly expressed views over the course of his life, he appears to have been, at heart, an Emersonian transcendentalist who believed in "man's perfectability" and was open to the "eclectic spiritualism of his time." See Grandin, *Fordlandia*, 40, 251.

82. Steven Watts, *The People's Tycoon: Henry Ford and the American Century* (New York: Vintage, 2006), 323–324.

83. Ralph Waldo Trine, *The Power That Wins: Henry Ford and Ralph Waldo Trine in an Intimate Talk on Life . . .* (Indianapolis: Bobbs-Merrill, 1928), 11. Not surprisingly, the adaptation that Trine and Fairbanks discussed never came to fruition.

84. Trine, 11–12.

85. Trine, 12–13. See Trine, *In Tune with the Infinite* (New York: Collier, 1970), 15.

86. Trine, *Power*, 13 (emphasis in original).

87. Trine, 15. In summarizing Ford's comments, I retain his exclusive use of the masculine pronoun to avoid excessive emendation of the quoted material and to highlight the gender-biased nature of his comments as they pertain to issues of power and social organization.

88. Trine, 16.

89. Trine, 16.

90. Trine, 21.

91. Ford professes to believe that the "globe has been inhabited by intelligent people millions of times," these prior civilizations experiencing both tremendous technological progress (he believes "they had the automobile, the radio, the airplane") and, eventually, "mortal" decline. See Trine, 76.

92. Trine, 16.

93. Trine, 78–79.

94. Trine, 12.

95. Trine, 17–18.

96. Trine, 18.

97. Fairbanks, *Making*, 9. In the "Author's Forward" to this second book, Fairbanks distinguishes its main purpose from that of the first: "In *Laugh and Live*, my sole purpose was to emphasize our first duty toward ourselves, which consists in doing our level best at everything we undertake, and making the best of every situation that arises to confront us." The implication here is that *Making Life Worth While* aims also, or even primarily, to address ethical obligations and collective challenges. Indeed, this book is more topical, reflecting on a range of pressing social issues (from world war to technological change) from a positive-thinking perspective.

98. Fairbanks, *Laugh*, 9–10.

99. Fairbanks, 12.

100. Fairbanks, 12–14.

101. As Heather Addison explains in *Hollywood and the Rise of Physical Culture* (New York: Routledge, 2003), "physical culture" was the period's "umbrella term for those activities that attempt to modify the size and shape of the body to improve health or appearance . . . includ[ing] dieting, muscle-building, and aerobic exercise" (1).

102. See Gaylyn Studlar, *This Mad Masquerade: Stardom and Masculinity in the Jazz Age* (New York: Columbia University Press, 1996), 21–29. Roosevelt first used the phrase "the strenuous life" in an 1899 speech advocating aggressively expansionist United States foreign policy: he saw imperial control of the Caribbean and Pacific as the next step in the unstoppable march of the "Teutonic" or "English race," an extension of the evolutionary competition that had resulted in the "winning of the west" by and for white Americans. Because such territorial expansion depended on military prowess, the physical condition of white American manhood was a central concern for Roosevelt. Like many of his contemporaries in the late nineteenth century, Roosevelt believed that modern urban life repressed boys' and men's "primitive" instincts, cutting them off from invigorating, purifying spheres of activity and leading them to become "overcivilized," feminized, and/or dissipated. As the feminist historian Gail Bederman has shown, "the strenuous life" quickly lost its specific connection to foreign policy and became a more general signifier of the ideal of a "virile, hard-driving manhood" to be regenerated through physical culture. See Bederman, *Manliness and Civilization: A Cultural History of Gender and Race in the United States, 1890–1917* (Chicago: University of Chicago Press, 1995), 184–187, 192–196. See also Kristen Whissel, "The Gender of Empire: American Modernity, Masculinity, and Edison's War Actualities," in *A Feminist Reader in Early Cinema*, ed. Jennifer M. Bean and Diane Negra (Durham: Duke University Press, 2002). 141–142; and Addison, *Hollywood*, 12. Note here that Fairbanks's boys' book is most extensively grounded in the strenuous life ideal; it is an extended argument against "excessive civilization," which calls for a return to wilderness activities that revive the American "pioneer" spirit.

103. Fairbanks, *Laugh*, 9, 14 (emphasis in original). From the standpoint of orthodox "mind-cure" philosophy—in which it is asserted that sickness and injury can be dispelled by thought—Fairbanks's program falls into contradiction.

104. Fairbanks, 42–43.

105. Fairbanks, 13.

106. Fairbanks, 29, 43.

107. Fairbanks, 23, 68, 73 (emphasis in original).

108. Fairbanks, 129 (emphasis in original). Here we see a good illustration of Studlar's central point in her definitive study of the gender dynamics of Fairbanks's star persona: that the ideology of masculine "character building" through athletics was central to Fairbanks's films and off-screen self-representation. My account of Fairbanks's motivational texts (which Studlar mentions only in passing) is meant, at the same time, to build on and complicate Studlar's scholarship by highlighting the important, but so far overlooked, influence of positive thinking or mental science on his ideas about society. This influence, I contend, provides a crucial context for understanding the utopian aspects of Fairbanks's discourse about cinema as well as the collectivist concerns of the more lavish, period productions (like *The Thief of Bagdad*), to which he turned after 1920; lacking this context, Studlar's chapter on Fairbanks necessarily focuses more on his earlier films and struggles to tease out the main themes of the later ones.

109. Fairbanks, *Laugh*, 68, 71.

110. Fairbanks, 68–70.

111. Fairbanks's discourse of cleanliness reflects the larger consumer culture's emphasis on the ruthless scrutiny of physical appearance by one's peers. See Roland Marchand's discussion of "the parable of the first impression" in print advertisements for personal hygiene and grooming products during this period in *Advertising the American Dream: Making Way for Modernity, 1920–1940* (Berkeley: University of California Press, 1985), 208–217.

112. Marchand, 21, 26 (emphasis in original).

113. Marchand, 19, 21 (emphasis in original).

114. In his conversation with Ford, Trine describes the "great wealth" that Ford has "accumulated" as an ultimately insignificant benefit that has accompanied his "big human service" throughout the years; Ford agrees that wealth is "only a means to [the] end" of expanded "power." See Trine, *Power*, 13.

115. Trine refers to the "law of attraction" and the "law correspondences" interchangeably, highlighting the Swedenborgian, neoplatonic basis of his thought. He offers this succinct summary of the operative law: "We are continually attracting to us, from both the seen and the unseen side of life, forces and conditions most akin to those of our own thoughts." See Trine, *Infinite*, 26–31. A central tenet of mental science from its earliest articulations, the "attraction" theory remains crucial to contemporary versions of this ideology (like the "prosperity gospel" and "the Secret"). See Fenwicke L. Holmes, *The Law of Mind in*

Action: Daily Lessons and Treatments in Mental and Spiritual Science (New York: Robert McBride, 1919), 78–80; and Barbara Ehrenreich, *Bright-Sided: How the Relentless Promotion of Positive Thinking Has Undermined America* (New York: Henry Holt, 2009), 59–73.

116. Fairbanks, *Making*, 145.

117. On what it means to "actualize" the self, see Trine, *Infinite*, 135.

118. Creel, "Close-Up," 732–734. See also a 1920 magazine article that casually mentions "'Doug' Fairbanks . . . out on 'location,' hurling Mexicans over his shoulders," as an example kind of thing that the visitor to Hollywood is liable to witness. "A Visit to Movieland," *Forum*, January 1920, 18.

119. Creel, "Close-Up," 732–734.

120. Studlar, *This Mad Masquerade*, 51–52.

121. Fairbanks, *Laugh*, 66.

122. Fairbanks's use of "debris" recalls Jungmeyer's characterization of Hollywood extras as "stolid" entities and "castoffs."

123. Charles K. Taylor, "The Most Popular Man in the World," *Outlook* 138, no. 17 (December 24, 1924): 683. As the following discussion of the film stresses, the stated moral of *The Thief of Bagdad* is "Happiness Must Be Earned."

124. Taylor, 683–684.

125. Taylor, 684.

126. Taylor, 684.

127. Taylor, 683–684.

128. By way of context, it is interesting to note that on more than one occasion, Fairbanks offered his fans the advice to "get out in a field and throw stones." For Fairbanks, who was most fond of physical activities that recalled childhood play, such throwing contests involving stones (objects that cost nothing and are always ready at hand) could simultaneously provide exercise and release from the constraints of respectable adult society. See Fairbanks, "How I Keep Myself Running on 'High,'" *American Magazine*, August 1922, 34. See also Studlar, *This Mad Masquerade*, 47–48, 268n145.

129. Taylor, "Most Popular Man," 683, 685.

130. Fairbanks, *Making*, 15.

131. Fairbanks, 45 (emphasis in original).

132. Fairbanks, 45–46 (emphasis in original).

133. Fairbanks, 46.

134. Fairbanks, 43 (emphasis in original). For some of the star's other references to film as universal language, see Fairbanks, "Let Me Say This for the Films," *Ladies' Home Journal* 39, no. 9 (September 1922): 117; and "A Huge Responsibility," *Ladies' Home Journal* 41, no. 5 (May 1924): 36.

135. Fairbanks, *Making*, 46 (emphasis in original).

136. Fairbanks, 53, 139–144. Along with other major stars like Charlie Chaplin and Mary Pickford, Fairbanks was one of the faces of the Hollywood film industry's support of the war effort. As Vance explains, in 1918, Fairbanks appeared in "short films to promote the purchasing of war bonds" and participated in major Liberty Loan drives. At the New York City drive, he "spoke . . . at the junction of Broad and Wall Street to an estimated twenty to thirty thousand people." Representing what Vance calls Fairbanks's "first real exposure to mass adulation," this appearance was documented in a series of famous photographs of the star standing on a high perch trying to communicate with a vast crowd people—Fairbanks, once again, as crowd-man. See Vance, *Douglas Fairbanks*, 46–47. Even before the United States entered the war, Fairbanks signaled a desire for intervention, playing a fictional character with "'belligerent ideas' in the cause of 'preparedness' alienate his pacifist fiancée" in the film *In Again, Out Again* (Douglas Fairbanks Pictures, 1917). See Studlar, *This Mad Masquerade*, 14–15.

137. Fairbanks, *Making*, 52–53, 157.

138. Fairbanks, 17–18.

139. Fairbanks, 18. On the problems of "inertia" and "indolence," see also Fairbanks, *Youth*, 72–87.

140. Fairbanks, *Making*, 18. Fairbanks's Cain is essentially the repressed, enervated urban boy in strenuous-life discourse, who lacks invigorating outlets like scouting.

141. Fairbanks, 53.

142. On Fairbanks's use of the term "preparedness" in his self-help books and on its usage in the debate about American intervention in World War I, see Curtis, "Douglas Fairbanks," 236.

143. Curtis, 157.

144. Curtis, 155–156.

145. Curtis, 157 (emphasis in original).

146. Curtis, 155.

147. Curtis, 156.

148. Curtis, 46.

149. Curtis, 91–92 (emphasis in original).

150. Curtis, 92.

151. Lindsay, *Progress*, 187.

152. William R. Leach, *Land of Desire: Merchants, Power, and the Rise of a New American Culture* (New York: Pantheon, 1993), 257.

153. Lindsay, *Progress*, 218.

154. Lindsay, 173–174.

155. Lindsay, 255.

156. Lindsay, 222, 239.

157. Lindsay, 186–187.

158. Lindsay, 230–231.

159. Lindsay, 230.

160. See Harriet Works Corley, "The Deuce with Reducing," *Photoplay* 28, no. 2 (July 1925): 131. This article uses the story of Comont's casting to illustrate the point that avoiding "physical culture," paradoxically, can also be a pathway to screen success.

161. Lindsay, *Progress*, 230.

162. See Walsh, *Each Man*, 165. Having relatively less screen time than his two rivals, the Indian prince receives only passing mention from Lindsay, who finds him a character of "reasonable dignity": an "intermediate figure" there to provide contrast to "the absurdity of the effeminate Persian and the fearful, senile fanaticism and power of the Mongol" (*Progress*, 231). Noble Johnson, an African American actor, played the role of the Indian prince. A pioneer of black independent cinema, Johnson went on to have a long career in Hollywood, playing bit parts across the industry's spectrum of racial and ethnic "types." See Donald Bogle, *Bright Boulevards, Bold Dreams: The Story of Black Hollywood* (New York: Ballantine, 2005), 18–28.

163. Lindsay, *Progress*, 249. See John Higham, *Strangers in the Land: Patterns of American Nativism, 1860–1925* (New Brunswick, N.J.: Rutgers University Press, 1955), 165–175. Lindsay's usage of the phrase "Yellow Peril" in his writing on *The Thief of Bagdad* appears to be straightforward, his way of glossing what he finds frightening about the Mongol prince character. The issue of Lindsay's attitudes toward "Yellow Peril" discourse across his body of work is beyond the scope of this chapter. Suffice it to say that Lindsay also uses Asian invasion scenarios in idiosyncratic, overdetermined ways in a pair of speculative fictional narratives, "The Golden-Faced People: A Story of the Chinese Conquest of America" (in *The Crisis* 9, no. 4 [November 1914]: 36–42); and *The Golden Book of Springfield* (New York: Macmillan, 1920).

164. Lindsay, *Progress*, 231.

165. See Yunte Huang, *Charlie Chan: The Untold Story of the Honorable Detective and His Rendezvous with American History* (New York: W. W. Norton, 2010), 136–145.

166. Lindsay, *Progress*, 174.

167. Lindsay, 187.

168. Lindsay, 169.

169. Lindsay, 184.

170. Lindsay, *Art*, 260.

171. Lindsay, *Progress*, 250–251.

172. Lindsay, 250.

173. In asserting this connection between the imagery of masses of white-robed knights and racial ideology, I draw on the scene's intertextual resonances with two earlier films, where it is registered in more obvious ways. In the climactic scene of *The Birth of a Nation* (Griffith Feature Films, 1915), the Ku Klux Klan drives African Americans from the streets in a display of optical whiteness that Lindsay famously described as an "Anglo-Saxon Niagara" (*Art*, 47). In what looks like an even more direct precedent for *The Thief of Bagdad*, Fairbanks's own *Robin Hood* opens with majestic images of what an early intertitle calls "England's knighthood . . . depart[ing] on the Holy Crusade."

CONCLUSION

1. Benjamin Hampton, *A History of the Movies* (New York: Covici, Friede, 1931), 429.

2. Hampton had worked as an independent film producer from 1917 to 1922 and had styled himself as something of a "spokesman for the industry" in a 1921 magazine article assailing Hollywood's production of "sex pictures." See Hilary A. Hallett, *Go West, Young Women! The Rise of Early Hollywood* (Berkeley: University of California Press, 2013), 154–155. In the preface to *A History of the Movies*, Hampton thanks Hays, James Quirk, and other industry leaders for giving him access to their files during the course of his research and portrays his project as an extension of Ramsaye's. See Hampton, *History*, 3.

3. Hampton, 427.

4. Hampton, 427.

5. Hampton, 427.

6. Hampton, 427.

7. Hampton, 427.

8. Hampton, 428.

9. Hampton, 430 (emphasis in original).

10. Hampton, 430.

11. Hampton, 430.

12. Hampton, 430.

13. Hampton, 428.

14. Hampton, 429.

15. Hampton, 429.

16. Hampton, 429–430.

17. John Durham Peters, *Speaking into the Air: A History of the Idea of Communication* (Chicago: University of Chicago Press, 1999), 1.

18. Mark Zuckerberg, "Building Global Community," February 16, 2017, https://www.facebook.com/notes/mark-zuckerberg/building-global-community/10154544292806634/.

19. Zuckerberg.

20. Zuckerberg.

21. Zuckerberg.

22. Zuckerberg.

23. Zuckerberg.

24. Zuckerberg.

25. Zuckerberg.

26. Zuckerberg.

27. See H. G. Wells, *The Outline of History: Being a Plain History of Life and Mankind*, vol. 1 (New York: Macmillan, 1920); and *The Salvaging of Civilization* (London: Cassell, 1921). See also Hendrik Van Loon, *The Story of Mankind* (New York: Boni and Liveright, 1921).

28. The first quoted phrase comes from Wells, *Outline*, v (emphasis in original). The phrase "one great epic unfolding" is from Wells, *Salvaging*, 110.

29. Wells, *Outline*, vi.

30. Wells, *Salvaging*, 80. In 1929, Wells published "an unconventional novel," written in the form of a film treatment, which tells the story of an enlightened monarch who rejects nationalism and lays the groundwork for a world state based on economic planning and the elimination of war. Both the screenplay and Wells's didactic introduction highlight cinema's power as what he calls "a means of expression, exceeding in force, beauty and universality any that have been hitherto available for mankind." Wells, *The King Who Was a King* (Toronto: Doubleday, Doran and Gundy, 1929), 3. On *The King Who Was a King* and Wells's complex relationship to cinema more broadly, see Laura Marcus's excellent *The Tenth Muse: Writing about Cinema in the Modernist Period* (Oxford: Oxford University Press, 2007), 44–67.

31. Edward S. Van Zile, *That Marvel—the Movie: A Glance at Its Reckless Past, Its Promising Present, and Its Significant Future* (New York: G. P. Putnam's Sons, 1923), 4. Van Zile was a newspaper editor who wrote fiction, poetry, and drama but had never written on film before this publication. See "Biographical Sketches," *Book News* 14, no. 163 (March 1896): 327; and "General Gossip of Authors and Writers," *Current Opinion*, 16, no. 6 (December 1894): 514.

32. Hence why the question of how social media could foster common knowledge—what Zuckerberg calls a "shared sense of reality"—proves so confounding in "Building Global Community."

33. Evgeny Morozov, *To Save Everything, Click Here: The Folly of Technological Solutionism* (New York: PublicAffairs, 2013), 36.

34. Two important qualifications are in order here. First, the question of which works count as "firsts" within the field of American film history is complicated. Second, Van Zile's status as a "historian" is debatable.

Robert Allen and Douglas Gomery's authoritative *Film History* treats Ramsaye's *A Million and One Nights* as one of two points of origin for "the writing of film history in the United States," the other being Robert Grau's *The Theatre of Science: A Volume of Progress and Achievement in the Motion Picture Industry* (New York: Broadway, 1914). Their decision to pair the texts as coequal "firsts"—despite the significant anteriority of Grau's work—speaks to the fact that Ramsaye's book subsequently exerted a much more significant influence on the discipline. This disparity is likely attributable to a number of factors. Obviously, Ramsaye's study is substantially longer: given the significantly later date of its publication, Ramsaye has much more material to cover, and he does so in greater detail. Likewise, the timing of Ramsaye's afforded him a more confident, authoritative perspective on his material, a sense of telling a complete story about a medium that had arrived at maturity, solidifying its position on the global cultural landscape. Significantly, Ramsaye's book was put out by a major publisher, whereas Grau's had been sold by subscription. Notwithstanding these differences, as Allen and Gomery demonstrate, Grau's text shares major themes and historiographical techniques with Ramsaye's: both narrate film history in terms of the exploits of individual inventors, entrepreneurs, and artists—the medium's "great men." Allen and Gomery, *Film History: Theory and Practice* (New York: Knopf, 1985), 51–60.

I include Van Zile in this discussion of early film history because his work opens with a series of chapters that trace the development of the medium from its origins to its present level of complexity, because his more theoretical discussion of the medium's "significance" is so steeped in contemporary historiographical trends, and because he covers so many of the same themes as Ramsaye and Hampton. At the same time, I grant that Van Zile's work as a historian is decidedly lacking in rigor. Whereas Ramsaye had examined a range of primary sources, including "court records (especially around patents litigation) and interviews with pioneers from cinema history," in crafting the articles that became *A Million and One Nights*, Van Zile's historical remarks are drawn entirely from secondary sources, especially Frederick Talbot's *Moving Pictures: How They Are Made and Worked* (Philadelphia: J. B. Lippincott, 1912), from which he quotes liberally. See Dana Polan, *Scenes of Instruction: The Beginnings of the U.S. Study of Film* (Berkeley: University of California Press, 2007), 97. Note also that Ramsaye's book emerged from a series of twelve articles that *Photoplay*'s editor, James Quirk, commissioned him to write; the series, "The Romantic History of the Motion Picture," ran in the magazine from April 1922 to March 1925.

35. Van Loon, *Story of Mankind*, 459. See Van Zile, *That Marvel*, 3–17; and Ramsaye, *Million*, v–xiv.

36. Van Zile, 147.

37. Wells, *Salvaging*, 1, 4–5. On this aspect of Wells's thought, see Simon James, *Maps of Utopia: H. G. Wells, Modernity, and the End of Culture* (Oxford: Oxford University Press, 2012), 160.

38. Van Zile, *That Marvel*, 4.

39. Ramsaye, *Million*, 1.

40. Van Zile, *That Marvel*, 130.

41. Hampton, *History*, 429.

42. Hampton's stance at the end of *A History of the Movies* is exactly that of Wells's in his *Outline*, which Simon James aptly describes as "a Whig version of history [written] from a nonexistent present." Both writers insist upon telling a story of irresistible human ascent belied by a contemporary situation that suggests regressive tendencies. See James, *Maps*, 182.

43. Gilles Deleuze, *Cinema 1: The Movement-Image*, trans. Hugh Tomlinson and Barbara Habberjam (Minneapolis: University of Minnesota Press, 1986), 148, 151.

44. Deleuze, 144.

45. A "part-talkie" mainly operates like a silent film with a recorded orchestral accompaniment, using intertitles to advance the narrative and to indicate characters' speech. On this phenomenon, see Donald Crafton, *The Talkies: American Cinema's Transition to Sound, 1926–1931*, vol. 4 of *The History of the American Cinema* (New York: Charles Scribner's Sons, 1997), 171–179, 273–276. As Crafton's research indicates, silent versions of films like *Noah's Ark* and *Uncle Tom's Cabin* would also have been distributed for exhibition in theaters not yet wired for sound-film exhibition.

46. Advertisement reprinted in William K. Everson's *American Silent Film* (New York: Oxford University Press, 1978), 25. Miriam Hansen's reference to this reprint suggests that it might have dated from between 1912 and 1915. Hansen, *Babel and Babylon: Spectatorship in American Silent Film* (Cambridge, Mass.: Harvard University Press, 1991), 317n56.

47. Images of an "exhibitors promotional handbook," advertisements, and souvenir programs appear in the University of Virginia's terrific multimedia archive, *Uncle Tom's Cabin and American Culture*. Links appear on the page devoted to the 1927 Universal production, http://utc.iath.virginia.edu/onstage/films/mv27hp.html.

48. The quoted phrases come from a story titled "Where Do They All Come From?" in the *Uncle Tom's Cabin* pressbook, which is included in the special features of the Kino Video DVD edition of the film.

49. David Pierce, "'Carl Laemmle's Outstanding Achievement': Harry Pollard and the Struggle to Film Uncle Tom's Cabin," *Film History* 10 (1998): 465–466.

50. Pierce, 462–463.

51. "Pollard Explains Why He 'Revamps' Harriet B. Stowe," Universal Pictures Publicity Notice, 1927, http://utc.iath.virginia.edu/onstage/films/1927/fipnup27et.html.

52. Ryan Jay Friedman, *Hollywood's African American Films: The Transition to Sound* (New Brunswick, N.J.: Rutgers University Press, 2011), 54.

53. Thomas Cripps, *Slow Fade to Black: The Negro in American Film, 1900–1942* (Oxford: Oxford University Press, 1977), 159–162.

54. Universal Pictures Publicity Notice, December 1, 1926, *Uncle Tom's Cabin and American Culture*, http://utc.iath.virginia.edu/onstage/films/1927/fipnup27dt.html. The publicity notices contained in this archive show that from the moment it announced it was going into production on the Stowe adaption, the studio's top priority was to reassure the public that the film would do nothing to "discredit" the American South (past or present). Thus director Pollard, sounding somewhat like Griffith before him, ends up in the absurd position of casting white racists as the victims of intolerance: "If our screen version should help to heal the wounds left by Mrs. Stowe's book, I feel confident Northerners would be the first to applaud; if the motion picture screen can establish itself as a medium for spreading the gospel of tolerance and understanding, it will have achieved something far finer than its present aim of mere entertainment." See "Pollard Explains."

55. Universal Pictures Publicity Notice, December 1, 1926, http://utc.iath.virginia.edu/onstage/films/1927/fipnup27dt.html.

56. Note that in the film, Eliza escapes Kentucky only to be recaptured and sold down the fiver, ending up with Tom at Legree's. This final scene reunites her with George Harris (Arthur Edmund Carewe) and Harry (Lassie Lou Ahern), who enter with the troops.

57. Despite its Kentucky location, the Shelby estate is depicted as a Deep South cotton plantation, teeming with singing and dancing slaves, in the fashion of numerous Hollywood melodramas from the period.

58. "Pollard Explains."

59. Pierce, "'Carl Laemmle's,'" 462–463.

60. "Pollard Explains."

61. It is important to note here that the producers were interested in staking their film's claim to superiority over all other film versions, extant and in production. They well knew that the hoopla surrounding the release of their film would likely prompt the rerelease of older versions, which would compete for audience share. On this point, see "Laemmle Issues Defiance to Owner's of Old 'Uncle Tom's Cabin' Prints," Universal Pictures Publicity Notice, 1927 (?), http://utc.iath.virginia.edu/onstage/films/1927/fipnup27ft.html. See also Pierce, "'Carl Laemmle's,'" 469.

62. "Pollard Explains."

63. "Liberate" is not hyperbolic here: the pressbook includes a story titled, "Freeing 'Uncle Tom' from Shackles of False Tradition," *Uncle Tom's Cabin* Kino DVD special features.

64. Universal Pictures, "Special Pictorial Supplement" to *Uncle Tom's Cabin*, 2 of 3 unnumbered pages, http://utc.iath.virginia.edu/onstage/films/1927/mv27spshp.html.

65. "Special Pictorial Supplement." In making sense of what "real" means in this context, it is worth remembering that the Shelby mansion is a fictional structure invented by Stowe and that, even as the studio insists on the "duplication" this structure on the production lot, the actual film relocates this setting (and redecorates it accordingly).

66. John Drinkwater, *The Life and Adventures of Carl Laemmle* (1931; repr., New York: Arno Press, 1978), 171.

67. Drinkwater, 172–173.

68. Agnes Repplier, "The Unconscious Humor of the Movies," *Atlantic Monthly*, November 1925, 603.

69. See, for instance, the pressbook stories, "Architectural Perfection Demanded in the Movies," "Fascinating Facts and Figures from Featured Film," "The Magnitude of 'Uncle Tom's Cabin,'" and "$27,400 a Day for Nearly Two Years," *Uncle Tom's Cabin* Kino DVD special features.

70. "Architectural Perfection," "Magnitude," and "$27,400."

71. Deleuze, *Cinema*, 144.

72. Walter Benjamin, "Light from Obscurantists," trans. Rodney Livingstone, in *Selected Writings: Volume 2, 1927–1934*, ed. Michael Jennings, Howard Eiland, and Gary Smith (Cambridge, Mass.: Belknap/Harvard University Press, 1999), 655.

73. Benjamin, 656.

74. Benjamin, 656.

75. Benjamin, 656.

Index

About the Author

RYAN JAY FRIEDMAN is an associate professor in the Department of English and directs the Film Studies Program at The Ohio State University. He is the author of *Hollywood's African American Films: The Transition to Sound* and contributed a chapter to the collection *Early Race Filmmaking in America*. His scholarship has also appeared in *Quarterly Review of Film & Video*, *English Literary History*, and *Arizona Quarterly*.